REVISED AND UPDATED

An Intelligent Life

A Practical Guide to Relationships, Intimacy and Self-Esteem

Julian Short

RANDOM HOUSE AUSTRALIA

A Random House book
Published by Random House Australia Pty Ltd
Level 3, 100 Pacific Highway, North Sydney NSW 2060
www.randomhouse.com.au

First published by Random House Australia in 2005
This edition published in 2010

Addresses for companies within the Random House Group can be found
at www.randomhouse.com.au/offices.

National Library of Australia
Cataloguing-in-Publication Entry

Short, Julian.
An intelligent life.

ISBN 978 1 74166 970 1.

1. Psychotherapy. I. Title.

616.8914

Cover illustration by Nanette Backhouse
Cover design by SASO Design
Internal illustrations by HL Studios
Text design by Maggie Dana
Printed and bound by Griffin Press, South Australia

Random House Australia uses papers that are natural, renewable and
recyclable products and made from wood grown in sustainable forests.
The logging and manufacturing processes are expected to conform to
the environmental regulations of the country of origin.

To my children, Tim and Tess,
and in memory of my father

Contents

PART 3   Intelligent Love
The Qualities, Pitfalls and Management of Different Types of Relationships

PART 4   About Us
The Things We Do and the Way We Are

※

Preface

LIFE IS SIMPLE. It's not always easy, but it's simple. *An Intelligent Life* invites you to think about your life in a slightly different way, but I think you'll find it's worth the effort. Once you clearly see what makes you feel and act the way you do, you'll be more at peace with yourself – especially because you'll find it easier to understand other people and see why they do the things that they do.

The forces driving emotions and behaviour are not all that complicated, even if they do take a bit of explaining. Understanding them and managing them intelligently makes the world an easier place.

A life lived intelligently maximises your chance of happiness. If you choose to act on the principles you find here, you can have much more of a sense of control as well as greater intimacy, self-respect and equality in your relationships.

This book is intended as a manual to give you the skills for living your life in a way that will let you feel as good about yourself as you possibly can. As you read, you'll see it's about being intelligently self-interested, which I must hurriedly add is not the same as selfishness, which is never intelligent. Behaviour that is truly in your best interests is good for other people as well.

In *An Intelligent Life*, I've made no attempt to be inspirational, just practical; there is no glowing tribute to positive thinking or any offer of a path to cosmic consciousness. You may find my advice hard work in places, and even a little confronting, but to understand yourself and manage life most easily, you need to look at the negatives as well as the positives.

I have tried to speak directly to you as the reader, writing as if I am describing you and your feelings. At times this will mean I'm way off the mark – appearing to suggest you might do or feel something that is totally foreign to your nature – but I'm still confident you will be able to recognise bits of yourself and identify a few people you know, and even some you love.

In describing human nature and behaviour, I have also been obliged to deal with the gender of pronouns. As the English language doesn't offer a satisfactory solution to the problem, I have generally settled for the masculine to cover both sexes, although I have sometimes used the feminine form in areas I felt would be most usefully seen as being from a woman's perspective. I hope you will recognise that by failing to regularly discriminate between the sexes I don't mean to discriminate against either.

My thirty years as a psychiatrist have only confirmed the blindingly obvious fact that self-liking is the foundation for happiness, just as a poor self-opinion underlies most emotional problems. Experience has also shown that even the happiest people are not always as secure as they'd like to be, or as confident as other people think they are. In life, that's fine, because a degree of self-doubt is not a problem and can even be a good thing – a little anxiety about ourselves makes us try harder and fuels our concern for others – but too much self-doubt is destructive.

If you're a superstar it might be easier for you to have a high self-opinion, but if you have an intelligently designed model for managing your world, you can learn how to be insignificant, how to fail, make a mess, or just be plain wrong and still like yourself, because happiness is about more than achievement or status.

The quality of your relationships is the key to a healthy self-esteem, which in turn is the key to happiness. Most of us secretly believe that money could buy a great deal of happiness, but even a huge fortune won't do the job if we fail to follow the rules for intimate and dignified relationships.

During my years of clinical practice, whenever someone sat up in his chair and looked at me with obvious understanding, I wrote down what we had been saying. So for a long time I have been collecting the ideas that seemed to seize people's imagination and motivate them to change. These are the principles of relationships, intimacy and self-esteem, and together they are the essentials of *An Intelligent Life*.

PART 1

~

Mostly Theory

The Principles and Background to
Living Intelligently

CHAPTER 1

✧

The Origin of Feelings

WE ALL WANT TO FEEL GOOD. We want to feel relaxed, secure, strong and worthwhile. We want to feel creative and in control, attractive and loved. If we could guarantee feeling this way we'd almost certainly be happy.

This is the way we want to feel, but we know perfectly well that what we want to feel and what we do feel are not always the same thing.

Feelings are strange creatures; everyone has them and we live with them all day, every day, but sometimes they can have a life of their own. We've all felt anxious when we knew there was no need to be, and we've all had angry conversations in our heads, bitterly running through a confrontation that never happens. Is there anyone who hasn't burnt with embarrassment at something they think they've done when no one else has even noticed it?

You have very little direct control over your feelings, but sometimes they can seem to control you. Unfortunately, your biggest influence on your feelings is your capacity to make them worse. It's painfully easy to dig up an unhappy memory or construct an angry fantasy, dwell on it for a while and make yourself thoroughly miserable. On the other hand, if you decide you want to be happy, you can count your blessings, think of happy times and list all your qualities and achievements – but sometimes that can feel like whistling in the dark. Being positive is a great way to go about life, and it's much better than wallowing in gloom; but you are not nearly as effective at making yourself feel good as you are at making yourself feel bad. 'Don't worry; be happy' has to be the most given, least followed, and probably the most useless piece of advice in the world.

Trying to manage feelings can be hugely frustrating. You can know one thing yet feel another as your emotions struggle with your logic. Your self-esteem is simply your happiness with yourself. The poorer your self-esteem and the lower your self-confidence, the more easily negative feelings can overwhelm ordinary good sense. Life would be so much simpler if positive feelings could take over as easily as negative feelings seem to be able to.

You can know, logically, that you are a reasonable, worthy human being, but still feel you're not. If you feel bad and try to rationally think through why you feel as you do, you will see the division between your thoughts and feelings very clearly. If you put in enough effort, you can have considerable control over your thoughts – which are the things you say to yourself in your head. You can tell yourself you are fine and you can see perfectly easily why you should be positive and shouldn't be so upset, but your feelings still run amok; a law unto themselves.

In the model for life I hope to help you develop, you will need to think about yourself in a slightly different way. You need to look at yourself as an individual, but always as existing in the context of people around you.

You are not, and never will be, independent of other people. You will always care what other people think of you. *You can only really know yourself through your relationships – and managing these relationships is the best and most reliable way to manage your feelings.*

We all feel the need to be independent, or at least to look that way, so these notions may be mildly heretical, but I hope I can show you why they are true and why understanding them is an important step to being happy. I also hope to be able to show you that the forces driving your emotions really are easily understood, and if you can see what makes you love, fear, rage and despair, you are closer to having some control over these feelings. Knowledge gives you power – or at least that all-important sense of control.

Life really is quite simple, because you only need to know one fact:

Unless you are facing physical injury or death, there is not a single human emotional problem that is not caused by either the reality or the perception of:

rejection, separation and loss of love

or:

weakness, belittlement and loss of power

There's nothing more. Emotions and relationships may look much more complicated because there are lots of variations, but they are only variations on one or both of these two themes. No human has any other emotional problem, because we have only two primary emotional needs:

- we need belonging
- we need territory

Again, that's all there is! You can survive physically without them, but it would be a pointless and painful existence.

I appreciate it may seem to be asking rather a lot to hope that you will accept such a simple view, but I can strengthen the argument by offering some ideas on the origin of our emotions, which evolved as our brains were shaped over millions of years through the survival of the fittest.

Physical survival was probably all our ancestors had to worry about – unless, of course, it was mating season. They had immediate needs for food, water, shelter and oxygen, but in the longer term these were not enough. Survival also depended upon two additional factors:

- belonging to the herd
- territory for hunting and mating

Belonging

Baby mammals die very quickly if they are separated from their parents. They need love, but long before they were adult our ancestors could no longer rely on their parents. Their mothers had younger children to care for and at the best of times fathers are rarely much use in the animal world. For safety, our adult ancestors needed to belong to their clan, group, tribe or herd. Having evolved to live on the savannah, where there aren't many trees to climb in an emergency, a lone animal is very vulnerable. If there's a large carnivore around, let's say a tiger, the safest place to be is in the middle of a group of friends. Unfortunately, to find safety in the herd, the herd has to accept you. It's not enough that they are your own species; if you don't belong because in some way you fail to meet the requirements of the group, you have a problem. If you don't smell right or look right, your own kind become more dangerous than any tiger. If the group decides you aren't good enough to belong, they'll kill you.

Putting it all together, being alone is pretty scary. If our ancestors were separated from the tribe because they were lost or left behind, they faced death in the jaws of a tiger. Worse still, if they were different enough to be actively rejected by the herd, the tiger probably began to look quite attractive compared to the group that was probably going to kill them.

This is the background to our need for acceptance and our fear of rejection, but we have another primary need; the urge for our own space.

Territory

Once their acceptance by the tribe was secure, long-term survival also demanded our ancestors mark out their own territory and then be strong enough to keep out competitors.

Without territorial control, no one gets to be an ancestor. Without the strength to fight and hold his own territory a meat eater will starve. There's too much competition for resources. While herbivores don't seem to fight over the dinner table, once it's mating season, the gentlest animal becomes a raving lunatic, fighting everything in sight. Even if an animal without territory didn't die of hunger, he was much less likely to pass on his genes, and so become an ancestor, because he would be less able to mate or raise young successfully. Females are as disinclined to team up with a weak and powerless male on the savannah as they are in a bar. While males guard sexual and hunting territory constantly, female animals are less territorial until they have young, when they become ferociously protective. A powerless female could never protect her young long enough for them to grow up, so a weak female becomes just as much a biological failure as a weak male. Weakness meant death from starvation and a much poorer chance at successful reproduction.

We still carry copies of genetic programming for survival that served our ancestors for the millions of years since they left the trees. If you appreciate this, you are on the path to understanding the ebb and flow of your feelings and why people do what they do.

We are all hungry for love, acceptance and belonging. Rejection can still feel like death.

Everyone wants the strength to control their own little patch, or a bigger patch if they can get away with it. Weakness, powerlessness and losing can still threaten us profoundly by making us feel small and unsuccessful as people.

Remember how you felt when you first wanted to ask someone out or needed to speak in public? Have you ever felt the discomfort of not being able to look someone in the eye? Ever felt awkward with someone very tall, very famous or very good-looking? If you haven't, are you sure you've never tried to make yourself bigger by reassuring yourself that you're as good as the next person, or that you really don't give a damn what other people think of you?

What are now emotional needs were once necessities for physical survival. The strength of the emotion you feel if you are rejected or belittled comes from ancient programming still resident in your modern brain. *Once upon a time, loss of love, rejection, weakness and loss of territory all meant death. Now it just feels that way.*

If you can live with the logic so far, the next statement follows reasonably easily: *every single waking act that is not looking after your physical survival is devoted in one way or another to the ultimate goals of getting as much love as possible, while simultaneously getting as much of your own way as possible.*

If that makes sense to you, it's not too hard to see how important an influence your relationships must be on your emotions.

Ideas

- Feelings can have a life of their own and you have very little direct control over them, except perhaps to make them worse.

- All human emotional needs originate in two necessities for survival: the need to belong for reasons of safety, and the need for the strength to be able to fight for territory.

- What are now emotional needs were once necessities for physical survival.

- We are profoundly threatened by rejection or weakness because once they meant death. Unloved or belittled, we feel we are destroyed, even if our logic says we don't need such a strong emotion.

- There is not a single human emotional problem that does not stem either from a fear of rejection and loss of love, or a fear of weakness and loss of individual power, control and dignity.

- You don't need to be rich or beautiful to like yourself, but you do need a system for maximising love and belonging, dignity and individuality. You can do this through skilful care of your relationships.

CHAPTER 2

ॐ

Self-Esteem Is a Sundae

IF YOU'RE SHORT OF BREATH, starving or cold, you will be totally focused on your body. You'll give very little thought to your affectionate relationships, your hairstyle, or whether someone has used your coffee cup. When your life is not under threat, other emotions will demand and get your attention.

You have a sense of your own existence that is much more than your physical body. Your sense of being you is much bigger and more diffuse than the flesh that you can see and feel. I shall call this sense of yourself your spirit – not with a mystical or metaphysical implication, but merely to acknowledge that you have the sense of an emotional self as well as a physical self.

The survival needs of your spirit are derived from the survival needs of your body. Belonging has become love; territory has become individuality.

I choose to use the word love in its broadest sense. Rather than confining it to only the most intimate relationships, I use love to cover every form of fond belonging. Certainly, you can hope to find love in the arms of a mother, a brother, a friend and a lover, but it comes in a hundred other varieties, too. There is a sense of love in your attachment to family, groups, clubs, teams, churches, religions, tribes, nations, or even a flag. If you have the gift of empathy you can find love in your bond to a tree, a mountain or an animal.

Love is all the variations on the theme of warmth, safety and belonging through attachment to those whom you identify as your own. Love blends you securely with the herd.

Your territory as a human being is harder to define; it is all the obvious material things and places, but it is much more than your car, your garden, your place in the queue, or even your personal space. You have a sense of personal territory, which is your individuality, which is defined by your philosophy, ethics, morality and all the things you believe to be good, right, holy and true.

Your individuality is the territory of your spirit, defining you as separate from the herd.

For our ancestors, strength was the physical power to fight for, hold, and even extend their territory. Now, living in a civilised society, physical strength is very rarely necessary for protection of physical territory, and illegal as a means to extend it. Strength now means strength of character.

Strength is still the ability to hold, and even extend, our personal or spiritual territory. The strength and power of your individuality is defined by your creativity, dignity and integrity. It is your stature as a person; your potency, distinction, autonomy and the effectiveness of your self-expression.

Strength means being able to stand up for yourself and assert your beliefs, even at the risk of rejection, resisting the temptation to give up your individuality for the safety of conformity in order to please and secure your place in the herd.

Unfortunately, terrified of being weak, some people feel they have to win and they confuse strength with stubbornness. It is my hope you will discover that *An Intelligent Life* will offer you useable skills for effective self-expression without aggression.

Strength is the ability to assert your individuality without aggression.

A diagram can sometimes show an idea better than words. Think of your self-esteem as an ice cream sundae – how could you have ever thought anything else? The sundae of self-esteem has two scoops: love and individuality.

Love and individuality make two scoops of the sundae of self-esteem

Good self-esteem is a full sundae with two full scoops which is well-balanced.

To feel good, the sundae of your self-esteem has to have a reasonable size and it needs to be roughly balanced. Unfortunately, to really enjoy your ice cream, a massive great scoop at one end of the bowl can't compensate for nothing much at the other. A well-balanced sundae has two generous scoops of roughly the same size, sitting securely in the bowl.

If you try to fill the whole bowl with a single scoop, it just doesn't do the job. Everything else is swamped and it doesn't fit properly. Too much at one end overflows the sides and just makes a tacky mess.

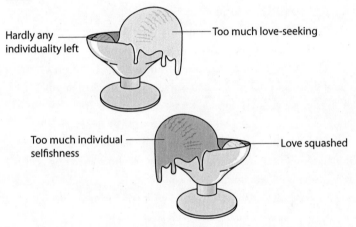

Hardly any individuality left — Too much love-seeking

Too much individual selfishness — Love squashed

For an adult, a mass of love is not enough without dignity, and all the power in the world is useless and joyless if no one loves you. In the pursuit of love, you could try to be the most warm and wonderful person in the world, but if you don't preserve your individual dignity, you will not feel great. Then again, if you aggressively demand too much and push your individual desires, you will be distinctly unlovable. At any one time you may get more of your share, but in the long term, the imbalance means you are unlikely to feel good about yourself. It is not intelligent to be selfish.

Happiness requires a balance. If you feel rejected, you need to pursue love with dignity. If you feel put down, you need to restore your dignity in an attractive fashion.

Within a life lived intelligently lies one inescapable fact: *love and individuality may be central to our self-esteem, but neither has any meaning without reference to other people.* We do not exist in a vacuum, and we can never be truly independent of one another.

Our emotional existence depends on other people. We need other people around us to complete our sense of who we are, just as the hole in a doughnut is defined by the dough around it or an island is defined by a surrounding sea.

To get the greatest pleasure from our achievements, we need them to be appreciated and validated by others.

Our pleasures are heightened and our pains diminished by being shared. Other people can bring us our greatest happiness and, of course, our greatest despair. Other people let us know we're alive, and through other people we learn how we feel about ourselves.

I am hoping to show that while being happy to order is incredibly hard, you can indirectly control your feelings in a very positive way through understanding and well-chosen actions within the setting of your relationships. I want to walk you through this, point by point, to show you the logic of each step.

Let's assume your life is progressing in a reasonably predictable way and there are no major external forces – good or bad – to swamp you with feelings. In other words, if you have not just won the lottery or suffered your boyfriend running off with your best friend, happiness is really your happiness with yourself.

1. The value you place upon yourself is your self-esteem, which is your opinion of yourself.

2. Any judgement you make of yourself will be in terms of two primary emotional needs: belonging and territory.

3. In judging yourself, you will be deciding whether you can see yourself as loveable enough to be secure in your belonging, and simultaneously as strong enough to protect the territory of your individuality.

4. Thus, self-doubt is questioning whether you can risk being yourself, that is, daring to assert your individuality and take the chance of other people rejecting you.

5. Your self-esteem is decided by how clearly defined you feel as an individual, and how loved and lovable you feel for being that individual.

6. In your assessment of your own worth as a person, your judgement of yourself is really you looking at yourself.

7. Therefore, your judgement of yourself is made as if you were another person looking at you.

8. In effect, your self-esteem is your judgement of other people's judgement of you.

9. The way you behave in your relationship with other people will decide how they react to you and then you will see yourself in the mirror of their reactions.

10. Thus, managing your relationships is your best access to your feelings about yourself, because other people's responses will decide how you see yourself.

You may still feel it is heretical to say your happiness depends so much on other people, but it's worth considering the idea. Discard it if you are sure the principle is wrong, but please don't dismiss it because you would hate it to be true. *Your relationships are everything. You see yourself in the mirror of other people.*

Obviously, your past experiences and your individual genetic programming must have some influence on your life. If your childhood was just too tough, the bedrock on which you must build your self-esteem will be much more crumbly than if you came from a childhood full of love and respect for you as an individual.

Your parents were the only people who ever had the power to simply hand you a near-perfect sundae on a plate. If they failed to do so, or you failed to receive the message that you as an individual are good, lovable and worthy, you will have more work to do than others. Despite this, if you have planned your life intelligently, you will have a system for finding most love with most dignity, allowing you to largely override the effects of an unhappy childhood or an unfortunate genetic legacy.

If you have a problem, try to fix it. If you can't fix it, get as much love from other people as you can, with as much dignity as possible.

Whatever problems you have, you need to manage yourself skilfully within your relationships. If you are bankrupted, you have cancer, your children are misbehaving, or your boyfriend has slept with your best friend, you certainly deserve sympathy, yet these are the very times when you must pay most attention to the way you relate to other people. For it is during awful times, above all others, when you need to be the best partner, friend, parent and adult you can be. You won't fix an unfixable problem, but you will feel as good about yourself as possible. The idea is simple. It's not easy to do, but it can be done.

Ideas

- Your spirit needs love and individuality for its survival.
- With enough love and individuality, the sundae of your self-esteem will almost certainly be big enough for you to be happy.

- A mass of love is not enough without individual dignity, just as any amount of power, money and achievement is useless if no one loves you.

- Your judgement of yourself is actually you looking at you, as if you were another person judging you.

- The result of your self-judgement is your self-esteem. If you like what you see, you will be happy.

- *An Intelligent Life* describes an active process for taking charge of your emotions; not directly, which is near impossible, but through skilled management of your relationships, to set up a mirror in which to see yourself positively.

- You can take charge of the past if you don't let it interfere with the quality of your relationships in the present.

- A healthy, happy person is never truly independent of other people. Care of yourself is care of your relationships.

- If your self-esteem is poor, you are unhappy with yourself, but it's still perfectly possible to be happy about happy things. If your self-esteem is good, you have the ability to feel good about yourself even if you are unhappy about things. A good self-esteem maximises your chances of being a happy person.

- If you want to feel good about yourself, you need the skills to enable you to feel loved, loving and lovable, but at the same time you must preserve a sense of individuality, dignity, strength and control.

CHAPTER 3

࿊

The Gang of Three

THIS IS THE MOST COMPLICATED CHAPTER IN THE BOOK, because I'm
trying to explain the psychological logic behind a system for managing your feelings. I wish it were as simple as positive thinking or just
picturing something you want to make it all come true. In my effort
to get the ideas across, I have repeated the hardest concepts, sometimes in a couple of different ways. If you have read a paragraph and
you don't really understand, please keep reading to see if the next
few clarify the idea for you. On the other hand, if the repetition gets
boring, I ask you to forgive me.

Managing your responses

It doesn't matter how well you manage your world, things will
happen that will make you feel bad. Stuff happens. The real question is whether you are just going to feel bad about the events or
about yourself as well.

By definition, negative experiences, past or present, will make
you feel bad. Feeling unhappy about these is part of normal living.
Some negative experiences will have an extra dimension that has
the potential to make you feel bad about yourself too. Feeling bad
about yourself is true unhappiness.

If your lover leaves you to work overseas, you'll feel bad. If he leaves you for your best friend, you'll feel worse. If you're betrayed by your partner as an adult, after being abandoned by your father as a child, you'll feel absolutely terrible.

At some point, self-dislike starts to creep in. The intensity of any emotional pain is not simply a function of the cause, but also the level of self-dislike you experience.

Whatever you do, if you lose love you will have pain. That's unchangeable, but the ultimate emotional damage depends less on the nature of the event, or even on your background, and much more on the way you behave in response to being hurt.

Your long-term happiness is not a feeble hostage to the events of your life. You can't control the past, and bad things will happen as a natural part of life, but you can control their effects on the present and your future. You do this by exercising your ability to choose how you react when things go wrong.

An Intelligent Life is designed to give you a set of guidelines for managing your responses.

Your reactions to events have a greater final effect on your self-esteem than most problems have in their own right. It is this fact that means you can have control over your long-term happiness or unhappiness, even if your childhood was miserable and the present seems almost as bad.

The events you can't control; the self-esteem you can. *Control of your emotions comes through your capacity to manage your actions. It's critical that you appreciate I am not saying you have to act happy when you are sad, or not be angry on occasions when you have every right to be angry. It is usually perfectly appropriate to show these emotions; even if you are wrong and the feeling isn't merited. It is the way in which you show your emotions that matters.*

If you feel anxious, angry or despairing and you thoughtlessly allow your feelings to drive your behaviour in a way that puts pressure on your relationships, you will always feel worse, because you have acted to make yourself feel worse. In other words, having a tantrum may be briefly satisfying as a way to communicate how put out you are, but it does more harm than good. Hardly rocket science, but quite an important concept.

On the other hand, if you have a well thought out model for living you can safely be yourself; that is, you can express your individuality by showing your feelings – both negative and positive. Do it well, and at the same time as you are protecting established relationships, you might even earn a measure of respect. It's your relationships that matter every time.

If you can behave in a way that is lovable and loving, dignified and individualistic, especially in the middle of a disaster, other people and you yourself will tend to respect you. It is possible to choose ways of responding to situations that will lead others to signal they feel you are worthwhile. The original problem may remain, but your feelings about yourself can be dragged into a happier position if you discover you can have some control over the way people respond to you. Respond intelligently and you will see a genuinely more positive image of yourself in the mirror of other people.

If you have a preplanned system that makes sense and feels right, because you can see it is potentially more effective in making you feel as good as circumstances allow, you might be able to prevent yourself throwing a tantrum when disaster hits. You can learn to behave in a fashion that is unaffected, not manipulative, is truly expressive of who you are, and at the same time designed to make others like you.

Knowing you can be genuinely liked for who you are and to feel confident you have the skills to get this feeling from others, is the basis of emotional security. The approach I am offering is based on the idea that, functionally, there are three parts to being you:

1. your feelings

2. your thoughts

3. your actions

Your feelings are the part of you over which you have least control, but as they cause the most difficulties, they are the part you most want to manage. Indeed, that's what this book is all about.

Your thoughts, that is your self-talk or the conversations in your head, are more manageable, especially if you have the right information to help you structure them.

Your actions are the aspect of yourself over which you have most potential for control. This is especially so if you have the motivation of hope that comes from knowing how to intelligently serve your own interests, which, I hope to show you, is quite different from being selfish. If you want to feel predictably, and not just accidentally, good, *that is, to be able to reliably manage your feelings, you must use your thoughts to drive actions that will produce positive responses from other people. You can reasonably hope that well chosen behaviour, well directed by logical thinking will influence other people's responses and the three will form a group of forces, which in combination has the potential to override feelings of self-dislike.*

It's important to explain why this can work. Human beings have a strong distaste for inconsistency; it makes us feel awkward and uncomfortable if we are obliged to choose from a number of possibilities that conflict, in that they can't all be simultaneously correct. When this occurs we call it *cognitive dissonance*, which we tend to deal with by going with the strength. If you're looking for Eldorado and you find three signs pointing north and one south you'll hesitate, but you'll probably go north.

I am proposing that if events are not going well and you feel bad about yourself, you can harness your human tendency to follow the majority to escape the dissonance of incompatibility. This is why it's possible for a pressure group to drag your feelings in the direction you would prefer.

I have called this pressure group the Gang of Three, not because I'm into silly names, but, like the Sundae of Self-Esteem, I couldn't think of anything better. The Gang is made up of two aspects of your inner life over which you have control: your thoughts and your actions, and they are joined by the reactions of other people to your actions.

Remember, the three functional parts of you are:

1. feelings

2. thoughts

3. actions

The aim of the exercise is to use your

- thoughts

- actions

- other people

to manage the out-of-control bit of you; that is, your feelings.

Let's look more closely at the gang members in action.

Gang member number one is your thoughts, that is, an *intelligent conversation* inside your head.

> 'I feel incredibly angry and hurt at the moment, so this is the very time I must be careful not to be aggressive and belittling, or sickly sweet and acquiescent. I must use the words and body language of a dignified, self-respecting and kindly adult. If I can't or don't want to conceal how distressed I am, I still must play an adult role, even if a clearly upset one ... '

> 'How do I do this?'

'I must try to act intelligently, even if I don't feel great.'

'Does this mean I have to fake being happy when I'm sad, or pretend to be relaxed when I'm tense?'

'No! It means I can show my discomfort, but as much as possible in ways that are likeable and dignified, which means not making myself or others look small or terminally unattractive.'

'It's perfectly okay to have negative emotions, but I need to act like a person who appears to be positive enough about himself to believe he is still a worthy human being, even if he feels disgusting at the moment, because what others think of me is terribly important to my self-esteem.'

'So, right now I must act as if I like myself, even if privately I'm not so certain that I do.'

'At the very least, I'm going to practise damage control. It's bad enough feeling bad; it would be worse feeling bad and then doing more damage by behaving stupidly.'

I appreciate this is fine in theory, but, unfortunately, you may have already had an attack of rage and now be wondering what to do. Obviously this is a little trickier, but later I shall try to show you how to apologise for what you have done, without apologising for having had the feeling that triggered your temper outburst. Your feeling might actually have been perfectly justified, even if your response was over the top. Apologising for bad behaviour is a great idea, but you must never apologise for having a feeling, because that would be apologising for being you.

Gang member number two is *intelligently planned action*. You choose bodily and verbal behaviour that expresses your feelings in a way that strengthens your individual dignity and preserves your attractiveness as an adult. You do this by using likeable, kindly techniques for assertion, emphasising adult equality and taking responsibility for your feelings. These principles are the essence of *An Intelligent Life* and they are examined step by step in Part 2.

If you are anxious, you own the feeling and you should never try to set someone up to take care of you.

If you are angry, assertively define your different point of view and never attack the self-esteem of the other person.

If you are hurt, you act as an equal, never boasting, never belittling and never trying to make someone guilty.

Naturally, you will not manage to be so constantly virtuous, but you don't need to be perfect to be loved, lovable and dignified. You simply need to try to start a trend in your behaviour.

When you regret your last foolishness, you may resolve not to do it again and then promptly repeat it, but if you try to salvage an awkward situation by applying some well thought through principles, you might be able to do so in a more attractive fashion. You do not need to get it instantly right, although obviously it is more important to do so with acts of cruelty or transparent selfishness.

Thus the second gang member, your actions, is dignified and attractive behaviour which has been driven by rational planning from the first member; your thoughts. This doesn't mean you feel good at this point; because you still feel hurt, angry and dismayed. You have simply lined up your thoughts and actions against your feelings, maximising the chance they will be joined by the third member of the pressure group.

Gang member number three is the *positive response of other people*. To repeat the concept yet again, if you react well in a difficult situation, other people are more likely to respect and may even like the way you have chosen to respond, even if they dislike what you originally did.

As an obvious example, once he was caught, if a recent and

seriously over-sexed American president had chosen an act of self-respect and said: 'I was really stupid and I'm sorry I was so stupid!' he'd have been a hero and the world would have been spared his successor. He also would have felt a lot better about himself.

Others judge you by what you do, but they are most influenced by your recent behaviour. Combine your best with your most recent and, provided you then stay with the good behaviour, you can often earn high respect and with it self-respect.

Damage control

Here we are talking about influencing the actions of others, so obviously I have to acknowledge you do not have the same potential for control over people's reactions as you have over your own. Individuals can have their own particular agendas that may be quite invisible to you, and these can sabotage the best-laid plans. Despite this, I think I shall be able to show you it is possible to recognise when other agendas are at work, even if you have no idea as to what they may be.

Having acknowledged the difficulty, I shall push on with the idea that we can influence others to help us feel better about ourselves. I still think you will find it's logical and, honestly, this is the hardest chapter in the whole book!

Ultimately, you are what you do, not what you think or feel.

If you act well, other people looking at you will most often respond positively. You will see yourself in the mirror of their reactions and not solely through your own negative eyes.

Remember how people reacted when you burst into tears and hid for hours in your bedroom after you felt unfairly criticised? The longer you waited for them to realise how they had wronged you and to come begging your forgiveness, the more hurt and angry you became. Remember how awful you felt and how the feeling lasted into the next day and beyond, and how you had to keep on needling them to feel you had any power at all?

Imagine bursting into tears in the same circumstances, but managing to shrug and smile sadly, saying: 'I really wish this didn't make me cry, but I feel so bad to think you see me this way.'

Remember, to live intelligently you are not pretending you do not have negative emotions, it's about choosing how you will behave when you have those emotions. No matter how controlled you would like to be, you may be so upset that there is no way you can stop yourself crying, but that's okay. Your tears are not a problem; it's how you handle yourself during and afterwards that counts. Every bone in your body might want to run to your room and slam the door, but instead, picture yourself continuing to say to the people who have hurt you, 'Okay, I'm a big girl, I can wear this. I'm not sure I feel you're being fair, but I'll survive. I'd like to convince you that you shouldn't think about me this way, but now may not be the best time to try.'

This is simple to describe and understand, but the style of approach would fit a range of difficult situations. Admittedly, it would be hard to do, but it is far from impossible if you knew the principles on which the response was based, and we shall come to technique later. Remember, we're talking about circumstances in which you might previously have had a tantrum and sulked for hours. You've been in this situation lots of times before and, to date, it's almost always been a disaster. *You know you will be hurt again in a very similar way, so you could pre-plan a different pattern of response.* The problem is the same, but you'd feel so much better if you managed it in a more dignified, and therefore more likeable, way.

I'm not pretending that choosing intelligent behaviour will make you feel great, but you have not made yourself feel worse. By practising damage control, you have lessened the intensity of your bad feelings. You've avoided sulking in your room and you've diminished the loss of dignity when no one came to get you. You've also saved yourself from the hours of brooding afterwards, endlessly revisiting how much you have been wronged, deliberately signalling with your irritability as you dig a deeper hole for yourself.

Road rage is all too frequent an opportunity to change your feelings. If someone drives like an idiot and pushes in front of you, you can lean on your horn and tail-gate him for half a mile down the road to teach him a lesson. He enjoys your powerlessness as much as you hate it and you're still steamed up half an hour later. If you blow him a kiss (best, of course, if he sees it) you won't feel the same pressure to blast your horn or run him off the road and your mood will settle much more quickly. You'll feel better because you'll actually feel more powerful and therefore less belittled by having your piece of territory on the road invaded.

By choosing alternatives to slamming a door in fury or teaching someone a lesson on the road, you can make the whole event smaller. You can look after your spirit well, maintaining the dignity of your individuality while preserving relationships as warmly as you can. You may not care about the guy on the road, but you look much bigger to your passenger and, most importantly, to yourself. Remember, all we ultimately care about is love and territory.

Crying is not pathetic until you try to escape from it by pleading to be understood or by behaving aggressively. Leaning on your horn is generally what you do when you feel powerless, which makes the aggression pathetic. We all do it, but that doesn't stop it being pathetic. By choosing alternative behaviours, you might even feel proud of yourself for the way you managed to prevent an emotional crisis becoming a behavioural disaster. How would you have felt if it were you who got stopped for dangerous driving as you were showing the idiot not to mess with you?

Here's looking at you, kid

If you behave well, others may judge you well, but of course there is more to it than this, because you have a deeper knowledge of yourself. You are going to be much less kind to yourself than other people will be. You might reasonably protest that no matter how much I say about the value of other people liking you, it's still not enough to make you like yourself. You know you have a mix of ideas and negative feelings continuously circling in your head, and you may be hurt, angered or ashamed. These feelings seem too deep to believe they could be influenced by simply behaving differently, but I would like to suggest that it's not so illogical that this could happen.

Because you judge yourself as if you were another person looking at you, you will still tend to judge yourself by the same criteria that others use; that is, you will mostly judge yourself by your actions. Again, what you do is what you are. The person other people see is actually much more the real you than your biased view of yourself.

Remember, your self-esteem is your judgement of yourself, so even if no other person actually sees what you do, you still observe yourself as if you were another person looking at you. *Thus you have the potential to act in a way that sets you up to like what you see in yourself.*

If I've lost you, please hang around and read on.

I am proposing that you have an *Observing Self*, which is you looking at yourself as if you were on the outside, either approving or disapproving, but your Observing Self is not as simple as your relationship with yourself. When you examine yourself, it is the *they* and the *them* who look at you; it's the vague mass of people you don't know, but somehow they are out there and you feel they might be criticising or judging you. These people don't exist in the way that you feel you know them, but are forever resident in your head.

Your Observing Self is made up of the social values of your culture; mixed up with parents, teachers, policemen, heroes and friends who have passed through your life. It includes people you admire and whose approval you'd like, as well as those whose criticism would sting. These people watch you from inside and decide if you are good enough to belong to the herd, the group or the family, yet strong enough to survive as an individual. It's not just you; everybody has such people inside them.

Although your Observing Self is looking at you from within your own head, it can still feel as if you are being watched critically from the outside. Fortunately, even though your Observing Self includes your conscience, it is more than your conscience. Your Observing Self can approve, give medals and be proud of you, while your conscience shuts up and sits silently by when you do well, but seems to enjoy giving you a hard time when your behaviour, or even your thoughts, are not quite up to its standards of virtue.

Using the Gang of Three

The estimation of your own lovableness and strength by your Observing Self is, by definition, your self-esteem. That's you looking at you and estimating your own worth. Get your behaviour right and you can still like yourself, even if the circumstances continue to make you feel bad and there is no other person there to see you do the right thing.

This means that the third member of the Gang; other people, has two components. The real people with whom you live every day and also the *they* and *them* who live in your head as your Observing

The effect other people's reactions have on your reactions, and your own self-observation

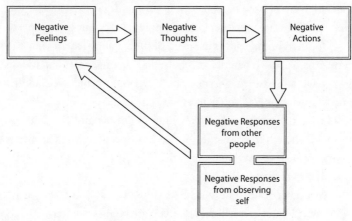

Letting negative feelings drive actions

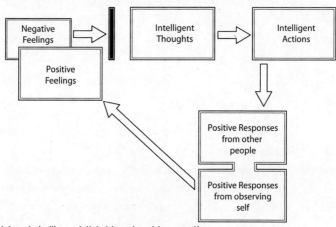

Using intelligent thinking to drive actions

Self. If you want to like yourself, you need to be liked both by other people and by your Observing Self. I think you will find *An Intelligent Life* can give you a practical system for pleasing the people who are inside as well as outside your own head.

Now that I have tried to define the Gang of Three and how to use them in words, perhaps a diagram will be a help (see opposite page).

If you can use the Gang of Three to good effect, the benefit to your feelings is real, solid and lasting. This is all your own work; quite different from a compliment you have fished for, or reassurance from a kindly aunt. It is not something good that happens by chance, or approval from someone who would tell you that you looked good if you had two heads. The result is something you have chosen and controlled yourself.

Our childhood is the only time in our lives when simply being given love has the power to make us feel durably good about ourselves.

As an adult, you can't hope to feel good about yourself simply by osmosis. Being offered a million dollars to believe you are worthwhile, or being told you are beautiful a hundred times, won't make your self-esteem any better if you don't feel you have had an active part in earning the compliment. Thus merely being the passive recipient of love is not enough; we need to feel some control of love ourselves and to feel we have our own active process that can reliably make us lovable. If somebody you love tells you he loves you, it will help, but it will not solve your problem if you don't feel lovable yourself. In fact, you're in danger of asking for reassurance again and again, even to the point of being irritating. If someone you admire tells you that you have done well you might feel better, but it could just as easily make you feel foolish and uncomfortable.

This is the paradox of low self-esteem: although we need love and pursue it so vigorously, merely being offered it is unlikely to convince us that we are lovable.

We need to master an effective system; something we can do and control that will get us a reasonable certainty of acceptance and respect. We may long for love, but if love comes our way and we don't feel we have earned it, we are in danger of deciding the love we want so much and have tried so hard to get is illusory and not to be trusted.

If someone were to compliment you on your looks when you have just emerged from bed in the morning, you'd find it very hard to accept and, indeed, you might wonder if you were being mocked. On the other hand, if you are told you look pretty good after you have washed your hair and put on your make-up, it's easier to believe and the compliment can actually make you feel better about yourself.

Your make-up is a reasonable metaphor for well-chosen and lovable behaviour. Certainly, it's an additional layer, but you are still you. It's not fake, even though you chose it deliberately to make people like you more. Putting on your make-up is a fairly reliable way to feel better with other people. It's a proven system that's under your control and you know what to do and how to do it. At this point the metaphor breaks down, because to feel securely good about yourself, good looks might help, but they're not enough. You must make use of the Gang of Three.

Recruiting the Gang of Three is not just positive thinking, but positive action, intelligently directed.

Living intelligently means linking your thoughts, actions and other people in a logical system for managing feelings in a positive way. The approach suits every situation and its effects are reasonably predictable and reproducible. It's not wishing and hoping, submitting to other people to please them or hoping they will do the right thing by you simply because you've done the right thing. It's not random. This is taking active control.

You are not pretending to be happy, relaxed and unconcerned; you are trying to behave like someone who may be unhappy, horribly stressed and apprehensive, but who still likes himself. As ever, your happiness is secured by skilful management of your behaviour within your relationships.

Obviously there are things you can do to feel better that do not appear to directly involve other people. You could mow the lawn, cook a glorious meal, read a book, build something, or climb a mountain. But if you look at these things, you can see they still fall into the two great categories of enhancing belonging and consolidating or extending territory.

Mowing, reading, cooking, building and climbing are all creative and it's not hard to see that creativity is an aspect of territoriality. You are marking out your patch with the mower – and think how satisfied you will feel if you can define a perimeter. You don't get the same quality of pleasure from doing someone else's lawn, even if you're paid for it, unless, of course, the payment is love and approval. Reading a book expands your knowledge and experience and hence enlarges the territory of your spirit, even if vicariously, while building or cooking are making something that is clearly a piece of you. What could be more territorial than conquering a mountain? If you don't believe a meal is a piece of the person who created it, try telling your mother that dinner wasn't great and check the response! By rejecting her dinner, you are rejecting her.

Mowing, reading, cooking, building and climbing are also valued by others as activities, and so earn love. Other acts can earn disapproval from some or many, but unfortunately for the amoral, the vulnerable or the fanatical, there can be a sort of satisfaction in brutality, throwing a bomb or even graffiti. In his destructiveness, a thug is very definitely leaving his mark and he may earn a fragile acceptance within his gang or terrorist cell. Even belonging to a herd of thugs has value for a person so weak or so disturbed as to think acts of violence are an expression of individuality.

Whatever might be your way of expressing your individuality, if you do it and you feel valued for it, you will tend to feel a little better about yourself.

A good self-esteem is within everybody's reach, because every sane person can choose how to behave, even if he can't directly choose how to feel.

If you want to feel good, you've got to act good. The grammar is poor, but the concept is invaluable.

That's it. Again, that's all there is. I don't think there's another way. By adopting the simple guidelines for an intelligent life in the coming chapters, I believe you can reasonably hope to be happy.

Ideas

- Your feelings, thoughts and actions are the three functions of being you. Your thoughts and actions are directly controllable, your feelings have a life of their own.

- You have very little direct control over your feelings. If you want to influence them in a positive way, you must make a consistent group of thoughts that can drive actions, and that in turn are most likely to recruit the positive responses of others.

- The principles of *An Intelligent Life* are guidelines for maximising the quality of your relationships, even when things aren't going well and you feel bad. By following the rules, you can avoid converting feeling bad into feeling bad about yourself.

- If you manage yourself well, other people are likely to signal in their responses that they see you as worthwhile. Their positive responses can join your judgement of yourself by your Observing Self, strengthening your self-esteem.

- Acting well is acting intelligently, choosing behaviour that will simultaneously get most love and most enhance your individuality. It is not pretending to be happy, it is acting as if you are happy with yourself, even if you are visibly unhappy with events.

- Acting well won't usually solve real-life problems, but it is a predictable, reproducible system for managing yourself and your feelings in any situation. You are not relying on good luck, positive thinking or passively hoping people will do the right thing. You are taking active control of your emotional life.

- If you have behaved badly, an apology is an excellent idea, but you must never apologise for having a feeling, because that would be apologising for being you.

- A child can absorb love from her parents and believe it; an adult needs to feel she deserves it in other people's eyes. A child should never have to feel she deserves her parents' love. It must be there even when she knows she's grubby and naughty.

- Inner change depends on the way you act in the external world.

- What you do is what you are and it is by your actions that both you and others will judge you.

CHAPTER 4

✧

Kindness and Dignity

IF IT WERE TRUE that we need to feel we have an active part in being lovable to feel secure and happy, it is important we understand what we mean by being lovable.

The ultimate measures of human worth are kindness and dignity. If you try your best to act with these in mind, you and other people will like you. If you have made a deliberate choice to act this way, you know you have had an active part in creating that liking.

Every human being wants to be liked and respected, but sometimes a person who doubts himself becomes embarrassed or even angered by signs of being liked. He is then liable to push people away, believing that if he is liked, it's under false pretences. He fears being shown up as a fraud if he can't meet what he imagines are the expectations that come with being liked or valued.

If you are rich, brilliant or beautiful, people will inevitably be interested in you and attracted to you, but for them to really love you, you need something that will survive bankruptcy, academic failure or your failure to be a supermodel. *If you have been kind in the service of love and dignified in the service of your individuality, and you recognise you have done this by choice, you have a good chance of being liked and liking yourself in a real and enduring way.*

That's all. Nothing else but kindness and dignity count in the long run. It's as simple as that.

Merrily down the stream

An Intelligent Life is based entirely on the notion that kindness and dignity are:

- Good for you
- Options available to everyone
- Easy goals to reach

My aim is not to push you towards moral perfection, but to offer a user-friendly means for getting as much love as possible while getting as much of your own way as possible. This is a skill worth having because this is the way to be happy.

It may not be simple coincidence that the principles of *An Intelligent Life* are also the style of behaviour generally regarded as ethical by a civilised society. From an evolutionary perspective, cooperative behaviour amongst individual members of a group is the best strategy for individual survival.

If you are willing to consider my proposition that the evolutionary background to self-esteem and happiness is being a loved and potent individual within your tribe, we can take the understanding further. We have all evolved from the same line of apes and our daily lives are still shaped by the forces of evolution that selected our ancestors for survival. We can each paddle our own canoe, but we are all carried along by the same stream. Fifty percent of our genetic material is the same as a banana, and more than 98 percent identical to a bonobo chimpanzee. If we are so close to such apparently different organisms, it stands to reason that you and I have exactly the same physical and emotional needs as every other member of our species and, originally, to every other mammal. Our individual differences are tiny ripples on the surface of a great river of similarity. What you feel, I feel. The strength, timing and expression of our feelings may differ, but our passions and vulnerabilities are the same.

Thus other people's emotional needs are easy to understand because they are the same as yours and our greatest similarity is our need to love and be loved, which has an enormous effect on our ability to live together.

A web of need

Essentially, everybody wants to like everybody else.

Belonging, liking and love are the forces that hold people together. We feel safer in a group, just as our ancestors felt safer in their herd. Love and belonging form the network that holds a group together.

If I like you and John likes me and I know Susie likes you, then Susie will probably like me and John will like you. This means we have a solidarity and our sense of belonging to each other means we will tend to stay together and defend one another, because in doing so we are protecting ourselves. This is the function of a tribe.

Self-interest motivates everybody to want to like everybody else – and that will include you, if you will let them. People love to give love because it makes them feel good. Pets are a perfect example. What possible gain is there for you to rub your dog's tummy? You collect several squillion bacteria and his breath stinks, but you enjoy patting him and telling him he is a good boy. You gain the peace and satisfaction that comes from any behaviour that strengthens emotional bonds.

Giving love makes you feel good because it satisfies a basic evolutionary need for the safety of strengthened belonging. Giving love does you good, calming you and reducing feelings of tension.

Sometimes it's easier to show love to a dog than to your human partner because your dog's acceptance and gratitude for your love is guaranteed. This is the other side of our love of love. We are almost as afraid of rejection as we are needy of love, because rejection once meant death.

Our fear of rejection is central to at least half of our emotional difficulties; the other half I would obviously argue is a fear of belittlement and loss of territory. *It is biologically impossible not to fear rejection, but it is crucial to learn to understand and manage the way you behave in the face of your fear; to reduce, even if you can never remove, the risk that it will happen to you.*

Fortunately, the normal human need to love and be loved means healthy, empathic people prefer to be kind if they can. To reject someone makes most people feel almost as uncomfortable as being rejected themselves. Out of self-interest people try not to reject other people and would rather say 'yes' than 'no'. Everybody wants love, and everybody feels better if they give it.

Reading this, you might think of Auschwitz or the killing fields of Pol Pot. You may be distinctly aware that neither your selfish next-door neighbour nor your ex-boyfriend fills you with thoughts of love. In answer, your neighbour and your one-time boyfriend may have allowed territorial selfishness, that is excessive individual expression, to override their natural preference to be loving. They have paid a price in losing your love, even if they don't seem as concerned about that as they probably should be.

Fear, alienation, anonymity and cultural non-conformity spawn aggression and violence in a thug. Some of the horror springs from direct territorial conflict, but most comes from the primitive urge to attack those who don't belong to your herd. Acting in a mob we are at our very worst, especially when we give our group a name and an identity, wear funny hats and hold torchlight processions. In a mob we can lose some of our individual natures. Discovery of an enemy or a difference can liberate the most hideous behaviour in apparently healthy individuals who have sacrificed their individual identities and integrity in the interests of belonging to the herd.

Despite your neighbour and the Nazis, put two healthy, happy human beings together and each wants to like the other, because each wants to be liked. This means we should feel quite secure with other people of our own culture, but obviously we don't do it automatically.

If your self-esteem is poor you will probably judge others as seeing you as negatively as you see yourself. You know you wouldn't hold a person like you in much esteem either, although, as an aside, it's a fair bet you wouldn't be as rejecting of him as you fear he would be of you.

You may start off being perfectly acceptable to other people, but a poor self-esteem can push you to actions that reinforce the feeling. If you feel bad about yourself, unless you know and play by the rules of an intelligent life, you are in danger of behaving in an insecure and defensive way that is unattractive enough to invite rejection. It's possible to make a reality of what was initially a misplaced fear of rejection or belittlement.

The dilemma of life lies in the conflict between your naturally selfish desire to have as much territory as possible and the equally natural desire to love and be loved. If you're too afraid of losing love you'll never feel safe enough to ask for something for yourself, and you'll feel anxious or guilty if you get your own way. If you pursue your own way excessively you'll be seen as selfish and no one will like you, increasing the chance you'll behave aggressively. The solution to this dilemma is finding a balance between these two apparently incompatible needs. Do it skilfully and you have the full sundae of self-esteem.

The importance of space

To be lovable to yourself and others you need to be generous, caring and supportive, and do so with dignity and without compromise of your individuality. This means respecting other people's physical and emotional territory as best you can, while clearly and firmly defining yourself and your needs as a person. Because not everybody will play by the same rules, there will be times when you may be forced to tread deliberately, although as gently as possible, on trespassing toes. This is another way of saying there will be times when you've got to mark out your patch very firmly or you would feel utterly compromised if you didn't.

This is much simpler than it sounds. It starts with a little self-knowledge, which allows you to clearly define the territory of who you are.

Your principles and values define you more clearly than anything else. The closest you will ever come to knowing yourself is to know your own values. The things you care for most passionately will tell you most about who and what you are.

Your ethics and morality are called spiritual values and they maintain your sense of being a whole person. Your values are your individual emotional or spiritual territory and, like all territory, there is a natural tendency to defend it and hold on to it.

If you have no ethical values, or you have them but don't care to protect them, you won't have a problem. Then you have no integrity to preserve, but you will have very little sense of individuality. There is no law that says your values have to have social or aesthetic value – they can be as attractive as Mussolini's, but they are still the territory of yourself.

If you are willing to live with the concept that your moral philosophy defines you, you may appear to have a wide range of beliefs and therefore a lot to defend. In practice, the issues you hold to be truths can be simply divided into *core values* and *peripheral values*.

You have a small inner sanctum of ideals that is the heart of your spiritual existence. Outside that, and potentially distinct from it, is a broad band of values that is still a part of you, but less essential.

You probably haven't many core values. You might love your children and family beyond all else; you might wish to never knowingly hurt another living creature, particularly a fellow human being, and perhaps you would object violently to wrecking the planet, but beyond these, you might well feel there isn't much worth getting really worked up about.

If you stick rigidly and stubbornly to your core values, while being more flexible with your peripheral ones, you can preserve your individuality with dignity, earn very little disapproval and possibly be well liked, at least by those whose liking you would want. This is the behaviour of a person with high self-esteem.

Core values need defending to the death. Peripheral values can be compromised or bypassed.

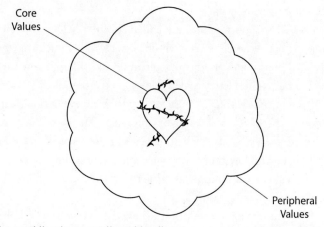

Your spiritual or emotional territory

When the only space left in the car park is reserved for the disabled, it's probably not just your fear of being caught that stops you taking it. You may be late and desperate for somewhere to park, but the violation of your core values would simply be too great. If you see someone parking his car in the same spot, his self-esteem is probably just fine because his ethics don't extend so far. Your values matter, so you couldn't have parked there.

By contrast, you might find yourself talking to someone who mercilessly mangles the English language. You may be offended by his grammar, but if you correct another adult you may be belittling him. If you can recognise your distaste for bad grammar is a peripheral value and your wish not to hurt is a core value, then you will have no problem deciding what to do.

Make a clear distinction between core and peripheral values and it's much easier to get your priorities right in judging how to respond to other people. It also allows you not to be oversensitive and take too personally the things people do to you.

A high level of self-respect allows you to change your mind or abandon an argument because you can judge what's essential to your individual dignity and what's not. In addition, by choosing to defend a smaller perimeter, you reduce the area into which someone can deliberately trespass or accidentally stumble. This in turn puts you in a good position to avoid aggression because you are very much less likely to attack or to feel attacked.

If you like yourself, you will be a happy person and have few conflicts with other people. You don't need to make a stand very often, because knowing the difference between core and peripheral values frees you to give in; you can lose without loss. As a happy person you don't need to fight to protect every difference, even if you would fight to the death over your core values.

Ideas

- You will never be truly independent of other people because care of yourself is care of your relationships. If people do not like you, you will not be as happy as if they do.

- The basic physical and emotional needs of every human being are the same. We all want the same things, although their form may differ.

- Everybody wants to like everybody else, for healthy, self-interested reasons, programmed by survival of the fittest. Love in its various manifestations is the force that holds people together, so we feel safer in a group, just as our ancestors felt safer in their herd.

- People love to give love because it makes them feel good.

- Healthy people hate to hurt because it makes them feel bad.

- Everybody is afraid of rejection, but happy people don't expect it.

- The dilemma of life lies in the conflict between wanting your own way, but wanting to be liked at the same time.

- Your principles and values – the things you hold to be good, holy and right – define you more clearly than anything else. They are the territory of your spirit.

- If you give away your core values, you cease to exist. If your sense of existence is vulnerable, you may be tempted to defend your peripheral values as if they were core values, but you will fight many pointless battles.

CHAPTER 5

✧

Feeling Bad

YOU ARE THE CENTRE OF YOUR UNIVERSE. Your feelings may be facts to you, but the rest of the world can sometimes see things very differently. When there's a big difference between your truth and the truth as other people see it, you can feel really bad. Feeling misunderstood feels like being belittled and rejected. It makes us feel anxious, angry and sad.

If you intend to live most happily, you need to understand how you think and feel, so it makes sense to have another brief look at the evolution and biology of human emotions.

Emotions are the flavour of experience and perception. Facts draw outlines and then emotions colour them in. No sensation gets into your consciousness without the addition of emotional hues. Although some events are more highly coloured than others, all facts are tinted, and some tainted – at times to the point of being unrecognisable. Objectivity in its true sense, that is observation without bias from emotion, just doesn't happen.

Roughly speaking, the frontal lobes of your brain manage the rational judgements of an adult human being. This is the part of your brain that allows you to have conversations with yourself. When your frontal lobes are not overwhelmed by disease, drugs, alcohol or emotion, they allow you to make subtle emotional and empathic decisions in your interaction with other people. Your frontal lobes know that emotional problems are better solved by waiting, assessing, negotiating; by kindly and dignified action.

There is another part of your brain which is a very close copy of the same region in the brains of other apes – presumably your ancestors of millions of years ago. This ancestral brain is called your limbic system, and sits deep in the substance of your cerebrum. I refer to this as your 'survival brain', because it carries the emotions of life and death, programmed by survival of the fittest in the jungle or on the savannah.

Your frontal lobes are perfectly capable of recognising that smashing, screaming or running away are not wise responses to an emotional threat, but sometimes knowing this is not enough. Your survival brain has no words; it deals in feelings. When you perceive danger – real or imagined – your survival brain has the potential to force its messages of fear, anger or despair into your consciousness, overwhelming the rational, adult judgement of your frontal cortex.

The wordless demands of survival are what we call emotions, and they once drove behaviour essential to staying alive. Because survival demanded an instant response, emotions can override judgement. Your survival brain fires from the hip, and is much less concerned with peace and happiness than it is with managing danger.

I'm not forgetting there are positive emotions as well, but they're hardly a problem. Positive emotions make us happy. Pride, passion, lust, respect, self-confidence, gratitude, amusement, hope and determination also grow from mixtures, in varying proportions, of our love, needs and our territoriality. When people and the beauty of the world make you feel good, just enjoy it and don't ask questions. *Good news looks after itself.* Sadly, you have no chance of a life free from negative emotions. You will very likely experience events that are so unpleasant you'd be unusual if you didn't feel terrible. As we've seen, you can choose clever or dumb ways of reacting to problems: if you apply the concepts of an intelligent life, you control the bits of your world that are controllable and then the uncontrollable bits don't hurt quite so much. By definition you can't make your own luck, but you can have a damn good try. It's simply that bad news needs more attention.

Logic from the front often loses to passion from below.

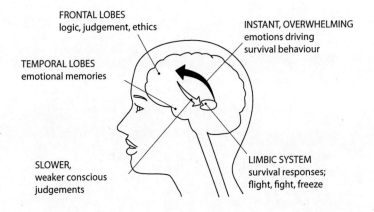

There are feelings associated with our fear of physical injury or death, or our desire for food, water, shelter or sex, but beyond the emotions of our obviously physical needs, every other emotion relates to our need for belonging and our need for territory. If you are willing to consider this as true, it's not a great leap of logic to see that every negative emotion springs from our fear of rejection and weakness.

Negative feelings have three basic divisions:

1. fear
2. anger
3. sadness

These three divisions obviously spring from the three basic responses to threat:

1. flight

2. fight

3. freeze

Whether you run away, stand and fight, or freeze and go to ground depends on your species, your judgement of the magnitude of the threat, past experience and the genetic programming of your temperament.

There are lots of labels for negative emotions, but they all belong to one of these three groups:

1. fear, anxiety, nervousness, concern, worry, terror and panic

2. anger, irritation, frustration, antagonism, rage and aggression

3. sadness, disappointment, despondency, grief, gloom, despair and depression

Other negatives are a mix of two or more of these primary negative emotions. Guilt is fairly obviously an amalgam of anxiety and anger; shame has the addition of more sadness. Depression, grief, despair and disappointment are labels for different levels of sadness, with variable mixes of anger and anxiety.

Some feelings can be a mixture of positive and negative. Anger and anxiety aren't inevitably negative; righteous anger gives purpose and direction.

Some people, in fact a lot of people, look for the stimulation of fear. They talk about an adrenalin rush and ride roller-coasters or jump out of aeroplanes in order to achieve it. If you think about it, the feelings in your body when you are sexually aroused are not very different from the early stages of anxious arousal.

Both fear and anger evolved to activate an individual in its own defence – to fight or run – but if the action they motivate doesn't effectively escape, control or remove a threat, an angry or frightened creature becomes exhausted and disorganised. If nothing works, eventually determination, motivation and hope melt away, leaving only frozen despair. At some point, in some individuals, this can evolve into depression, which is a system failure, leads nowhere and can never be positive.

Hope itself, a positive emotion, contains elements of anxiety and even a background of sadness. You only need hope when there is danger of loss.

Anxiety (flight)

Anxiety is the primary emotion of survival. It's Nature's early-warning system. The sensations of anxious arousal in your body are the first stage of a system of self-protection. Your survival brain sends messages of such intense discomfort that you would do almost anything to escape from them. Evolutionary necessity doesn't allow you to simply turn down the volume of your anxiety at will; anxiety has evolved to be so horrible that you run away from the emotion before you meet the tiger. Once he has his teeth into you, you might just as well relax and let life flash before your eyes.

You have to escape the situation that provokes the feeling. For your ancestors trying to survive on the savannah, it was easy to know what to do, although not always so easy to do it, but once they knew the threat had passed, they could relax. It's easier to stay alive now, but our survival brains don't let us off the hook. We can still feel we are in danger even when there aren't any tigers around, couldn't possibly be and never have been.

Imagine being a person with a sense of low personal worth – either because your genetic programming handed you the feeling, or because your parents didn't give you enough love, or both. You will automatically have a high level of anxiety because you have to live with a constant expectation of rejection or belittlement. The actual truth of how others see you is less important than your perception, because your identity is defined by your truth about yourself, not necessarily by commonly accepted reality. The more anxious you are, the more likely you are to read minds according to your own negative text, and not according to the rules for an intelligent life.

You don't have to be defective, you just need to think you are. Once you are gripped by the paranoia of low self-esteem, it's painfully easy to detect other people's negative judgement.

If there is no hungry tiger around to make sense of why you feel anxious, you'll start to feel anxious about being anxious. You only make it worse if you believe you shouldn't care what other people think. You become anxious that your anxiety will show and make you look different and deficient. This is the feedback loop of anxiety: you become anxious in case others see how anxious you are, which increases the chance that you will look anxious, because you are convinced that strong, worthwhile, lovable people shouldn't be anxious.

To your survival brain (or the limbic system of your paleocortex, if you like a more scientific sounding name), there is no semantic quibble between anxiety and fear; they are the same. The feeling in your stomach when faced with a tiger is remarkably close to the feeling you get when you are going to speak to a large audience, are working up the courage to approach a sexually attractive person, or are waiting backstage and wondering if you'll forget your lines. If you have to make a presentation at a conference or a meeting it's very hard to relax until you've done your bit.

Anxiety can be a good thing. It can make us reluctant to disappoint people and motivate us to be civilised and considerate towards each other. Provided we manage it skilfully, the anxiety that comes of self-doubt makes us try harder, makes us nicer people and strengthens our relationships with other people.

At low levels of arousal, anxiety is alerting and motivating. At higher levels it can enhance performance, literally making us sit up and take notice. But as arousal increases to the point at which we label it anxiety, it becomes painful and ultimately sabotages performance. The most common experience of this is in a person whose self-esteem is vulnerable and so believes he must do brilliantly just to be good enough. This is how first-class students fail simple exams.

Anxiety makes us try harder, but it can trip us as well.

Anger (fight)

Anger is the original motivator: it makes the weak powerful. Anger is usually the first response to a territorial threat, which might be to the physical territory of your own space, or the spiritual territory of your beliefs and philosophy. It may not be the only emotion, the predominant emotion, or even recognised at all, but it will always be there if you sense belittlement or trespass.

Anger is easier to understand if you make a distinction between anger, aggression and violence.

Anger is the inner feeling. The emotion has to come first to drive action.

Aggression is threatening behaviour designed to scare an intruder away from your territory. If you can protect your hunting or mating grounds without fighting, you are ahead of the creature that has to fight because even the winner of a fight can get hurt.

Violence is actual physical attack.

If your territory is under threat, there's a natural progression from the inner feeling of anger, through aggressive signalling and then to violent attack. This all made perfectly good sense in the process of the fittest surviving, but it's different in civilised life. There is no rule to say you can't be angry, but if you signal it with aggression or violence rather than intelligent assertion, you're telling the world you feel weak and vulnerable. Aggression and violence in any form will eventually earn you rejection, so you will always lose.

Territory is not just your physical or moral patch; mating gets caught up in territoriality because mating is not only about love. It's too easy to see your lover as your territory and then become aggressively protective. The territoriality of sex and reproduction can lead to the jealous control that destroys loving relationships.

Anger can also be provoked by rejection. It's easy to understand why, if you can accept that rejection once meant certain death and still feels like it just a few million years later.

If your boyfriend is clearly interested in your best friend, as far as your survival brain is concerned rejection is rejection. Whether it is from a parent or a partner, your life is in danger if you are rejected. In the light of this primitive truth, attacking makes good sense; you are trying to stop something that could kill you. If you feel small like a child and so have a child-like need of your partner, you will be even more prone to terrified anger and aggression.

Anger is not all bad. Healthy anger gives you the strength and motivation to deal with threats of moral or physical encroachment, and obviously there will be times when you must be angry. *There are also rare occasions when aggression or physical violence is necessary and justified, but it will always be in response to situations of physical danger and never, ever when the threat is emotional. Throw something, and your validity goes with it.*

Anger may not be great as a feeling, but it beats the vulnerability of anxiety and the helplessness of despair. Anger at least makes you stand up straight. Being aggressive can give you the illusion of power, or even dignity, while anxiety or despair only seems to offer weakness and ignominy. Because of this, people often try to avoid their sadness or anxiety by getting angry, so we see irritability in someone struggling with depression, or fear and aggression in someone trying to avoid feeling guilt.

The Three Negative Emotions Come in a Pie

The same total volume of negative emotion can be altered in its proportions by choosing the size of the pie slice. Some people deliberately choose the brief power of anger in a struggle in order to reduce the emotions of anxiety and despair, which make them feel so much more vulnerable.

At lower levels, the emotion that can grow to anger is experienced more as an increased energy to fuel competition, which always symbolises territoriality and a healthy, normal desire to be in control. We all want things to go our way, but fortunately the need to be loved and accepted stops most of us from being too aggressively competitive.

One of the nice things about being a human ape is that it is not necessary to be the biggest to do well or even to win. In contrast to other animals which are obliged to compete for the same patch and partners, an individual human has the potential to hold his own bit of territory and also have a sexual partner, even if he isn't the biggest, the best and brightest. Other animals may have no option but to establish power through aggression or violence, so there can only be one winner; the rest must be unhappy losers.

Once equality becomes an option, as it does amongst humans, it is possible to be content with your status, even if you aren't a winner. Aggression and violence thus become even more unnecessary.

Sadness and depression (freeze)

If the danger seems too great to possibly escape from, if fear can't make you run fast enough, or if anger hasn't made you strong enough to fight, eventually you will give up. Some animals freeze as a first line of defence, paralysed by fear. Sadness and despair are a sense of helplessness in response to outside forces over which you have found, or you believe, you have no control.

Depression has a different flavour and is more than sadness. Depression is an inner loss, when self-love has evaporated and there's a feeling that it can never be restored. Depression eats you from the inside because it is more than losing something external.

Sadness, despair and depression can all be provoked by loss, which may be love lost through rejection or death, or a loss of power and dignity; perhaps a collapsing business, or failing an exam. These examples represent the loss of a piece of yourself, but depression then goes further; it is a feeling that you personally have been irreversibly reduced and with your loss, you have lost your worth.

Depression is a loss of self-esteem or self-love. It can obviously be triggered by external events, but it differs from sadness, which is much more able to acknowledge a potential for resolution with time. Depression is timeless because its presence is determined by the very act of living, which some depressed people choose not to do. Sadness feeds on the death of something outside you and so ultimately decays and disappears, but depression lives on malevolently while you do. Depression ulcerates your spirit, while sadness is emptiness, but with a chance of being filled again.

It's possible to feel depressed even when everything is fine around you, or it can happen after events that don't seem serious enough to explain why you keep on feeling so bad for so long. If friends, lovers and family can't comfort you, you may have the disease of depression, which will need medical treatment.

If you feel more or less continuously down and this is not your usual character, or your self-esteem has fallen but you can remember once you thought yourself to be a reasonable human being, you may have a biological depressive disorder. You may feel you have a very good reason to be depressed, and you may be right, but just because you have a good reason to be despondent it doesn't mean that events haven't pushed you beyond sadness.

In the disease of depression you have a biochemical deficiency in the connections between your frontal lobes and your survival brain. You have an under-supply of neurotransmitters, which are chemicals essential for the passage of electrical messages from one nerve cell to another. The best-known neurotransmitter is serotonin. Depression can be triggered in almost anybody exposed to too much pain for too long, so perhaps some people just burn out earlier. Whatever is happening, although no one yet knows how or why, when you run out of serotonin, you run out of self-love.

You can have a milder form of the illness, too, in which other people's kindness and love can top you up, liberating you to forget yourself and feel good, at least for a while. In a more severe variant of depression nothing can lift your spirit, nobody can fill the empty worthlessness you feel, and it is hard to feel love for anybody or from anybody. In this situation there's a danger that your melancholic disease could be fatal.

You might feel terrible and start to wake in the middle of the night, then have trouble getting off again. You might feel agitated and lose your appetite for food and sex. You may lose weight, energy and motivation, so nothing much feels worthwhile. Depression means you can't be bothered, or can't find sufficient self-confidence to do something that should make you feel better, and you probably wouldn't be able to concentrate or remember properly what to do anyway. Or you might feel too tired and apathetic to be agitated – sleeping twelve hours a day and developing a huge appetite for all the wrong foods.

If you are a woman, you are very likely to have, or have had in the past, serious pre-menstrual tension. If you have been miserable and irritable for ages, you might realise it has been since one of your babies was born, even though you felt fine during the pregnancy and now have everything to live for. If the only reason you haven't killed yourself is that your children need you, there is real help available.

If these awful things are happening to you this book might be helpful, but it probably won't be enough. Helpful as they can be, you may need more than an understanding of the principles of living set out in *An Intelligent Life*, or the dozen other books you may have read, or all the herbs, vitamins, exercises and natural therapies you have tried.

Just because you feel you ought to be able to control your feelings doesn't mean you can. In fact, if you are the sort of person who feels you should be self-reliant and does not habitually blame others for your misery, you are all the more likely to have an illness that you can't fix by willpower or understanding alone.

If a psychoanalyst wants to lie you on a couch and tell you how much you hated your mother, look for another opinion. We all have things in our past that we can feel horrible about, but it doesn't mean that they are the cause of your depression. Do yourself and everyone around you a favour, see a doctor and ask about antidepressant medication. There is a good chance that medication could make you feel vastly better, even after years of being down.

Antidepressant medication cannot and does not change you as a person. Illegal drugs can make you happy any time, but antidepressants cannot make you happy when you should be sad. All that medical treatment of a depressive illness can do is liberate you to be as miserable as you should be in the circumstances. Medication can't and won't alter your personality or distort your perception of reality, but it can give you a clearer view of the facts. You could find that the weeping, helpless outsider you have become and whom you dislike so much might start to turn into someone you recognise again; someone who can actually do something about the things you don't like in your life.

If you have the disease of depression, antidepressant medication can save your spirit and even your life, but it is possible for your sense of despair to be a result of mishandling your relationships and not, or at least only minimally, the biochemical abnormality of depression. If this is the case, you have some hard work ahead of you, and unfortunately antidepressant medication might just give side effects and no benefits. Your job is hard, and this book is designed to help you, but please don't forget that you are probably the least suitable person to make your own diagnosis, so look for professional, medical advice.

Ultimately, whether you are depressed as a result of overwhelming stress, depressed because of a specific biochemical disease, or depressed, anxious and angry because you are not handling your life and relationships as intelligently as you might, you must always be aware of the two basics of emotional survival. With or without medication, you must learn to live in a fashion that secures both love and dignity, because without them, there is no escape from sadness.

Ideas

- There are only three options in the face of threat; flight, fight or freeze.

- Anxiety is the primary emotion of survival. It is nature's early-warning system.

- Anxiety has evolved to be so horrible that you run away from the emotion before you meet the danger.

- A poor sense of self-worth guarantees feelings of anxiety.

- Once you are gripped by the paranoia of low self-esteem it's just too easy to detect other people's critical judgement.

- For most anxious people, the fact that they are anxious is the only real evidence they can find that there is something wrong with them.

- Anger is usually the first response to a territorial threat, which might involve the physical territory of your back garden or the spiritual territory of your beliefs and philosophy.

- Anger can also be provoked by rejection, because rejection once meant certain death and can still feel like it. You naturally get angry with someone who's doing something that will kill you.

- There is no reason to believe a normal human being, or any other creature, wants to be violent. We do not have a primary drive to be angry just for anger's sake, as if there were an in-built badness.

- People sometimes use anger to override fear or despair, because anger feels better.

- Sadness and despair are a sense of helplessness in response to outside forces. Depression is an inner loss, when self-love has evaporated and left a feeling that it can never be restored.

- Antidepressant medication cannot change you as a person, but it can let you be the real you instead of the diminished creature that depression makes you. All that medical treatment can do is liberate you to be as miserable as you should be in the circumstances.

჻

CHAPTER 6

Unhappiness Is a Poor Self-Esteem

YOUR RELATIONSHIP WITH YOURSELF can't be separated from your relationship with other people.

A sense of low self-worth always means you believe, or at least half-believe, that other people don't value you either. If you have this feeling, you are more likely to feel anxious, angry or sad than somebody who believes he or she is worthwhile.

Some people don't actually realise, or more accurately don't allow themselves to realise, that they are struggling with a poor self-esteem. They know they are often hurt, but they're convinced people are insensitive and don't care about anybody else. They know they always seem to be having fights and that other people never admit they are wrong and never apologise. They see everybody as being quick to blame them, criticise and exclude, but slow to forgive or welcome. They know everything about everybody, but miss the point when it comes to looking at themselves.

It is really important to recognise a simple and basic truth. *A person who is nasty to you – who is arrogant, distant without reason or is angry at a level much greater than you deserve – always, absolutely always, dislikes himself.* He doesn't dare recognise his own self-dislike; instead, he thinks he sees it in your eyes and then responds to you the way he sees you, not the way you are.

Your behaviour in relationships is the making or breaking of your self-esteem. If you don't value yourself, you will become oversensitive or defensive. This means you will see rejection or belittlement either when it was not meant at all, or as being much bigger and more serious than it was meant to be. In short, if your self-esteem is poor, you are in danger of seeing and reacting to any possible negative assessment as if it were lethal.

Don't forget, rejection once meant death to your ancestors and still feels like death to your survival brain. An oversensitive person gets into a mess because he senses danger without adequate reason. Perceiving rejection or put-down, his survival brain has pushed him into acting with an urgency that would be fine for staying alive in the jungle, but is much more forceful than necessary in a civilised world.

A touchy, vulnerable person gets anxious too soon, angry too easily, or slips into despair without sufficient cause. He may become arrogant or clingy, trying to cope with his anxiety, or his anger might push him to act in a resentful, prickly or openly aggressive way. If his defensive behaviour doesn't change things, he will become distant, passive or totally helpless, as he freezes into the immobility of despair.

Action and reaction then feed each other in a growing personal disaster. He may have completely misunderstood a situation, but *nobody acts irrationally according to his own truth.* To him, his reactions make perfect sense, but unfortunately other people see things differently and don't understand or don't like the way he is behaving. They see him as needy, bad-tempered or lazy and respond accordingly. This then confirms his view that other people don't like him, which either deepens his own self-dislike, if he recognises it, or makes him angrier and more defensive if he doesn't.

As a sane person, his understanding of a situation should have been much the same as that of anybody else, but primitive emotions of survival have overwhelmed his logic. As a result, his fear and his anger have taken over his behaviour and he then behaves in a way that sets him up to make a reality of the rejection or put-downs he misperceived earlier.

Behaviour can turn feelings into facts either way, but unfortunately it is much quicker and easier to cause damage than it is to repair it, even if people do prefer to like and forgive.

Fortunately, you don't have to be perfect to be loved or to love yourself. There is plenty of room for manoeuvre and a lifetime of mistakes and bad memories doesn't have to destroy your self-respect, but somewhere there is a limit. Too much mismanagement of your relationships, especially if you don't understand why, can pull you down. To make matters worse, it's possible to be vulnerable to self-doubt even before you start, either because of a genetic programming in temperament to be oversensitive to rejection, or if your family background didn't offer you enough love to build the foundations of automatic self-love.

Whether it's our DNA, our family or our own misjudgement, we all carry emotional baggage. The people we've hurt, the utter fools we've made of ourselves, our insensitive and sometimes self-destructive acts – most of these awful memories could have been avoided if we'd understood a few simple rules. Hopefully, the good outweighs the bad, but there are moments most of us would be very pleased to rearrange, and there's a lot we wish we'd known a long time ago. Unfortunately, these are wishes that will never come true.

The things you've done and the things that have been done to you are an unchangeable reality. To make them worse, bad memories have a habit of being clearer, sharper and more intrusive than good memories, and the more painful they are, the more real and immediate they can feel. Fortunately, these are feelings, not facts.

Bad feelings, like bad memories, tend to take up more time and need more work than happy ones. It's not always clever to try denying the bad, the sad, the angry and the anxious with blindly positive thinking or glowing self-affirmations that you struggle to believe yourself. Intelligent living means acknowledging the negative so as to manage it better.

You don't need to be making a mess of your life to have regrets. They can be large or small, justified or unjustified, but if you are willing to give the ideas in this book a try, the very least you can hope is to avoid adding to the collection. Do so consistently and with a little daring and you will probably be very happy, even if you're not particularly clever, beautiful or rich and there are one or two bits of your past you'd prefer had never happened.

You need to begin by accepting there are some things that will never be right. Cruelty, neglect or bad luck leave marks in your brain, especially if they happen when you are young. Some of these scars will endure. You can blame them and you might be totally justified, but being right about it not being your fault isn't enough. A satisfying explanation can certainly help you feel better, but you will still need to draw a line under what has happened and attend to the present.

There is no need for pain from your past to be much more than a memory. It only becomes a solid reality if you let it control the way you behave in the present. *The way you feel today is far more influenced by the way you handle the present than by what happened in your past.*

This is an instruction manual for the present and the rules apply whatever problems, pains or regrets you may have. Even if your life has been just fine, the principles of *A Model for Living* are worth knowing because the way we have evolved has made us clever and adaptable, but left us emotionally vulnerable. We often don't need much of a reason to be unhappy.

Ideas

- Your relationship with yourself is inseparable from your relationship with other people, and your management of your relationships makes or breaks your self-respect.

- Some people don't actually realise they are struggling with a poor self-esteem. They adopt the role of a victim and a victim is safe because he's not responsible.

- Someone who treats you badly without reason is always a person who dislikes himself.

- Nobody acts irrationally according to his own truth.

- Bad luck, bad treatment or bad genes may truly be the origin of unhappiness, but they do not have to be the final deciders.

- The way you feel today is far more influenced by the way you handle the present than by what happened in your past.

- Feeling bad and feeling bad about yourself are not the same.

- Mishandling your relationships is the most certain path to self-dislike.

PART 2

Mostly Practice

*A Series of Practical Steps towards Assertiveness
and Self-Respect*

CHAPTER 7

ک

Happiness Is a Good Self-Esteem

A SELF-RESPECTING PERSON likes himself, but it is visible in openness, not confident certainty. He knows he'll feel bad if he's rejected, but he also knows the world won't end if that happens. He wants approval and feedback, but he isn't desperate, doesn't look desperate and doesn't make other people responsible for his happiness. He makes it clear he wants to give love to those whom he sees as lovable, and that he would like love from them, but not as payment or obligation. Much as he wants love, he won't compromise his dignity or his principles to get it. He behaves like a person who doesn't expect to be rejected; on the contrary, he looks as if he believes he'll be liked and respected.

If the attitude of a self-respecting person towards another were put in words, it would go roughly as follows: 'I like myself well enough and I think you will like me. I hope I shall like you and I'll make every effort to do so, unless I find your ethics are just too different from mine. If you don't like me, I'll be distressed and I'll do my best to get you to like me, but not if I have to violate my own morality or dignity to avoid upsetting you. If ultimately you do not like me, I'll be unhappy, but I shall not be angry and I'll certainly survive.'

When your self-respect is high, many things about you become automatic and obvious. Here are some of the most obvious characteristics of self-respect:

- You have a strong, clear and distinct individuality and you feel approved, accepted and even loved for your differences.

- You feel like an adult amongst adults and treat others as equals.

- You take responsibility for yourself; being pleased when the world treats you well and sad when it doesn't.

- You live your life in hope, not expectation.

- You want to win and you try very hard, but you don't invest all your worth in winning.

- You know love and individuality are vital to your wellbeing, but you know that ultimately love is more important than getting your own way.

This level of comfort doesn't always come easily, and even as a person with a high level of self-respect, you frequently need to recruit the Gang of Three. You never forget that your thoughts and your behaviour are under your direct control, even if your feelings are not. To manage your feelings, you use your knowledge of human emotion to behave in a way that is designed to win the approval of other people – including your Observing Self, who is really you judging yourself as if you were another person. Your thoughts, actions and favourable reactions of others can generally pull your feelings into line.

You have to start with thoughts based on your knowledge of human emotional reactions, so a dialogue in your head in difficult situations might go roughly like this:

'The way to manage my feelings is through action. If I wait until I feel good before I start to act as if I like myself, I'll wait for ever. So ...'

'It doesn't matter what I'm feeling at the moment, it's what I do in response to my feelings that plays the biggest role in the emotional outcome. So ...'

'I must try to consistently play the role of a kind and dignified person because ...'

'Kindness and dignity are the final deciders of human worth. Therefore ...'

'Other people will like me more and ...'

'If other people like me, I am in a much better position to like myself. So ...'

'Although I want to get my own way as often as possible, I've got to balance my individualistic desires against my need to be loved. So ....'

'I'm always going to try really hard to win and do well, because it's a lot easier to be happy if I succeed. But ...'

'I don't have to win, because not winning isn't the same as losing. All I need to be is equal. So ...'

'I don't have to be perfect to be liked. So ...'

'I've got room to move, make mistakes and still like myself.'

Thinking about yourself and your relationships in this way leads very naturally to the behaviour of self-respect:

- Behave as the person you would like to be and to be seen to be.
- Behave like a person who likes himself.
- Act with kindness and dignity as often as you can.

- Treat everyone you meet as worthy, equal adults.

- If in doubt, administer love.

- Follow the golden rule for building and preserving your self-esteem: *always treat other people as if you believe they like you.*

The rest of this book is devoted to the fine tuning of these simple rules.

CHAPTER 8

٣

The Balance of Assertiveness

THERE IS NO DOUBT THAT PEOPLE would prefer to like each other, but life is not quite as easy as this. Love may be the best thing around, but being nice is not enough. People won't value you as an equal if you are constantly warm and giving but won't take anything for yourself and can't say 'no'.

Once, staying alive meant having the physical strength to hold your own territory. Now, emotional survival and happiness depend not only on secure belonging, but still require you to have the skills to mark out and defend the territory of your opinions, ethics and rights.

Because not everybody is skilled at managing their sundae of self-esteem, you will occasionally meet people who don't seem to realise it is not in their long-term interests to be selfish. These people may appear to have forgotten, or perhaps have never known, that they would prefer to be lovable, and they will sometimes try to trespass on or even take over your territory in a most unattractive way.

In a world of imperfect people, to survive the psychopathically selfish you need either legal protection or somewhere to run. To live with the rest of humanity, because everybody is competitive to some degree, you will still need techniques for skilful arguing and you will always need the ability to assert yourself, even with the kindest and most self-respecting people.

If you have no ability to stand up for yourself, or you can't do so without aggression, neither you nor anybody else will value you.

Assertive skills and effective arguing are the next step in *An Intelligent Life*, but you must never lose sight of the fact that ultimately love is more valuable than power.

Competition between equals

To feel good about yourself, you need to feel you have a presence in the world. You need a sense of place, of some influence and a belief that you have a degree of control over the events of your life. Inevitably, you will want some influence within your relationships, but fortunately you also have a need for approval, which usually lays a civilising hand on a desire for too much power and control over other people.

To be happy, you need to feel you have some ability to secure and even to enlarge your territory, and still be liked while you do it.

Trying to control and change other people is risky, whether in an intimate relationship or not. We all try to do it, and the need to feel some power with others is not shameful. However, there is a great difference between gentle competition at one end of the spectrum and absolute domination at the other. *Healthy people want power with people, not over them.*

If you are going to jockey for position in a civilised and therefore likeable way, you should appreciate your power is limited and you should never expect or try for total control. Real power is only what others allow you because they see you as having earned it, rather than something you've taken by force. The best use of power is to remain equal, not to dominate.

A relationship between two people is like two balloons being blown up in a box. The faster and harder one is expanding, the less room there is for the other one. Once one person takes the initiative and his power expands, the other has the potential to be diminished by being pushed into a corner.

A person who is feeling squashed and put down but has no system for healthy assertion to protect her own space has only three choices. She can:

1. Withdraw and leave the box.
2. Accept a deflated role.
3. Needle the other to deflate him.

We have all developed techniques that are variously successful at influencing people, allowing us to either take just a little more territory or prevent being trespassed upon ourselves. These methods are based on either giving or withdrawing love, or conceding or grabbing for territory. They are designed, in our own minds at least, to serve our own interests. If we do it well, that is we are able to balance our needs for love against our wish for power, the world seems a safe and manageable place. If we fail, we feel insecure, diminished and threatened, and we are in danger of becoming either anxious, angry or sad.

Winners can be losers

When people don't get their own way there's always a risk of aggression because not all that many people are totally satisfied with their lot; most want a bit more, sometimes at someone else's expense. Gentle competition can quickly become controlling and intrusive. Aggressive people are obvious invaders, trying to take over somebody else's territory. Aggression is a violation of borders and designed to intimidate, but it invites active dislike and therefore has no place in a well-planned life.

Assertion is effectively holding your own territory; defining yourself by it. Trying to take over someone else's territory is aggression.

When you behave assertively, you are clarifying what territory you believe is yours and in the process you will automatically tend to define the other person's position.

Assertion means standing at the very edge of your territory of truth or belief to show where you end, where the border lies and where the other person begins. Assertive behaviour denies another person the opportunity to trespass into your territory, but equally it doesn't attempt to trespass on somebody else.

As an adult in a civilised society, the territory you define and defend is usually not physical territory, which civil law should do for you, but the moral or spiritual territory of what you believe to be true, right and fair. There can be a great sense of pressure to back down in order to please people, preserving love and approval, but you can pay dearly if you say 'yes' to avoid conflict when you should probably say 'no'.

To assert yourself you need to make your point sufficiently firmly to preserve your sense of identity, but gently enough not to alienate people. People struggling with their self-esteem often make the mistake of believing they should be more powerful than is humanly possible.

Self-doubt can make you believe:

- You should win arguments to be an effective person.

- If someone tries to trespass on you, you must have been seen as weak (the background to road rage).

Believing you are weak if you don't win arguments or can't control others is lethal to self-esteem. Mostly you can stop a trespasser without aggression, but sometimes when you are dealing with someone who is trying to control you, the best you can hope for is to hang on to your own integrity. In the real world there will be people with more power than you, whether you like it or not. When you are powerless, all you may be able to do is choose to act with assertive dignity, which is still possible even while you are being trodden on. *Assertion is not putting somebody in his place; it's putting yourself in your place.*

To be aggressive or violent is to both signal your sense of weakness and to weaken your argument. If you genuinely feel potent, you don't have to dominate or belittle anybody, because big people don't need high horses or big guns. Big people can give up territory, back away, apologise, even forgive, and if they can't forget, they can still decide that shutting up may be the best choice. It is perfectly possible to defer to people to please them or because it is not worth the trouble to do otherwise, and still do this in a dignified way.

The art of assertiveness includes saying 'yes' as often as you can. Civilised, effective and reasonable people do not go around constantly asserting their rights. Maturity is knowing what's worth defending. As I suggested earlier, a healthy self-esteem means that you have a small set of principles that you'll defend to the death, but outside the territory of these core values you're flexible, because your sense of self is not threatened by modifying what are merely peripheral values. A good sense of worth liberates you to accommodate and to give in to please other people, if you judge it will make you more comfortable.

Healthy self-respect knows instinctively that in broad principle it is better to err towards being conciliatory than difficult. While your ancestors undoubtedly wanted both, safety in the herd was probably more important to survival than triumph over territory. When there is a tiger around you are much better off lost in the anonymity of belonging to the herd than being proud, individualistic and eaten.

When the chips are down, pleasing people has a lot going for it. Love and belonging are ultimately better than power.

If you are a seal battling for a piece of the beach, or a rutting stag, being a sensitive, caring guy isn't really an option. As a human being, if you want to battle, that's fine, but you will have to live with more tension. Aggressive preservation of your individual territory will rub people up the wrong way, and they won't always like or respect you for it. This is going to put you on the alert, which is the same as saying it will make you tense, anxious or stressed, because your evolutionary programming says it is dangerous not to be liked.

If you are getting lousy service in a restaurant, healthy assertion doesn't automatically mean that you should get carried away with the defence of your rights. It is terribly easy to see the poor service as much more of a put-down than it really is. Your dinner may be slow in coming, but it's unlikely that the staff are selecting you personally to ignore.

If the waiter is ridiculously busy, choosing not to complain or even offering him sympathy may be more grown-up response, which will leave you feeling better and might even speed up the arrival of your dinner. Obviously there will be times when you really are getting a raw deal and the waiters are simply slack, but the atmosphere of hostility you create by complaining may not be worth the assertion of your rights, even if you have every right to do so.

It's worth remembering that people tend to do more for someone they either like or fear. In a restaurant, the waiter has all the power so you should fear him, because he can spit in your soup. Your chance of intimidating him into quicker service is smaller than the risk of collecting something nasty in your dinner if he doesn't like you.

Intelligent assertion is flexible; you need to feel strong enough to complain if you want to, but also free to decide not to do so in the service of a pleasant evening. Assertive behaviour is appropriate to the time and the issue, not a rigid set of rules to be followed the moment you sense your rights are threatened. Behaving assertively maximises your chances of getting what you want, although it in no way guarantees it.

An assertive style leaves you with your dignity reasonably intact, even if no one hears you or takes any notice of you. You have been assertive if you can look at what you have done, even if things have gone horribly wrong, and you can truly say you acted with kindness and dignity. If you are aggressive, people will probably hear you shouting, but if they listen at all it will only be until you have gone.

Clearly, assertion is a process designed to advance, or at least hold your position, not to force a retreat. A person who gives in too easily, selling his adult dignity for the security of a child's role, is only too aware that he is unassertive. On the other hand, an aggressive, controlling bully is much less likely to appreciate that he is just as far from being effectively assertive as his child-like opposite.

Assertion is getting your own way as much as possible, but not losing your integrity while you do so. By acting assertively, other people will still like you and, just as importantly, you will be able to like you, even if you don't get your own way.

Assertive people can still lose, although rarely as badly as aggressive people. Assertive people lose well, in part because they have given themselves room to be wrong or fail. If you are assertive you will like yourself, therefore your worth will not be so heavily invested in being right or winning. If you have been aggressive in pushing your point and you are wrong, you have a lot further to fall and a lot more people keen to push you.

Merely being wrong will very rarely cause you to be labelled stupid. Being aggressively certain that you are right when you are wrong is guaranteed to earn you that title. You can also be fairly stupid if you are aggressively right.

This makes life a lot simpler. You do not need to be right to justify being assertive, and you don't need to have the correct answer to avoid being a fool. You merely need to act as if you believe in your right to offer an opinion or make a request, and then do it in a gentle and non-invasive fashion. This also frees you from the need to measure your assertiveness or your worth by your success. You may be impeccably assertive and still be ignored and misunderstood. Generally, the best you can rationally hope from behaving assertively is to increase the chances that you will be heard. The problem can remain unsolved – not all problems have solutions – but your way of approaching it may have been an absolute triumph. Never forget your options include a self-respecting 'can't', 'impossible' or 'too hard'.

It's easy to be right. You shouldn't have to be right to feel okay, although obviously it helps. Perfectly good, valuable people get things wrong and hate it, but not themselves. As a healthy person you never lose your capacity to be hurt, angry or dismayed, but your bad feelings don't include a decision that you are a worthless person just because your answer was worthless.

The art of assertiveness therefore includes the ability to be wrong and forgive yourself, recognising that other people are unlikely to be as critical of you as you may be of yourself. Unless you really push them with ill-chosen defensiveness, most people are quite keen to forgive you. Being wrong is not being bad, except perhaps in your eyes, so there is actually nothing to forgive. Other people's respect doesn't require you to be right, but it does require that you be wrong or right gracefully. Owning your own weakness is strong and looks strong.

A healthy self-esteem means an ability to balance power and love skilfully. Someone who likes himself well enough can monitor his own feelings and the feedback he gets from other people. If an assertive person makes a mistake and gives in too much, he will recognise the feeling of anger with himself or the beginnings of his resentment toward the person for whose approval he has compromised himself. Once he senses his own anger, before he converts his negative feeling into behaviour that harms his self-respect or his relationship, he will be able to reassert himself and so not need to be angry, or at least not quite as angry, any more.

If an assertive person has asked for too much, his own ethics or empathy will tell him he has overstepped the mark or he will respond to the early warnings of someone's anger or hurt and he can retreat. He will also have the flexibility to learn from his mistakes.

We all want a feeling of individual power, territory and exclusiveness, as well as a reasonable confidence of acceptance and approval. Thus we face a dilemma. Push your rights too hard and you invite disapproval, rejection and perhaps attack, even if you enjoy feeling righteous and tough. On the other hand, if you don't ask for anything you won't antagonise anybody, but then you won't have much personality, which will very definitely put people off. Assertion is getting the balance right.

Ideas

- Healthy people want power with people, not over them.

- If you can balance your needs for love against your wish for power, the world becomes a reasonably manageable place.

- Holding your own territory is assertion, while trying to take over someone else's territory is aggression. Assertive behaviour denies another person the opportunity to trespass upon you, but equally it doesn't attempt to trespass on somebody else.

- Assertiveness is putting yourself in your place, not someone else in his.

- Assertive behaviour is appropriate to the time and the issue, not a rigid set of rules to be followed the moment you sense your rights are threatened.

- Behaving assertively maximises your chances of getting what you want, although it in no way guarantees it.

- An assertive person loses well, in part because effective assertiveness leaves you room to be wrong.

CHAPTER 9

⁓

Assertive Self-Definition

ASSERTION IS MEASURED IN TERMS of behaviour, not intentions. All the things you might have said would have been more useful had you actually said them.

Most of us tend to revisit confrontations and conversations we would have preferred to have managed differently, searching for an alternative view of our performance or trying to rewrite history. As we play out past scenes in our heads they can feel so real they make us cringe with embarrassment. If we try to salvage our self-respect by rescripting the event in our heads, unfortunately nothing is really changing. Usually we feel worse as we pump ourselves up with retrospective anger or crumble under the weight of rerun embarrassment.

When we are simply not quick enough to think of the brilliant response in a difficult conversation, worrying about it later is useless, although of course that doesn't stop us doing so. We need to do a better job in the first place. Unfortunately, the sense of threat in situations where we should stand up for ourselves can be so overwhelming that we can scarcely speak, far less be clever. To have any hope of getting past the anxiety or anger that blocks our words, we need to have a system already in place for dealing with such situations.

Assertive techniques must be simple and applicable to all threatening situations so that they can be used automatically in emergencies. It's rather like driving: if something goes wrong, you can't afford to waste time debating whether to brake or accelerate.

A simple but flexible formula for negotiating, disagreeing or refusing must maximise your chances of winning, but it must also minimise your losses, given the excellent chance that you will not win, which I cannot emphasise enough is not the same as losing.

If you over-invest your own worth in convincing someone else that you are right, you are in trouble. You might have the intelligence of Einstein, the wit of Oscar Wilde and the cosmic truth at your fingertips, yet you will still not succeed in converting somebody to your way of seeing things. Wanting to be right is fine, and wanting others to agree with you is equally valid, but in order to do so all you can do is argue assertively and hope. If you expect others to agree just because you are right, you are doomed to frequent frustration.

If you over-invest in winning you may be obliged to squash someone else to thrust your ideas onto them, because if you lose, your survival brain fears you'll be annihilated. Your best chance of being heard, even if not agreed with, starts with learning to gently define the territory of your truth, a process I choose to call *assertive self-definition*.

Wrong can be right

To be assertive, you must spell out who and what you are. It's very easy to get your facts wrong when you have a disagreement, but you will never be wrong if you define yourself by describing your feelings. No one can ever prove you are wrong if you say you are unhappy, anxious or uncomfortable about something. They may argue about whether you are justified in feeling that way, but they can never prove that you don't feel it. Honestly describing and taking ownership of your feelings or beliefs is one of the few life situations in which you can be absolutely certain you're more right than anybody else.

If you truly believe the earth is flat and say, 'The earth is flat,' you are easily shown to be wrong. If you say, 'I believe the earth is flat,' you are absolutely, incontrovertibly right.

You can always be confident you are right if you describe yourself as having a feeling, even if you can't be confident of its justification, its cosmic truth or whether other people will agree with it. A little later, I shall try to demonstrate the words and technique for this approach.

The fear of being wrong stops lots of people from asserting themselves. Uncertainty can push people to aggression, trying to exaggerate their confidence where they feel insecure. Just as often uncertainty causes people to hold back so much they find themselves discounted, because they act as if they don't know what they want.

If you are offered the choice of going to the beach or the mountains but you say you don't mind, you may truly not care, or it may be that you are simply a wonderfully unselfish person. However, it is also possible that you are waiting for clues as to what the other person wants; to see just how much disapproval you would get if you chose the beach and then found he wanted the mountains. You may be hoping for the safety of consensus rather than risk what might prove to be the lonely individuality of stating your own choice.

'Would you like tea or coffee?'

'Whatever's easier.'

'Milk, sugar?'

'I don't mind.'

An exchange of this nature is terribly burdensome.

Truly not knowing what you want is fairly rare, but doubting either your right to want something or the security of your relationship if you dare ask for it, is common.

People who are not assertive enough sometimes have real trouble addressing issues that threaten their values and self-respect. They are held back by the questions that are not necessarily thought through properly, but still driving their behaviour: Have I enough personal credit to be safely, validly and openly angry about this? Will the loss of love if I object be worse than the loss of dignity if I don't?

If you feel bad and you want to hide the feeling, and you can trust that it won't sneak out and trip you, then that's great. Do it. If you are feeling bad and you can't or don't want to hide it, then you may be better off letting it out. However, this needs to be done in a way that doesn't make you feel worse.

If you can bring yourself to directly describe how you feel, you will make the best of a bad situation. By saying: 'I feel lousy,' 'I feel vulnerable,' or 'I feel angry,' you can actually make yourself feel better in a couple of ways.

First, you are being self-respecting. You are sending the message that you like yourself enough to offer a negative side of yourself, yet you still appear to believe that you have enough credit to be worthy.

Second, in defining yourself as feeling bad, you reduce the emotional pressure to hide how you feel.

The direct statement, 'I'm angry,' makes the fact that you are angry perfectly clear, which will be what you want to do. Anger is the emotion of territorial protection and it motivates action. It gives you a powerful drive to change whatever made you angry in the first place. There's no use in being angry without action, so at the very least you'll want to communicate it.

If you define yourself by directly describing your emotion – 'That makes me very angry!' – you actually lessen the pressure to show it in less effective ways, such as shouting, breaking things, sulking or cynically belittling someone. Defining yourself by clearly stating you are angry is an assertive act of self-respect. Anything else risks being aggressive, which weakens you and makes your opinion less valid.

Words are the most precise means for communicating not only the feeling, but the reason why you have the emotion. Shouting or sulking demonstrates the emotion very clearly, but relies on the other person working out why you are behaving this way. If they don't read your actions correctly, either mistakenly or by choice, then you will be even more upset.

Don't signal it, say it. You can say, 'I'm really hurt by that,' 'I feel afraid,' or 'I'm going to cry!' and it can be done without sending a message that some other person is responsible and should be guilty enough to do something about it. By defining yourself as anxious, but still an equal and worthy adult, you may not drag victory from the jaws of defeat, but you will seize as much self-respect as you can reasonably hope for from a bad situation.

Feeling something but not saying it may mean you genuinely do not want to hurt someone's feelings, but it can also mean you are afraid of rejection for having the emotion, or you have doubts about the legitimacy of your complaint. Of course, there are situations where not saying anything can be highly assertive and self-respecting, but you must be very careful if you try some other way to communicate your feelings other than words. Silence is easily misinterpreted. Make sure you haven't chosen a seemingly safer but actually manipulative way to send your message.

It is really very important to recognise that if you are a person whose basic values have always included a wish not to trespass on the rights of others, it is most unlikely you will suddenly become an aggressive, arrogant bore if you learn to be more assertive and say what you feel. In addition, as a sensitive person already concerned not to offend others, what you believe to be reasonable to ask is unlikely to be so outrageously unfair or selfish that if you express your ideas, you will be instantly labelled as self-centred and controlling.

To be assertive most definitely does not mean you lose your respect for other people's feelings, but it does mean you respect your own as well. Be careful not to use your deep sensitivity to the needs of others as justification for lack of assertiveness.

Despite this, sometimes it is not possible to say what you are feeling. Perhaps the person simply can't be there to hear you because you are acting the scene out in your head, or the person is too scary to face, like a violent parent. Perhaps the person is not an individual, but a corporation or a government department that has too much power over you. An organisation can feel like an unreachable, living entity when you are in helpless opposition and full of a sense of angry injustice. Then writing a diary can make a huge difference.

When you write down your thoughts it's much more like speaking to someone than when you have a conversation in your mind. Just sitting down to think something through is not always a good way to finish or focus your thoughts, especially passionately emotional ones; talking is best, but writing is almost as good. When you commit your ideas to paper you define yourself; it's like looking at your footprints in the sand or listening to your voice in a recording or in an echo. You become more solid; more real. You confirm your own existence.

When you are ignored, losing or depressed, the territory of your spirit is shrunken as if your existence is compromised. By describing your feelings in words, you are defining who and what you are and so making yourself more real. Even if your feelings only find their voice in a diary, your self-definition alters your relationship with other people. A diary always addresses things which are urgently present in your head to an audience or posterity or a particular person.

If you define yourself early, gently and skilfully in potentially threatening situations, you have your best chance of keeping your self-respect and your reputation intact. Assertive self-definition is an action designed to simultaneously define your individuality and maximise the good feelings other people have for you.

Ideas

- The techniques of assertiveness must be simple, require very little spontaneous cleverness and be applicable to all threatening situations.

- Wanting to be right is fine, and wanting others to agree with you is equally valid, but for these things to happen all you can do is argue assertively and hope.

- If you expect others to agree just because you're right, you'll be disappointed.

- Describing your negative as well as your positive feelings is assertive self-definition. Just don't expect people to fix you.

- Don't signal it, say it. If you are angry or hurt, say it with words, not actions.

- Truly not knowing what you want is rare, but either doubting your right to have it or doubting the security of your relationship if you dare ask for it, is common.

- To be assertive does not mean you lose your respect for other people's feelings or suddenly become aggressively arrogant, it simply means you respect your own feelings as well.

- You will always be right if you honestly describe your feelings. Although people may deny their validity, they can never prove that you do not feel them.

- Sitting down to think something through is not inevitably the way to complete a train of troubled thoughts; talking is best, but writing is almost as good. If you truly can't find or daren't face the person, a diary helps you order your thoughts and can have real value in the process of assertive self-definition.

CHAPTER 10

꒜

The Basics of Self-Respect

A GOOD SELF-ESTEEM ALLOWS YOU to feel valid enough to differ from other people and valuable enough to still be accepted if you do.

Most of us are not born to be assertive and the best parenting won't inevitably hand you techniques for managing situations where you need to disagree or stand up for yourself. The will may be there, but your performance can be sabotaged by the conflict between wanting your own way and wanting approval.

Despite this, people who feel good generally do behave assertively, conducting themselves as self-respecting, equal adults without really thinking about it. Self-doubt increases your self-consciousness and makes you more likely to feel pressured in human encounters that really shouldn't be all that demanding. Self-doubt also increases the danger you will fail to behave in a way that preserves both halves of your sundae of self-esteem. You can find yourself being either aggressive or just too nice when all you want to be is normal.

If you do feel uncomfortable after an interaction with another person, you may need to ask yourself three basic questions, the first of which you know already: 'Is this bad feeling because I feel rejected or is it because I feel belittled?'

When you feel bad, you will never go wrong if you use this as a starting point for self-examination. If a nasty feeling is not due to physical danger, pain or material loss, the reason for your unhappiness will always centre around issues of acceptance and rejection, power and weakness. Look beyond the apparently complicated problem and you will see that, real or imagined, loss of love or loss of territory underlies every emotional trauma.

Before you decide what action to take, based on the principle of taking responsibility for your feelings you should ask: 'Should I legitimately feel bad? Have I been unkind or undignified?'

Unfortunately, if you genuinely believe you have done something wrong and you deserve the rejection, the put-down or the guilt, there is no direct approach to changing the way you feel about yourself. You will simply dig a deeper hole for yourself unless you remember that beyond apology, the only way to minimise the damage you have done to yourself is to minimise the damage you have done to somebody else, if you can. After that, promise yourself you won't do it again and conduct yourself as a kindly, self-respecting adult from now on.

Whether you decide you deserve to feel bad or not, you must ask yourself the third question, which is simply: 'What are the rules for acting as a self-respecting adult?'

Fortunately, the rules aren't all that hard or complex.

1. If you want to feel like a self-respecting adult, you need to behave as one. If you want to feel good, you must act well, especially when things are going wrong.

2. If you feel bad but there's nothing more you can do to fix the problem, you need to remember that the best you can do in adversity is to behave with kindness and dignity. Then, at least, you will be a self-respecting adult who also happens to feel bad.

3. You must carry yourself as if you believe you are worthwhile and

equal, but never act as if you think you are better than other people. Your body and verbal language must not signal certainty you are right, but simply certainty that you are good enough to be wrong. This means acting as if you will not die if you were rejected, or if someone proves you wrong, not behaving so arrogantly as to pretend you wouldn't care. Beware of, 'Well, that's his problem!' A popular but vulnerable refuge.

4. You should say what you would like to happen and act as if you believe your wishes are probably acceptable. If you are in emotional pain, your pain should be either invisible or clearly spelt out with words. Remember: don't signal it, say it.

5. You would be much better off trying to force yourself into clearly saying that you feel bad and why, without self-justification or blame, while being careful not to become your own most enthusiastic biographer. Offer your vulnerability as self-defining statements and not as covert questions or indirect pleas for reassurance. It's perfectly okay to say: 'I'm feeling really threatened.'

   By contrast, fishing for reassurance or trying to diminish your responsibility in various ways is undignified and won't make you feel any better. 'I know you'll think I'm stupid'; 'I'm usually much better than this'; 'It always makes me nervous when people watch me'; 'I'm really tired today and I have a terrible headache'.

6. If you consider others' rights, you will never go far wrong, but trying to meet everybody else's wishes is quite different. Other people's rights don't need skilled interpretation; they are self-evident, unlike their wishes, which may be driven by a dozen obscure agendas. In short, respect other people's rights before your own wishes, but don't put their wishes before your rights.

7. You probably don't believe you can read minds, so make sure

you are not acting as if you can. All you can do is interpret others' feelings in the light of your own, so you are sure to get it wrong some of the time. If you are trying to anticipate what people want, you may win approval from a few, but you can find yourself in a whole lot of trouble if you misread someone's mind and decide they are against you. Wait until they tell you. You will never be able to fully trust your interpretation of other people's agendas, especially as it's hard enough to know your own. So don't try. Stick to the rules of behaviour that will always be right: act as the self-respecting adult who behaves with kindness and dignity. Do this and the worse things are, or the worse you feel, the more respect you will have for yourself and from others, which is the best and, I suspect, the only way to feel better.

8. Remember that, be it by accidental misinterpretation or by assertive necessity, if you don't please someone, it doesn't inevitably mean you are hurting them. If you use not hurting people as a life plan you will do well, but if you equate not pleasing someone with hurting him and then use this as a reason not to assert yourself, you are in danger of feeling powerless and resentful, as well as being seen as weak.

9. A self-respecting adult will support and feed the sense of self-worth of another person if he possibly can. Never use a put-down as a way of making yourself feel bigger or better. If you feel small, making someone smaller only feels good for a very short time. If you are truly angry with someone, perhaps belittling him might be justified, but regard it as a measure of last resort, because it puts huge and possibly irreversible pressure on your relationship.

10. Conversely, never put yourself down in an effort to please someone, trying to show what a good and humble person you

are and how relatively big the other person must be. A self-respecting adult never plays wounded and weak in an effort to make someone else guilty. People hate it and your observing self won't be particularly impressed with you, either.

'I thought you were going to call me.'

'You promised you'd be here by six.'

Springing the trap of guilt just makes people angry and has no long-term holding power.

11. For the same reasons, if you really have done the wrong thing, never take on the role of a contrite child. You can and should apologise and try to fix the problem, but you should not grovel. If you do so, you are taking refuge in diminished responsibility, trying to avoid the disapproval as an adult that you may richly deserve. Endless apology only shows your anxiety over rejection, not true remorse over your act.

12. Try to be honest, but remember that if you are brutally honest in the belief you are maintaining your integrity, you may be violating a more important value of not hurting someone unnecessarily. Put simply, it may truly be an awful meal, but think through your priorities before you tell the cook.

13. If you must tell lies to protect your self-esteem, make them lies of omission, not embellishments. You can never hope to be rehabilitated if you are caught making yourself grander than you really are, but it is more excusable to forget to mention some of the bad bits. Lies that make you look bigger than you are or help you escape responsibility are a disaster and quite incompatible with happiness, because they always undermine trust in your relationships. Lies that preserve the feelings of others are of a different order.

14. Don't send concealed messages. Don't use words that say one

thing but are designed to carry an underlying message. Hints, name-dropping or very long words may graphically illustrate your social importance, your intellect or how hard-working yet uncomplaining you are, but they are usually transparent manipulations, which people hate.

15. Give compliments if you feel they are deserved and receive compliments with thanks, even if you don't feel you deserve them or you're afraid you'll be seen as insufficiently humble. If you haven't the courage to agree, at least tell your admirer how kind he is to say such nice things. Never reject the gift of a compliment. Never deny someone the pleasure of being kind.

16. Finally, it is impossible to over-emphasise the golden rule for your every interaction: always treat other people as if you believe they like you.

The rules are simple, obvious and basic to survival in emotional emergencies.

Ideas

- If your discomfort is not due to physical pain or material loss, unhappiness will always come down to your perception of being rejected, belittled, or both.

- Beyond apparently complicated problems, loss of love or loss of dignity underlies every emotional trauma.

- If you want to feel like a self-respecting adult you need to behave as one.

- You must carry yourself as if you believe you are worthwhile and equal, but never act as if you think you are better.

- Respect other people's rights before your own wishes but never put their wishes before your rights.

- If you equate not pleasing someone with hurting them, and use this as a reason not to assert yourself, you will always feel belittled.

- Endless apology only shows you're afraid of disapproval: it does not demonstrate true remorse.

- Never reject the gift of a compliment. Never deny someone the pleasure of being kind.

- The golden rule for your every interaction is to treat other people as if you believe they like you. This will always be the correct choice. It will never let you down as first choice when you don't feel secure or you're not sure you understand what somebody means.

CHAPTER 11

✦

Saying 'No'

ALL REASONABLE PEOPLE PREFER To avoid arguments, but sometimes you simply must say 'no'. You may have to ask for things that are really yours; stand your ground; disagree or argue, either because you'll lose something material, or because your integrity would be hopelessly compromised if you didn't.

When you say 'no', you are inevitably displeasing someone, either by diminishing him or rejecting him and his request. In our abstract world, the idea can be a symbol of the person and to reject the idea feels like rejecting the person. If you say 'no' you must face the possibility of feeling disliked, or actually being disliked, irrespective of how skilfully you do it. In addition, as a civilised person, you will suffer an empathic discomfort if you feel you are disappointing someone, even if you're not really rejecting or putting him down – you're just saying 'no'.

If you hold on to your idea or your position, you may lose love and approval; if you let go you are diminished and lose something of yourself. Hence the distaste most people feel for arguments: either way you lose something.

Saying 'yes' when you know you should say 'no' is not an involuntary act. In your truth of that moment, there is more immediate reward in agreement than in refusal. By saying 'yes' you are offering a gift. When you give, you gain the feeling of virtue, love and acceptance that goes with generosity and being pleasing.

If you say 'yes' instead of the 'no' you would have preferred, you may also be trying to ease the guilty fear of rejecting, or avoid being rejected yourself. It may not be rational, economical or intelligent, but on one level of your consciousness it seems right. That's why you do it. Like a drug addict, have your anxiety relief now and worry about the consequences later.

If you give in to avoid conflict, unfortunately the conflict will still live on in the form of an argument in your head. If you have given in for approval, you are very unlikely to get the level of love and thanks you feel is appropriate for the degree of sacrifice you have made, so you'll feel used.

Feeling used is an extended form of failing to say 'no'. 'He used me' may just mean that you loved him more than he loved you, but it can also mean you gave more than you wanted to give at the time but hoped to get your money's worth later. There is considerable danger in giving too much, because if you decide to call in your debts the other person may not agree on the extent or timing of his dues.

If you have thought through the balance of profit and loss and you really don't want to say 'yes', it's not too hard to work out when you ought to say 'no'. If you know you will feel angry or belittled if you agree to something, then you should probably refuse.

Obviously, giving is good and, up to a certain limit, the more you can give the better. Sensible, rational people will tend to give a bit too much rather than too little, and anything you can do to make another person feel good that costs you little is a great investment. You are good and wise if you give as much as you can, but it must be short of the resentment barrier.

The limit of sensible giving is decided by the pleasure of both the giver and the receiver. If it's costing you too much in frustrated expectation, or the other person is being loaded with too much unwanted obligation, you've judged badly. So if you learn your new friend likes watermelons and you deliver a truckload on his front lawn, you may find he is not quite as grateful as you would like him to be.

An adult recognises that people are something like a cross between a Coke machine and a parking meter. It's no use looking and longing; if you want something from them, you have to put something in, but putting in excessive amounts doesn't necessarily get you more out. Even if the large amounts you put in are accepted, the machines take your money without even a thank you.

A gift of role-appropriate love is generally valued, but it is most valued if it comes from someone who appears to value himself. Giving too much always betrays a shaky sense of self-worth and devalues you, and also what you give.

The anxiety of rejection is a particular burden to people who regularly say 'yes' when they would prefer to say 'no'. They find peculiar difficulty in refusing, both because they fear their worth to the other person is so fragile that any relationship will be demolished by refusal, and also because to say 'no' feels just too aggressive. This can be complicated by real anger towards someone who makes a request they feel should not have been made of them; one they would love to refuse, but dare not.

All this becomes too confusing for some people, so they avoid and explain it by saying: 'I just can't bear to hurt people!' If you hear yourself saying this, make absolutely sure it is the sensitivity of your soul that is speaking and it is not an excuse to avoid risking your acceptability by asserting your individuality.

An equally poor device is to offer a very clearly reluctant 'Well … ok … .er … yes', hoping your hesitation and discomfort will be obvious enough to make someone guilty and oblige him to take his demands away, freeing you from the pressures of having to say 'no'.

The capacity to say 'no' without aggression implies a belief in your own worth and substance. To state your position in the face of opposition, disbelief or disapproval requires you to be willing to take a risk. By saying 'no', you will always be less liked at that moment, compared to saying 'yes', but if your self-esteem is reasonable, you'll survive. If your self-respect is not so robust, you will need to learn how to act as if it is.

Clearly, not wanting to do something is not necessarily the best criterion for saying 'no'. There are lots of things that you may not want to do, which are actually in your interests to do. You probably know instinctively that once you have done these things you will feel quite good, or at least not as bad as if you hadn't. The art of effectively saying 'no' starts with seeing if you can say 'yes' without too much cost. Never say 'no' just to show you're not a pushover.

Ideas

- Being nice is essential, but it's not enough.

- Rejecting someone's idea inevitably feels like rejecting the person.

- By saying 'yes' you might mean you are happy to oblige, but it could mean you have decided to either avoid conflict or buy approval.

- Anything you can do to make another person feel good that costs you little is a great investment. You are wise if you give as much as you can, but it must not be so much that you will be resentful if there is no payback.

- You should give to a point short of the resentment barrier, beyond which you will expect payback and be hurt or angry if you don't get it.

- The limit of sensible giving is decided by the pleasure of both the giver and the receiver.

- Never use guilt as a way to control another person; all you'll do is make them angry.

- Your ability to say 'no' without aggression shows you believe in your own worth and substance.

✌

CHAPTER 12

The Direction of an Argument

IT DOESN'T MATTER HOW CLEVER, diplomatic or pleasant you are, if you have any self-respect at all one day you're going to have an argument. This has to happen because looking after your interests inevitably has the potential to force somebody else to abandon or modify his own ambitions. It need not happen often and the conflict need not be intense, but it will always be a possibility and so you should know how to argue well.

Effective arguing is the art of getting what you want without forgetting that one of the things you will always want is to be liked. Once you launch into an argument, sooner rather than later you'll need to decide whether to defend your position at any cost or whether your relationship with your opponent is more important. A wise person makes a definite choice and doesn't try giving equal importance to both.

The direction you take will be decided by:

- How much you feel your principles will be violated if you let the argument pass.

- The value to you of your relationship with the person with whom you are disagreeing.

If in doubt, intelligent self-interest dictates it is better to compromise for love, because that is almost always a reversible decision. Punishing someone for disagreeing with you can leave an indelible mark.

If you do decide to hold your ground, you should make sure it is the message and not the messenger you attack, because you can find yourself saying unkind or belittling things that can never be retrieved. Claiming later that you didn't mean what you said is often hard to believe.

All confrontation is territorial dispute, therefore all arguments are power struggles to some degree. So it is good to know a little about the rules for establishing power.

Your interests are best served if you don't behave in a threatening way. If you argue gently, the person with whom you are in dispute is potentially liberated to put his time and effort into considering your point of view. In other words, if you don't force someone into defending himself against your attack, he might just listen to you. If you are excessively confronting, you greatly reduce your chances of even being heard, still less of getting an agreement.

If you don't launch into an attack, not only do you increase the chances of your ideas being heard, but you've also got more room to make mistakes. If you've offered your point of view gently and then you're proven wrong, the other person won't feel the same need to rub your nose in it. By considering the self-esteem of a person with whom you are disagreeing, your own self-esteem is safer because you won't be so disliked. If you don't win, it's only the argument you have lost, not self-liking or self-respect.

Skilled arguing aims not to lose but doesn't regard a win as essential, although still well worth trying for. Remember, not winning is not the same as losing. If you think about it, there are rarely any winners in arguments, if by winning you mean that another person accepts your truth and rejects what he had originally believed strongly enough to provoke the disagreement in the first place.

Many disputes become emotional contests without resolution. Usually the best that you can rationally hope for is to preserve your dignity by clearly defining your beliefs, while trying not to make an enemy out of the opposition. This is assertive self-definition, but irrespective of how well you do it the number of times you actually manage to change somebody's mind will not be great. As a result, it is wise not to invest too much of your own personal worth in the outcome.

Unfortunately, even if your method of arguing is beyond criticism, both in style and intention, somebody else may not play by the rules. You may find yourself at the receiving end of an argument that appears to be specifically designed to put you down. If you feel this is happening there are some rules to consider:

1. Most importantly, if you do feel you are being unreasonably criticised, don't forget how easy it is to see malice where none was intended.

2. If you are genuinely under fire, you will never go wrong if you are slow to see an attack. If you respond gently and politely to aggression but you continue to be abused, you have the option to enjoy the power of righteous rage, but if you choose not to exercise that right, you become increasingly empowered. In non-physical disputes, turning the other cheek has lots going for it.

   If you are rude to someone who deserves it, you help him to avoid facing what he has done wrong. He will be only too happy to be offended by your rudeness, because you free him to attack the way you are arguing and thus to avoid responsibility for his actions. By being aggressive you make it so easy for the other person:

'You're a total bastard (and he was) for doing that!'

'How dare you be so rude to me!'

Even if you have every reason to be angry, if you behave aggressively your right to anger is potentially invalidated and your point is diluted or lost. Structure your language so as to attack the argument or the behaviour, not the person.

Healthy anger is a response to an accurate perception that you or your principles have been violated, your rights diminished, your character impugned. An intelligent expression of anger is not an antidote for helplessness or a pathetic bid for power, but motivation to change what you see as wrong.

3. It is worth remembering that most arguments, disagreements and conflicts are not designed to reject you or destroy you. When they are arguing with you, some people will attack you personally and they will try to hurt you. You couldn't possibly avoid being affected by this, but you'll feel better if you can appreciate that such people have very poor arguing skills. They don't want to actually destroy you. They just want to weaken you a little bit, with the idea they can impose their point of view more easily. It's a bit like a healthy parent chastising a child; designed to change, not to break. The ease with which an idea is accepted as a truth is in part dependent upon the status of the communicator – one is more likely to accept nonsense from a person of high status, so the logic of belittlement is to increase relative status by making you smaller.

In addition to a natural desire to win an argument, it's a sense of personal threat, real or imaginary, that causes someone to attack or belittle you. They are not doing it because they see you as personally weak, bad or deficient, although it's so easy to feel that's what's happening. It's simply that they think they will look small if they don't win, and that making you a bit smaller will make them a bit bigger.

Being nasty is a weak way to argue, but it's usually only an attempt to manipulate you into a different position, not to destroy or totally reject you.

4, If somebody who is arguing with you is willing to be aggressive, but not to take the illegal step into violence, there is no such thing as domination, only your submission. *If you do not choose to submit to threat, you cannot be dominated.* If he's going to hit you, just agree.

5. Amongst humans, the winner is the one who displays most power with least aggression, even if brawn can beat brains in the short term.

   To look powerful, all you need to do is act as if you have a robust self-respect. If you can assert yourself effectively, you can often have the advantage, because people have a natural tendency to defer to such displays of power. If you act gently, you look powerful.

6. In a genuinely self-respecting person an ethical system operates. The exercise of his power is not limited to how great a trespass is possible, but by what he judges is fair and reasonable.

Many people wade into their disputes with little direction, blindly struggling to dominate without sticking to the topic or to any agenda. An effective argument can best be mounted from a few sound principles:

1. Know what you are really arguing about. Children's arguments are usually quite clearly, 'It's mine', but most adult disputes are over the less tangible territory of belief, right and privilege. Adult arguments, especially those between intimates, are more

likely to be over what appear to be trivial issues, but these always represent more significant struggles over love or control.

Disputing which end of the toothpaste to squeeze may really be an exercise as to who can impose his will, or a test of love: 'If she really cared about me, she would do what I have shown is logical.' To have your truth rejected is to feel rejected and belittled yourself.

If a fear of being weak or anger over not being loved enough is the true meaning embedded in a trivial argument, there is little point in wasting words on the mere logic of toothpaste-tube squeezing. You will need to address the underlying agenda.

2. People argue because their logic leads them to a different truth from another person's. A dispute should begin with your particular logic, but there is no point persisting for too long. It is naïve to believe that if you can get the other person to understand, an argument will be automatically settled. Assuming that you do know the cosmic truth and you have offered it with impeccable good sense, if your reasoning was not accepted the first time it was given, there is not much chance it will be accepted with further repetition.

3. An argument can get away from the original topic, tracking off on tangents, crossing and re-crossing its own path. As well as knowing what you are arguing about and how long to persist with logic, it is really useful to have a sense of how an argument should be structured.

If you make certain you are clear as to the direction you wish the argument to follow and the purpose for which you decided to argue in the first place, it will help you to stick to the topic. This has the advantage of reducing the chances of a dispute degenerating into personal attack.

An essential skill in the art of arguing is to keep returning to the original point, not allowing yourself to be forced into arguing something that was never the issue.

A poorly conducted argument can look like the track of a demented snail, meandering in any direction.

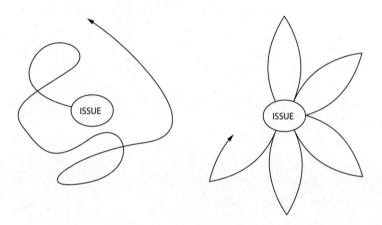

Better handled, an argument looks like a daisy, tracking away from its centre but always returning to the point you decided was the purpose of the argument.

Much of what I have suggested about assertiveness has been about how to lose. I apologise for this apparent negativity, but it has a clear purpose. People who fail to assert themselves or to protect their interests are generally afraid of being belittled by losing an argument, or of losing love by not agreeing or cooperating. They get so bogged down in their fear of negative consequences that they can be miles away from considering positive approaches that would lift their self-respect.

It is for this reason that these ideas may seem to be offered in reverse. By looking at losing before winning, I am trying to show that if you skilfully handle an argument, even with the worst possible outcome, you will not lose. An investor would be much more courageous in the market if he knew that breaking even were the worst that could happen.

Thus, the first step towards effective self-assertion is to understand that it is really very safe, because while you mightn't win, you cannot lose. By contrast, the systems that you may have used for years to manage confrontation or make your point might actually be quite risky to your security and self-respect, not to mention significantly reducing any chance you might have had of winning.

Ideas

- There are rarely any winners in arguments, if winning is defined as another person accepting your truth and abandoning what he had originally believed.

- Most disputes become emotional contests without resolution.

- It is a sense of personal threat – real or imaginary – that causes someone to attack or belittle you.

- Most arguments are not designed to destroy or reject you, merely to manipulate you into a different and weaker arguing position.

- In the absence of violence, you cannot be dominated unless you decide to submit.

- Aggression will never win an argument. Beating up Einstein won't prove him wrong.

- The subject of an argument may seem trivial, but it is always symbolic of bigger things. The universal agendas of love and power underlie every argument. No one truly argues over trivia.

- It is naïve to believe that if only you can get the other person to understand, the argument will be settled.

- An essential skill in the art of dispute is to keep returning to the original point, not allowing yourself to be forced into arguing something that was never the issue. An argument should look like a daisy.

- If you argue skilfully, the worst outcome will be failing to win.

❧

CHAPTER 13

The Anatomy of an Argument

WHEN YOU ARGUE EFFECTIVELY you don't try to take another person's position by direct attack. Instead, you offer your opinion as a Trojan horse.

To argue well, you must take your point of view to the edge of the other person's territory and leave it there, welcoming him to examine it if he wishes, while you quietly step back. With a little luck, if you offer the concept gently and the idea doesn't too clearly violate his core values or damage his self-interest, he may come from behind his wall of disbelief and take your idea inside for examination.

A win in an argument is getting someone to modify or change the territory of his truth and replace it with your truth. This structure offers your best chance of winning under these terms, but never forget, winning an argument is rare and not always necessary.

Clearly it is impossible to change another person's mind; he must do it himself and he will only do so if you provide the optimum circumstances:

- You offer acceptable logic.

- You do not threaten his security or his self-esteem.

- Ideally, you demonstrate to him that he will gain materially or emotionally if he accepts your point of view.

If the first step in self-assertion within an argument is to recognise it is safe for you to offer your opinion, the second must be to convince your opponent that he is safe. You need to show he will lose nothing – and may even gain something – if he considers your idea.

Intelligently managed argument, dispute, debate, disagreement or negotiation avoids attacking, and better still tries to enhance the self-esteem of the opposition. You obviously can't say his idea is correct, because your disagreement is the reason you are arguing, but you can acknowledge that other truths than yours might possibly exist, even if privately you don't really believe it. You can also remind someone that you know he is a reasonable human being, to make it clear you don't feel all his ideas are wrong. If you can make someone feel respected as a person, he may be a little more willing to listen to you and review his own position.

Obviously, if you are really angry, making people feel good about themselves may be the last thing you want to do, but not attacking their self-esteem is worth considering if your goal is to get your idea across rather than to simply demolish your opponent.

The vast majority of confrontations are not with people whose eternal dislike you would welcome or whose self-respect you'd want to destroy: try not to forget the wisdom of asking yourself whether ultimately the relationship is more important than the point.

Based on the theory of healthy assertiveness, it is possible to define a series of steps to take when you face a potential confrontation. The principles are flexible enough to apply in situations where you need to say 'no', and broad enough to use on occasions where you are asking for something the other person may not want to give. These concepts are applicable to disagreements over many issues.

Assertive step 1

'This is your idea, as I understand it …'

Clearly define the other person's argument by restating his position as you have heard it.

Ideally, you put no slant on the restatement at this point. The more your phrasing actually favours him and his view, the better you are serving your longer-term goal of selling him your version of the truth. If he sees you trying to reshape his view from the beginning, you are more likely to be locked out. Provided it is genuine, the more regard for another idea you can offer, the better, because you are not alerting your opponent to the disagreement that is going to follow.

By restating his argument, you also show someone he has been heard and his position noted. You validate and define him, affirming his individuality and thus supporting his self-esteem; obviously a good idea if you want someone to listen to you.

Assertive step 2

'This is your idea, as I understand it. I also see that your position must be reasonable because you are a reasonable person …'

In addition to strengthening someone by affirming his position, it is worth saying anything positive about the person. Make sure you err on the side of understatement rather than effusiveness. If you can't find anything good to say, say nothing, but if you can genuinely compliment someone, you might just be able to help him feel big enough to give in.

We all want to believe we are good – and nobody does anything with a single agenda. Every act has the potential for several layers of meaning. We all tend to promote our more virtuous motives to the top of the pile and ignore the less than noble ones that, if we were to recognise them, would threaten our sense of worth.

The man who embezzles money will say he did it to support his family, or that the person he defrauded deserved to lose it. Both these agendas may have existed, but in reality the most powerful force may have been his greed. If you are to have any chance of getting him to look at himself, you must first address the motives that may have genuinely existed and that in his mind head the list. If you choose to tell him he is a greedy crook, you'll get the satisfaction that comes from abusing someone you don't respect, but you have no chance of being heard. By acknowledging that he may have some good qualities, you increase the possibility that he will contemplate his less ideal motives.

Assertive step 3

'This is your idea, as I understand it. I also see that your position must be reasonable because you are a reasonable person, but ...'

The word 'but' is essential in defining one's territory. 'But' draws a line in the dust, clearly marking out the border between two opinions. It denotes where one truth ends and another begins. The degree of emphasis you give to 'but' is an important decider of how forcefully you wish to make your point.

Assertive step 4

'This is your idea, as I understand it. I also see that your position must be reasonable because you are a reasonable person, but I ...'

In the natural progression of assertiveness, by saying 'I' you do a number of things:

- You begin to define your position, clearly showing that a new or different territory of ideas lies beyond that of your opponent's thinking. The pronoun 'I' must immediately follow 'but' because just as 'but' shows where his territory ends, 'I' shows where yours begins.

- By clearly stating the territory of your truth, you take possession of and responsibility for the ideas that follow. If you say 'I' with some emphasis, you are assertively holding your point without aggressively crushing your opponent.

- By firmly taking possession of your different ideas, you will tend to reduce the reflex antagonism in someone who may feel that you are saying that he should think what you think. 'I' demonstrates that although your positions are different, you do not intend to push your ideas into someone else's territory.

At the same time you are saying that while you do not intend to invade, you still plan to bring your ideas as close to the borders as possible, separated only by the thin line of 'but'.

Assertive step 5

'This is your idea, as I understand it. I also see that your position must be reasonable because you are a reasonable person, but I feel ...'

Choosing the correct verb to follow 'I' is profoundly important to signal your lack of aggressive intent as you present your different ideas. 'I believe', 'I feel', 'I wonder', 'I think', 'I suspect', 'I imagine', 'I consider' or 'I propose' are not dogmatic. The words are gentle in their implication, with very little appearance of territorial ambition.

Soft, non-invasive verbs leave the other person room to move. The softness of these words does not make them weak; on the contrary, because of the paradox of civilised behaviour where aggression is weak and gentleness is strong, their very lack of aggression signals confidence and self-respect.

Expressions that are full of dogmatic certainty, such as 'I know',

'I'm telling you' or 'I want', are almost as invasive as 'You should know', 'You must believe', 'Try to understand', 'Believe me', 'I insist' or 'Can't you see?'

Phrasing like this obliges the person with whom you are disagreeing to mass his forces to evict you. You have much less hope of being heard and, as a result, your opponent may be left ignorant of the cosmic truth you are offering.

Assertive step 6

'This is your idea, as I understand it. I also see that your position must be reasonable because you are a reasonable person, but I feel another way of looking at it might be ... [short, clear explanation of your view]'.

Following the verb is the statement and explanation of your ideas. Clearly, you have to say what you want or what you believe, and you may need to explain that in detail. There is no harm in trying to justify something as part of your initial explanation, but your efforts should be to explain, not to extract approval or forgiveness for being different.

As I've shown, you should also try to give the other person as much room to move as possible; to make it clear you are still open to logic and persuasion: 'Please keep trying to sell this to me, I'd love to be convinced,' or: 'I'm wide open to a good idea.'

Brevity and clarity in your explanation are a big help if you want to effectively communicate your ideas, but avoiding dogmatism and showing some willingness to be less than totally confident are potentially even more helpful.

In keeping with this principle, there is an advantage to using words with low rather than high emotional impact. Words symbolising violence or words regarded as swearing reduce the validity of what you say. This applies at a more subtle level, too: 'not good' is more powerful than 'absolutely terrible', and 'unpleasant' may give your message more validity than 'hideous'.

Strongly emotional words draw attention to themselves rather than to your ideas. For high impact, use low-impact words.

The essence of the assertive technique is to keep your behaviour gentle and civilised. Aggressive, dominating, belittling or even theatrical behaviour will elicit either the same from the other person, or merely withdrawal. Either way, your chances of being heard are much smaller.

Assertive step 7

'This is your idea, as I understand it. I also see your position must be reasonable because you are a reasonable person, but I feel another way of looking at it might be ... [short, clear explanation of your view], verbal full stop.'

At the end of every statement of your position, your voice and your phrasing should contain an implied full stop. The definite pause, your lowered voice, silence, and the direct gaze of a verbal full stop clearly state you have finished what you are saying and that you regard your statement as complete and sufficient.

Remember, arguing is a territorial struggle and the verbal full stop denotes the margin of your territory, the end of your statement, and leaves the responsibility for any further dispute firmly with the other person.

In summary, an effective disagreement is one in which you have said the person with whom you are arguing is worthy and you have defined the territory of his ideas. You have separated your territory of truth from his with a line drawn by the word 'but'. You have gently taken responsibility for your differing ideas by saying 'I' followed by a soft verb. You have defined those ideas and rounded off with a full stop. The ball is now very firmly in the opposition's court.

The entire procedure could be summarised as: you're fine, and that's your idea, but I feel this way. Full stop and ball in your court.

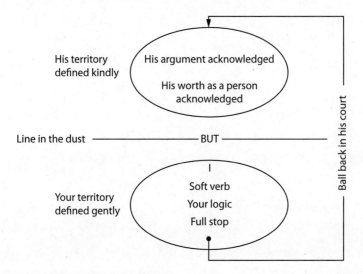

The anatomy of an argument

Ideas

- You will never convince someone by direct attack. Place your ideas at the very edge of your opponent's territory like a Trojan horse, but don't try pushing them through the door.

- To have any hope of convincing someone, he must be able to see that he does not lose too much and may even gain something.

- By clearly spelling out the differences between your view and that of another person, you are actually defining him and thus supporting his self-esteem, even if you disagree.

- If you can offer a genuine compliment to someone with

whom you are in dispute you can strengthen him, potentially helping him feel big enough to re-examine his point of
view.

- To argue well you need both structure and direction, with a
  clear view of your goal.

- Abusive, vulgar or exaggerated words draw attention to
  themselves and detract from your argument.

- For high impact, use low-impact words.

CHAPTER 14

꩜

The Structure of an Argument

IN THE PREVIOUS CHAPTER I offered the basic verbal structure of an argument and the principles behind it. So far, so good, but there is still more to arguing and negotiation.

Other animals are less well-equipped with language than we are and they are probably even more territorial than human beings. These two factors oblige them to make much greater use of bodily signalling to say what we can say with words.

While words are clearly a superior way to communicate, it would seem unlikely that we, as animals, could entirely replace physical signals with symbolic sounds. Predictably, the more threatened we are, the more we start to slide towards behaviour better suited to the jungle. As we regress, we have increasing difficulty communicating with language and we automatically start to signal more with our bodies. Punching someone very clearly says something, even if it doesn't say it very well.

The body language of effective dispute is simple if you understand the rules. Best practice suggests you signal self-liking and security about your own territory, at the same time showing no intention of invading another's. Your signals need to contain messages of confidence in your own power, but only the power to hold your own patch, not to take someone else's.

Arms bent, palms open towards the other party, a direct but unchallenging gaze and a conciliatory, unpatronising smile help deliver the desired message. By using body language like this, you signal that you feel powerful enough not to need to win in order to respect yourself. You show you have the ability to lose without feeling destroyed, and you are free from the empty and usually angry posturing necessary for pretending you don't care.

The appropriate use of eye contact is essential to effective debate. To assert yourself adequately your gaze must spend the majority of time within the triangle formed by the two eyes and mouth of the other person.

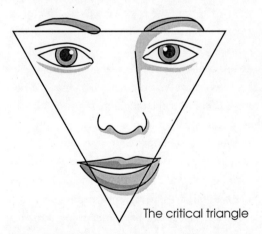

The critical triangle

A baby's early efforts at active communication centre on the eye–mouth triangle, and throughout life we respond as if the triangle were the centre of the person. So do other animals.

In theory, a direct stare without other gestures of aggression should merely signal the fact that you are willing to stand your

ground. However, in practice, directly staring into the eyes of someone when you're having a disagreement can be very hard to do
because it can feel like a hostile, awkward challenge.

If you can't manage the tension of eye contact and you drop
your gaze too easily, you will start feeling beaten, just as the person
with whom you are arguing will feel like a winner because you look
weak. Avoiding another's eyes and failing to engage sufficiently, or
moving your eyes away too rapidly, is taken as evidence of weakness,
cowardice or dishonesty. Fortunately, there are tricks to prevent
this. If you look at the side of a person's nose, at the same level as his
eyes, you will not feel the pressure of his gaze to the same degree as
you do if looking into his eyes directly. He will not be able to detect
that you are not looking him in the eye.

When the pressure of looking even at the side of the nose is too
great, shift your gaze to the mouth. The move away from the eyes to
the mouth is visible, but still signals interest rather than capitula-
tion.

You can make particular use of this system if you are doing the
talking, which is generally a more difficult time to look someone in
the eye than if you are the listener. If you can get to the point where
you can't take the tension of even the side of the nose or of the
mouth, you can ease the pressure when you are speaking by looking
down and away purposefully, apparently thinking deeply about the
issue and staring at a patch of ground off to the side, as if that's
where the issue resides. Then you must lift your gaze to the triangle
again.

Arguing with your body

Your body language can show that you do not regard a dispute as
something standing immoveably between you and your opponent;
something that must inevitably separate you.

Even in disagreement, it is possible to send a message of association between two people that is greater than their differences; a bond of equality and shared humanity that can be strengthened by your choice of language, gestures and even body position.

The way you position yourself can say a lot. Angle yourself in such a way as to suggest you see the argument as occurring in an area to one side, towards which you can both turn, rather than an obstacle between you.

You can turn your body half away, but keep your face directly towards your opposite and lean slightly in his direction. By doing this you send a message implying you are equals standing shoulder to shoulder, both looking towards a more peripheral problem. Your body half-rotated away, your head towards him, suggests a shared concern rather than the challenge of standing toe-to-toe, directly facing one another and staring each other down.

To help get your bodily-signalling right, it does no harm to try picturing yourself as someone respectful, kind and potent. I am not suggesting you have to feel or believe it, but by acting the role you will feel better in the face of disagreement and you might argue more calmly. Act as if you believe both your lives are bigger than the argument and its outcome, while avoiding being patronising, dismissive or superior.

The game plan

If you decide to pursue an argument, everything you do must maximise your own security and dignity, simultaneously offering as little threat, criticism, abuse or belittlement as possible to the person with whom you are disagreeing.

Even if someone is openly hostile and you simply match his aggression, you are at a greater risk of losing your dignity than if you were able to argue gently. This isn't saying much more than 'Turn the other cheek,' but the emphasis is on doing so as an intelligent option rather than a moral manoeuvre.

Please try to remember the impossibility of confidently knowing another person's agenda. Acting as if you believe you are liked, likeable and not under attack is not merely dignified and potent, it is also safe because it is so easy to misjudge another person's meaning as being hostile. You'll never go wrong if you treat someone as a friend, but you can make a terrible mess if you respond aggressively.

You may have mastered all these skills but still have your idea, belief or request rejected, and in the process you may be rejected too. You then need to decide whether the point is worth pursuing. If you want to press ahead, you must enter the next level of argument and employ a different style.

There are ways of arguing that you might have to consider if you are getting nowhere and you can't resist trying to do better. However, if you use these secondary techniques, you risk being seen as immoveable and even aggressive. So, the more you use them, the more you need to signal with voice and posture that you are still open to reason and conciliation, minimising any appearance of hostility.

If you have attempted to explain the facts as you perceive them and they are not accepted, they may need restating, but it should be in a contracted form. Ultimately you are saying something like: 'That is your idea and it may be perfectly valid, but unfortunately I see it differently.'

If your explanation was adequate but it wasn't heard the first time, there is not much reason to believe repetition will improve its reception. By this stage, you have probably passed the point when logic alone has much chance of influencing outcome; it is now a competition of personality, status or blind stubbornness, but not reason. Please try not to confuse stubbornness with strength.

In this more tense and even aggressive level of dispute, if somebody is obviously hostile to your ideas and therefore possibly to you, giving additional reasons to support your argument simply sets up a bigger target to be attacked. The more you reason and object, the more you make it easy for someone disagreeing with you to find the motivation to keep on arguing. By fuelling an argument in this way you expose yourself to a risk that sheer weight of words will persuade you to submit.

Because of the increased tension at this level of arguing, it is much easier to get your techniques wrong. By casting about for further reasons to strengthen your position and getting further involved in trying to explain, you may choose a genuinely weak supporting argument, even if your original position was sound. Then the attack immediately falls on the flaws in your logic and if that can be proven faulty you have badly weakened your original argument. 'He's better at arguing than I am and he always manages to turn it back against me' really means you've said too much and found yourself in a muddle.

Never forget, an argument should look like a daisy, not the track of a demented snail.

For the same reasons, it is important not to repeatedly interrupt. Let the other person talk himself out. If you interrupt, you provoke more vigorous argument to silence you. By waiting and saying nothing you leave an attacker to run out of steam until eventually he has to fall silent, starved of the response necessary to keep him going.

Don't fuel the fire of an argument by throwing twigs on it. Everybody needs feedback to maintain the vigour of their debate. Try to wait until your attacker runs out of words and then see if you can find the courage to hold his gaze and wait a further half-second before replying. If you can pause and then respond quietly and gently, there is potential for a considerable transfer of power, especially if you stick to the 'you ... but ... I' technique, giving only very short explanations or justifications for your position. To use this technique, you must stay absolutely, totally silent when someone is speaking, leaving him to exhaust his energy by talking himself to a standstill.

The same principle applies if someone tries to interrupt you when you are giving your explanation. The moment he makes a sound or moves to break into your flow, stop – even if you are in mid-word. If you are interrupted, don't show any expression of hostility. Don't roll your eyes or signal exasperation and above all do not compete by trying to talk over him. If you do this you will inject a new level of aggression into the dispute and motivate him to talk even more.

Say absolutely nothing while keeping your eyes in the triangle of his face. Try for an expression that signals total concentration on and even interest in what he is saying, even if it is infuriating garbage. While you try to look as if you are listening you may as well do just that, given there is a small chance he is right and you are wrong. As before, don't fuel his fire with any interruption of your own, leave him to talk himself to a stop. After a fraction of a second's delay, resume at the beginning of the sentence he interrupted.

If he interrupts again, repeat the procedure, taking great care not to signal impatience; in fact, ideally acting as if you had not said any of this before. It's possible to take an apparently naïve or ingenuous role when you argue. Reply as an equal, appearing to take each question, even with its barb, absolutely at face value, acting as if you have no thought that there might be malice or a desire to put you down.

Meanwhile your statement edges forward, stopping at every interruption and then inexorably moving on.

Unfortunately, no matter how gently applied, this approach is still fairly provocative, so if an argument has progressed to this point, the person you are facing might have become quite angry. If he shouts or swears you are in a particularly strong position. If you can speak quietly he has to slow down, lean forward and attend more closely to what you say. At whatever stage of the argument you find yourself, a soft voice contains the greatest human power and with it you can potentially oblige him to play by your rules.

Just do it

Having said and done all of this, no matter how well you learn to argue, you are still likely to feel unpleasantly aroused during confrontations: either anxious because of the threat of rejection that is always present in an argument, or anxious and angry because any challenge invites an attack, putting your survival brain on heightened alert.

You will be much more comfortable if you can accept the inevitability that you will feel tense in any confrontation and forgive yourself for a weakness you share with most other reasonable people. Don't ask yourself to be comfortable in an argument; merely ask yourself to do it well.

Despite being armed with the most potent of arguing techniques, a civilised human being won't look for confrontation if conciliation is possible. However, if you have a system in place for knowing in advance how to conduct an argument, as well as knowing what you are arguing over, you can reasonably hope to reduce your dread of confrontation and take on a disagreement if your dignity obliges you to.

If you have argued well, even if you haven't won (which you will rarely do), you will avoid the angry, repetitive, inconclusive conversations in your head to which you are doomed if you mess up the process of arguing. Lastly, if you think the other person might hit you, make absolutely sure you are not setting him up. The bitter satisfaction in being a victim can be quite seductive.

Ideas

- Best arguing practice suggests you signal self-liking and security about your own territory, while showing no intention of invading another's.

- Just because someone doesn't agree with you, doesn't mean he doesn't understand you.

- The appropriate use of body language, particularly eye contact, is important in effective debate. To argue well, your gaze must spend the majority of time within the triangle of the two eyes and mouth of your opponent.

- There are escalating levels of arguing technique, and the lower-level forces must be exhausted before you enter the secondary stages.

- Don't make the mistake of equating stubbornness with strength.

- If you interrupt someone's flow, you are likely to provoke a fresh attack to silence you.

- The more you justify, the more vulnerable you are to producing a logically weak argument, putting your whole case in danger.

- Avoid contempt, derision or exasperation, which simply weaken your position by giving the other person something to legitimately attack, as well as increasing his determination to disagree with you.

- If someone is rude, you are more potent the more polite you become.

- At whatever stage of the argument you find yourself, a soft voice contains the greatest human power.

- Listen silently and appear to be attentive. It might even be worth really listening, because the other person might just be right.

- If you have a system in place that allows you to know how you will conduct an argument, even if you don't know what you're going to say, you can reasonably hope to reduce the fear and risks in confrontation.

CHAPTER 15

کو

Surviving Criticism

MOST OF US ARE NOT VERY GOOD at being wrong, and when we are, we can end up responding in some unproductive ways.

People will admit to not being perfect, but they are often reluctant to specify exactly how. Confessing weakness or fault is generally a good thing to do, but it doesn't always have good motives. Confession can be used to offload guilt and abdicate responsibility: 'Now I've told you, I cleansed myself.'

Quite often an admission of fault only comes when someone is caught out and his back is against the wall. Someone in this position may confess, but he's more often angry than contrite. At other times, someone is confessing before anyone else can have a go. 'I'm the first to confess I make mistakes!' can often mean: 'So don't you start on me!'

Some naïve souls declare they welcome constructive criticism, but close examination usually reveals that the only criticism they accept is so constructive as to be indistinguishable from a compliment.

The art of managing criticism lies in acknowledging your failings, provided you can genuinely agree they exist, but simultaneously behaving as if you think you probably have enough in your bank of human credit to still be a worthwhile human being.

You do not need to be perfect to be loved, but you do need to look as if you have some love for yourself, which is not the way you seem if you are obviously grudging or defensive. It's even better if you seem to be making some genuine effort to change what you have agreed is a failing. It's worth noting that in addition to conceding they are not perfect, many people will assure you they recognise their faults. What they don't always mention is why they haven't already set about fixing the problems they have apparently recognised.

Room to move

Intelligent management of criticism means responding in a way that doesn't earn more criticism. If you are very skilful you might even convince your critic that he's got you wrong, but to do that you still need to get past the barrier of appearing defensive.

The optimal first response to all criticism is both to be seen to consider and ideally to actually consider the possible truth of the comment, even if you regard it as absolute nonsense, a gross injustice or an insult. If your initial reaction is to dismiss the criticism, or worse still to get angry, no matter how wrong or unfair it may be, you will be immediately labelled as defensive and therefore guilty as charged.

So, even when you are profoundly hurt, you must go through a display of a reasoned consideration of the criticism if you are to have the least chance of restoring your good name. Obviously, while you are doing this it might be reasonable to genuinely examine the proposition. If you do find there is any truth to any part of the comment, by conceding this you strengthen rather than weaken your ability to negotiate the parts that you find unacceptable.

Imagine the following exchange:

Critic: 'You are horrible: I know about you, you pull the wings off flies.'

Knowing full well that you never willingly do such a thing, you have two potential answers. Firstly: 'What nonsense, I've never done that, that's incredibly unfair!'

This may be true, totally justified and something you can say with pride. Unfortunately, as a civilised person, knowledge of your own integrity may not be enough. As well as knowing yourself to be good, you are highly likely to need other people to see you as good. Your response has done nothing to convince your critic of your integrity, but it has made you look defensive, which of course you very well might be, given the magnitude of the charge.

Your second possible answer could be something like this: 'Do you really think so? I'm upset that you see me that way. Please tell me, what have I done to give you that idea? I'd really like to know because it would be awful if it were right.'

This response gives you much more room to negotiate, even if you believe your most appropriate reply would be: 'That's total garbage!'

If you appear to have seriously considered what has been said, you are in a much better position to defend yourself effectively. Once you have done this, then you can start to backtrack: 'You know, I'm not sure that's fair. When I think about my track record, I can't think when or how I could have done that. I'm really upset by all this and I don't think you've explained why you said what you did.'

This approach may get a hearing if your critic genuinely believed the criticism. Of course, if there is a hidden agenda and he simply wanted to put you down because of his own vulnerability, it will have no effect. If your detractor won't listen, you now have reasonable grounds to protest at the way you are being treated, which then gives you more leverage to contradict what has been said.

You will often find yourself in a position where a critic will not negotiate a criticism that you remain convinced you don't deserve. When this happens, you need further techniques to manage the situation. There are two simple sentences that you can use in all situations of unjustified or unnegotiable criticism. They are unbeatable; you cannot lose if you employ them, but there is the usual caveat – this doesn't mean you can win by using them, if winning means convincing a critic that he is wrong. The sentences are:

'I'm sorry you see me that way.'

and:

'I'm sorry that upsets you.'

In making either of these statements you speak the truth, because obviously you are sorry to be seen in a negative way, or that an action of yours has upset someone.

By phrasing your response to criticism in this way you are neither apologising for what has been said about you, nor apologising for what you have done. You are merely lamenting the perception someone might have of you, or the other person's distress at that perception. You are not apologising for something you do not believe you should have to apologise for.

On the assumption you have considered a criticism and genuinely do not believe it to be justified, 'I'm sorry you see me that way', or 'I'm sorry that upsets you' can be repeated several times if the attack goes on. You can back up the words by using the techniques of body signals I have already outlined: a direct gaze into the triangle of the face, gestures of openness and a complete absence of irony from your voice.

Here is the alternative hypothetical exchange:

Critic: 'I know for sure that you pull the wings off flies. I think you are truly horrible!'

You: 'I'm sorry you see me that way.'

Critic: 'Don't give me that – you're an insensitive liar!'

You: 'What can I say? I'm really sorry you see me that way.'

Critic: 'No you're not! You don't care about anybody or anything.'

You: 'All I can say again is that I'm sorry you see me that way and that you're upset with me. I wish you could give me a chance of convincing you that I would never do such a thing.'

You have not solved the problem of having someone see you in a light you don't enjoy, but there may not have been much chance of correcting that anyway. If logic has a chance, use it, but if it is obvious there is no common ground, at least you have kept your dignity and practised a degree of damage control.

If you are too hurt or angry to go through the motions of even the briefest consideration of the comment, and if your need to block the criticism gives way to a desire to score points, there is another, much riskier alternative. A wild exaggeration of the comment delivered with a reasonably straight voice, avoiding the temptation to add too heavy a note of irony, effectively mocks your critic but leaves you less room to move, as you are not offering an inch of concession: 'Yeah, I get a real kick from trying to wipe out an entire species!'

Such a technique is fine, but it is very close to the margin between assertion and aggression, so you do need to be comfortable that you truly are above criticism.

Unfortunately, repeating, 'I'm sorry you see me that way ...' too often, or using gross exaggeration, can both easily be seen as belittling responses, because ultimately they are. If you do put someone down, he will find great and obvious satisfaction in jumping on you if you subsequently prove to be wrong, which you must never forget is always a possibility.

It's not a jungle out there

Whatever you do, even if you feel you've done it well, if you are criticised you will feel angry or hurt to some degree. Finding yourself criticised unfairly or given no right of reply, you have very little chance of totally avoiding one or more of the negative emotions: anxiety, anger or sadness.

The only way you can reduce the hurtful impact of some of life's less pleasant events is to develop as robust a self-esteem as possible, and to confirm it by behaving in a way that both you and other people will respect. A good self-esteem becomes self-fulfilling. To feel good about yourself, you need to act with kindness and dignity, and if you like yourself, that's the way you will be most likely to behave anyway. As a result, you are less likely to be criticised.

As we've seen, a poor self-esteem becomes equally self-fulfilling, because a person with a poor self-esteem will judge others as seeing him through the same critical eyes as he sees himself. This means he is in danger of seeing criticism, rejection or put-down where none was meant. This then makes him defensive, aggressive or clingy, which will attract the very criticism he was trying to avoid and further undermine his self-esteem, provoking yet more defensive behaviour.

If you want to like yourself, act as if you believe you are liked, treating everybody as if their intentions towards you are good, as far as you possibly can.

In theory this is fine, but what if somebody really is rejecting you or putting you down? What if you are the object of a clear and obvious attack? Sadly, during the course of your life there will inevitably be times of confrontation, cruelty and crisis in your relationships with other people. Fortunately, the principles of *An Intelligent Life* offer a few simple guidelines.

You need to do something pretty bad to force a secure and healthy person to reject you or put you down. If someone is putting you down, a quick scan of your conscience is very likely to let you know what you have done to offend the person. On the other hand, if you can truly see no valid reason for an attack, you may safely consider it might be the other person who has the problem. While you might be right, always keep in mind how easy it is to sense criticism when there is none. It's easy to be over-alert, reacting perfectly rationally in your own perception, but overreacting in other people's eyes.

Having considered this, if you are still convinced you are being rejected or belittled, you have examined your own behaviour and you're certain you don't deserve such treatment, the problem may truly be someone else's emotional difficulty – one of prejudice, jealousy or ignorance. You can then forgive yourself for feeling hurt (because it doesn't signify anything but your own normal human vulnerability), but do think carefully before publicly dismissing a critic with, 'Well, that's his problem!' It's powerless as a put-down and never convinced anyone.

If someone's foolishness is obvious, it may not need illustration. If it's not so obvious, belittling someone may be your way of grabbing a little power when you feel vulnerable. As a technique, dismissing someone holds real dangers because, again, you could be quite wrong in your judgement. Once you have committed yourself to an angry denial or to an attack, it's terribly hard to undo it.

If somebody openly attacks you, there is no debate about what that person thinks of you. As a reasonable human being, you cannot be indifferent to a direct attack or rejection, but you will know where you are. Open abuse doesn't leave you guessing whether you are being attacked; it merely leaves you with the necessity to work out why and what to do. You are also free to make up your mind as to whether you deserve it or not.

As a reasonable person, if you agree you deserve criticism you will ultimately feel best if you accept your guilt and respond with an apology and appropriate attempts at restitution. If you don't agree, the way you feel will be decided by your skills in arguing and self-assertion.

When you have time to think through events and consider your interpretation, how you respond to a direct attack is relatively easy. The hard bit comes during a conversation when you sense something negative – a cynical note in someone's voice, a gesture that might be a dismissal, or a compliment that might really be a mockery. Then you need to decide on the spot what to do, because there is always the fear that you will get it wrong and respond in a way that leaves you feeling alone and foolish.

Events move fast in the process of relating to other people. How are you to accurately and quickly interpret what somebody means and then work out what to say in the few moments available before a conversation moves on and the opportunity to defend your dignity is lost? Unfortunately, the answer is that you can't. But then nor can anyone else.

You might think you understand what is driving someone, or what their motives are, and you may be correct, but you still won't be able to rely on your ability to correctly interpret and then choose the right response in the time available during the flow of conversation.

To repeat a point made before, other people's basic needs are easy to understand because they want belonging and individuality, just as you do. But at what level another person is playing, or which need is getting priority during any one encounter, is just too hard to know. Like you, another person has many layers of reasons for doing something, and usually (again, just like you) he doesn't fully understand himself either. It is a totally unrealistic expectation to believe that you should be able to accurately work out other people's agendas.

Yet your emotional comfort demands that you have an appropriate response in ambiguous situations. So you will need an approach that has universal application and does not require you to understand all the nuances of someone else's thinking.

You need a system for responding that makes equality the worst outcome, not loss. It needs to be easily applicable, even when you haven't got time to think. It must work just as well in situations where you really are being rejected or put down, as in those where it is no more than your oversensitive imagination.

In everyday existence, not many problems are life-and-death issues that need to be instantly deciphered for survival, so your choice of action in situations of uncertainty should be governed by a very basic principle: it's a tragedy to see and respond to an attack where none was meant and as a result lose someone who likes you. A great way to make an enemy is to attack him. Consider the following exchange:

> Sue, who has always had a bit of a soft spot for John, but is quite shy, says: 'John, I really like your tie!'
>
> John has always liked Sue, but she has never seemed to respond very well to him, despite all his efforts to get her attention. Sometimes he suspects she thinks he isn't quite good enough for her.

This comment could be his chance to ask her out, but then he wonders if she is laughing at him, especially as he has never really trusted his own taste in ties. It would be lovely if she were being friendly, but he would look so small if she were putting him down and then she went and told other people he really believed his tie was okay.

Seeing the situation as too risky to chance being mocked, to defend himself John replies, with a flash of his deservedly famous repartee: 'Well, I don't like your perfume!'

In this exchange no one makes a fool of John except himself.

Consider another situation. Sue has complimented John on his tie and, unfortunately, in this case she really is mocking him, as he suspects. Despite the disconcerting awareness he may be an object of fun, he replies: 'Thanks Sue, that's really kind of you.'

Now Sue is in a spot. She shot an arrow but it missed. Sure, she can go to a mutual friend and chuckle that John really believes his tie is acceptable, but it's pretty small stuff. John has started to force her hand.

'Yes,' she quips, 'it goes with the colour of your eyes.'

Given that his tie is yellow and purple, he is now getting a fairly clear idea of her motive, but this is actually quite calming, because the uncertainty is fading and he knows better where he stands. However, he persists in the same vein.

'Well, I didn't realise that purple and yellow suited my eyes, but I'm delighted you like my tie.'

Sue is really in trouble now. He has taken control and she really has no option but to declare her hand: 'To be honest John, I think your tie's foul!'

This may not be particularly reassuring, but it is actually easier to deal with than the uncertainty of not knowing what an exchange means, and it firmly puts the power in John's hands. If someone is truly putting you down, turning the other cheek has great potency, smiting your enemy much more mightily than abuse or a blow. Now in control, John is in a good position to calmly respond: 'Well Sue, I'm sorry you don't like it, especially as I've always admired your taste in clothes.'

Hardly game, set and match, but pretty good!

Such tales simply illustrate that by acting as if you are disliked you can lose love that was previously yours, while by acting as if you are liked you can at worst leave in a neutral position, and you might even earn a grudging respect.

The great beauty of acting as if you are not being belittled or rejected, and indeed acting as if you believe you are liked, is that you do not have to rely on the accuracy of your judgement of the situation to make the right response. A whole lot of pressure is taken off you because acting in this way is genuinely likeable and dignified. So the obvious conclusion is that if you behave in a likeable fashion, you will find it easier to believe you are liked and so like yourself.

The value of behaving as if you believe you are liked, even if you suspect that you are not, can be summarised in a very simple grid.

| | | John's Actions | |
		As if she's on his side	As if she's mocking him
Sarah's Agenda	She really likes him	<u>Score</u> + + Because he has kept a friend – cell a. –	<u>Score</u> – – Because he has lost a friend – cell b. –
	She's really mocking him	<u>Score</u> + Because no friend but dignity intact – cell d. –	<u>Score</u> + Because they are even – cell c. –
	Final score:	+++	–

The reaction grid

If you add up the vertical columns of the grid, simple arithmetic makes it very clear which is the better behavioural decision.

Cell a. Treat someone who does like you as if she likes you and you consolidate a friendship. The best of all possible outcomes.

Cell b. Treat someone who likes you as if he doesn't and you lose a friend: the worst of all possible outcomes.

Cell c. Respond with aggression to someone who doesn't like you and you're probably about even, but you're hardly a winner because aggression signals vulnerability.

Cell d. Act as if you believe someone likes you, when in truth she doesn't. If you do act as if you believe you are liked, even if it turns out you are not, you can protect and even strengthen your own self-respect.

When you are in physical danger, it makes sense to shoot first and ask questions later. Hopefully you will never be in this situation, but your survival brain sees rejection or put-down as a death threat and can push you to react with a level of aggression that is suitable for protecting your life, but that is disastrous for your normal relationships.

Your survival brain is profoundly resistant to the idea of acting within Cell d, but away from our jungle origins and within the rules of civilised human behaviour, at worst you are equal and you might even earn reluctant respect from someone who had originally determined to pull you down.

Are you a bigger fool if you look gullible or if you attack and lose a friend?

Ideas

- If your initial reaction to criticism is to reject it, right or wrong, you are likely to be labelled as defensive and therefore guilty as charged.

- You must at least look as if you are considering a criticism before you have any real chance of defending yourself.

- If there is any truth to a criticism, by conceding this you strengthen rather than weaken your ability to negotiate anything you find unacceptable.

- There are two simple but unbeatable responses to all unjustified or non-negotiable criticism: 'I'm sorry you see me that way', and 'I'm sorry that upsets you.'

- The only mind to which you have access is your own, so your judgements in ambiguous situations are at best suspect and often plain wrong.

- When physical threat is not an issue, if you delay confirming that someone is truly rejecting you or trying to put you down, there is very little lost.

- It is the greatest tragedy to see and respond to an attack where none was meant and as a result to lose someone who likes you.

- If you treat someone as if you believe he likes you when he really doesn't, you lose nothing. You keep your dignity and you may actually regain some control of the situation.

༈

CHAPTER 16

Self-Defence

WE ALL TRY TO PROTECT OURSELVES. Sometimes we look after our emotions with a lot more energy than we give our bodies. None of us are so secure, so skilfully assertive or have such a good self-esteem that we don't ever need to protect our feelings.

If your self-esteem is good, your systems for securing love and dignity are likely to be effective, so you will need minimal self-defence. When people with a high level of self-respect do need to defend their emotions, the techniques they use make them feel better by increasing their sense of belonging and individuality.

Intelligent self-protection is like any other element of a life lived well: it doesn't draw attention to itself but merely sits in the background while you strive as effectively as possible for more love and dignity.

Because we can all feel threatened, we don't always protect ourselves very cleverly. Anxiety can sabotage good sense. Sometimes we fear an event, a situation or an encounter without good reason because we have never thought through the consequences to their rational conclusion. This can send us on a lifelong quest for control, even if we have very little idea as to what we are controlling, why we are controlling it or what would happen if we stopped. The more threatened we feel, the more rigidly stereotyped our behaviour becomes, and so the more we lock ourselves into our own thoughtless defences.

If you don't like yourself enough, you will tend to assume others don't either, so your feelings will be vulnerable and you are more likely to feel under attack or rejected. Locked into your own anti-self-prejudice, you are in danger of not getting close enough to people to hear what they really think about you, leaving you with only your self-critical voice by which to judge yourself. This is bound to be bad for you, because as part of any satisfactory system of self-protection, you must approach other people. Only in situations of intimacy can you hope to get accurate feedback or find effective ways to like yourself.

If your self-esteem is poor, it's easy to forget that other people are much more likely to accept you for what you are than you are to accept yourself. Many people recognise they are their own harshest critics, but they don't know how to change, or don't dare to change because they are afraid they have to watch themselves all the time.

Some people respond to their sense of rejection with aggression or even violence. They instantly lose out because any defence system that either takes you away from other people or obliges them to distance themselves from you is no good. Fortunately, most people are not so foolish as to physically attack other people, but there remains a wide variety of defensive responses, all designed to be protective, but which when overused or misused actually do harm.

The first instinct of secure people who feel threatened is to try to increase their sense of both belonging and strength. Insecure people do the same, but they tend to go about it in a self-defeating way because they are preoccupied with avoiding rejection and weakness.

Your genes and your background have handed you a mix of

characteristics. You will recall the sundae of self-esteem – one scoop of which represents love and belonging, the other individuality, dignity and strength.

Your personality may make you more a love seeker or a rejection avoider; or you may be predominantly a power seeker or a weakness avoider. These characteristics strongly determine your personality structure, the way you respond to the world and the way the world treats you. Based on this concept, these aspects of personality could be plotted on a simple diagram that represents the dimensions of people's protective styles.

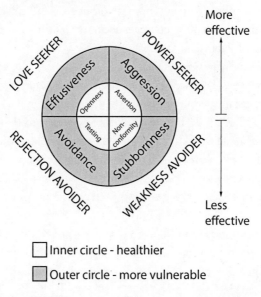

☐ Inner circle - healthier
▨ Outer circle - more vulnerable

Some personality styles

Obviously your individual personality style will affect the defensive systems you use. Despite the variation in emphasis, effective techniques for self-protection differ from ineffective ones in three very distinct ways:

1. They work. That is, you get more love and more dignity.

2. They don't make things worse. That is, you don't suffer more rejection or belittlement.

3. They are less extreme and less obvious.

Self-protective systems fall into five categories:

1. Looking for love.

2. Avoiding rejection.

3. Looking for power.

4. Avoiding weakness.

5. Avoiding everything.

The rest of this chapter is a broad overview of the way in which both happy and unhappy people try to protect their emotions. Because all defensive systems have their origins in healthy devices, I have highlighted the effective systems to contrast with the distortions and exaggerations of someone in distress.

Looking for love

Looking for love is the single best thing you can do in the service of your self-esteem. Any move that truly brings you closer to people is good for you. If you are willing to accept this, it reasonably follows that all effective self-protection must include the pursuit and maintenance of love.

No one has ever persuaded another person to love him. Love has to be given freely; it cannot be forced or extracted. Therefore love must be pursued with gentleness and dignity, which means without signalling either anger or desperation, even if you feel it.

Sometimes when you feel you are in real danger of rejection and want to do something about it as quickly as possible, the most active and positive thing you can do is nothing. Unfortunately, doing nothing does not sit easily with human nature, and fear or anger can drive some remarkably unproductive behaviour.

At one level or another, every sane person knows he wants and needs love, but some people forget the rules of the game and become clinging, pleading, wounded or angry. A pathologically dependent person is someone who has so overcommitted herself to another adult that she feels she will lose everything if her investment in the relationship is lost. She has neglected the necessity for preserving individuality and dignity, so she has truly sacrificed herself for love.

If a relationship comes to an end, a desperate person fears she will have no identity left, quite forgetting she had a separate existence before the relationship began and may have been a perfectly effective person. In her truth, there is nothing to do but cling or chase, hoping she will catch enough love to feed her starving spirit. There is a horrible inevitability in the way that desperately chasing love will chase away the last of any love she was trying so hard to catch.

To have love turned off in a relationship is usually devastating, even for the healthiest and most self-respecting people, but most of us are very wary of appearing to be too hungry for love or to be seen as jealously guarding it, even if we are. Neediness, like jealousy, signals a desperate fear of being alone, which almost guarantees rejection, as well as loss of dignity.

A person who signals no self-love is a bottomless pit of need and scares everybody away. If you want to be loved, being friendly and offering intimacy is clearly appropriate behaviour in the pursuit of your goal. Unfortunately, if a little bit is good, insecure people sometimes decide more will be better, resulting in excessive familiarity and intrusiveness. Sincere two-handed handshakes, earnest inquiries after someone's wellbeing, or loud and repeated declarations as to how wonderful it is to meet you will rarely convince someone to like somebody more.

Generosity is also an essential element in the healthy pursuit of love, but generosity can grow into excessive giving. Generosity is wonderful for you and those around you if you are a warm and giving person; one who gets pleasure from generosity and apparently asks nothing in return. Unfortunately, generosity can be overplayed in an attempt to get and hold love by keeping people in debt. The desperation of excessive givers is matched only by their urgent need to keep out of debt, returning fourfold any favour they receive.

An excessive giver is always in danger of feeling hurt and used. I have already alluded to the difficulties you will have if you deliver a truckload of watermelons to someone who likes the occasional slice. Effusive gratitude, talking too much, over-explanation of your reasons and motives, or repeated apology can all spring from an exaggerated urge to buy love with gifts. Sexual promiscuity, especially in females, may have the same origins.

Sometimes talking too much or giving an excess of detail is part of a desperate attempt to be understood. *For most of us, to feel understood is to feel as if we are loved and accepted, just as being misunderstood feels like being rejected.*

It's a sad fact of life, but there isn't much doubt that high status can help one's popularity. The better-looking, cleverer or richer you are, the greater your potential for finding love and the larger the population from which you can pick your lovers and friends. You can choose to deny it, but this may be more idealism than reality.

If you can live with this as a possible truth, clearly you should present yourself as well as possible, signalling your intellectual, financial or physical advantages, but it's vital to do your signalling in a low-key way and later rather than sooner. Ideally, you should pitch yourself modestly, hoping others will discover your full value.

It's tempting to add value with extreme modesty, but this is usually transparent. The reverse of this coin is boasting or paying excessive attention to your appearance, spending more than you can afford on clothes, cosmetics, jewellery or cars. From this point, it is only a short distance to lying in an attempt to present an irresistibly high-status package.

Exaggerated humility and exaggerated displays of status are techniques that will lose much more love than they can ever possibly win.

Your ability to behave in a way that helps you to feel accepted into a group is really important to your wellbeing. The rules of good manners guide you on a safe path through uncertain territory. They allow you to feel more secure, giving you reasonable confidence that you will not offend others. This is not conformity; it's civility.

Manners are the accepted rules of a society, which give you guidelines for dealing with unfamiliar people or threatening situations. People who are safe with each other still avoid being offensive, but they can choose how well-mannered they wish to be, depending on the level of their familiarity. The greater your sense of a difference between your status and the status of the person you are dealing with, the more likely you are to be formal. Your inner ape feels more comfortable if he signals deference to the bigger animal by being polite. This has its evolutionary background in trying to inhibit aggression if you accidentally trespass, which you are less likely to do if you are well-mannered.

If you feel vulnerable, overly polite behaviour and studied formality are a refuge from uncertainty. Excessively well-mannered people are protecting themselves from rejection by rigidly adhering to the rules, hoping they'll be safe inside them. Unfortunately, the stiffness of too much politeness gets in the way of intimacy, leaving such people a lot lonelier than if they were able to recognise they would actually be more acceptable if they were less deferential.

Some people (those preoccupied with avoiding weakness) are contemptuous towards socially approved behaviour. They are striving to show very clearly how independent they are. Many non-conformists believe their own propaganda, which can make them difficult to be around.

Having high standards and expecting a great deal of yourself is a perfectly rational way to think and behave. It is equally rational to hope for, but never to expect, equally high standards in others. *Expect a great deal of yourself but don't expect to be to be rewarded just because you have behaved well by your own criteria.* Hopes are fine, but expectations are risky. If you expect other people to behave in a particular way because you have done so, you may be disappointed and you risk giving in to displays of anger and hurt.

The much overrated Dr Freud described a defence system he called sublimation. Through this process he suggested anxiety and anger can be converted to fruitful activities and relieve the pressure of negative emotion. If you can paint beautiful pictures, exercise, perform acts of selfless nobility or just do things very well, you are employing effective defensive systems and you'll certainly feel better than if you choose to do nothing.

Religious faith is a powerful and effective system for finding love. It offers strength and reassurance to a majority of people on this planet. It gives a sense of being loved by a deity and love through belonging to a congregation or a group of fellow believers. It offers such a depth of protection that it is often strengthened after a massive personal tragedy.

Avoiding rejection

Anything that takes you away from other people is likely to be bad for you. Obviously there is pleasure in healthy solitude and contemplation, but happy people eventually head for home and their emotional attachments to people.

Fear of being seen as clingy can make people hide behind a distant exterior that might be mistaken for arrogance and superiority. Their pendulum of behaviour has swung too far the other way, trying to signal complete indifference to conceal the neediness underneath. The fear of being rejected for asking too much is replaced by the imagined dignity of looking as if they didn't care in the first place.

This is the very essence of an ineffective defence system; behaviour designed to help but just makes things worse. Often no defence was needed in the first place. *Remember, you are much more likely to be rejected for the things you do to protect yourself than for what you really are.*

Withdrawn, distant, angry people are nearly always people who fear rejection. Their behaviour signals either: 'I have so much self-love that I don't need your approval,' or, more directly: 'Go away, I don't like you!'

They are trying to say: 'I don't need you!' But they really mean: 'I don't want to need you, because I'm afraid you wouldn't want me.'

Some people are so terrified that their hunger for love will put them in a position where they will be weakened, they are determined not to be fooled into trusting, only to be rejected once they let their guard down.

Not valuing yourself automatically means not trusting other people to value you. It's very scary to need someone who you can't imagine would possibly want you. It may seem much safer to retreat into the dignity of appearing not to care; better still if you can believe it yourself. To avoid the lethal dangers of rejection, a fail-safe system is to avoid intimate relationships. Withdrawing from someone or pushing them away can feel like self-protection. At the same time, by putting pressure on someone to go, it can be used to test the security of the relationship.

Secure people run a gently critical eye over the behaviour of a person they are considering as a friend or a long-term partner. They assess what they see but accept that they cannot possibly be certain of what that person is really thinking, or of every aspect of his character. Because secure people know they'll survive even if they do misjudge someone, they are able to refrain from setting up tests because they aren't so hungry for certainty.

Frightened people often set traps, which others refuse to fall into because they hate being manipulated, or they design tests that people fail because they didn't know they were being tested and wouldn't have known the rules if they had. As a result, an anxious tester can test a relationship to destruction, always getting the negative result he fears. The unhappy logic behind this form of self-protective behaviour is fairly obvious.

If you were forced to climb down a cliff to save your life and you were offered a coil of rope but didn't trust its strength, you'd test it by trying to break it. You would put your foot on it and stretch it. The weaker it looked to you, the harder you would try to break it. At first glance this may seem a little bizarre – trying to destroy something that you want to support you and save your life – but people do it.

Worse still, if you had ever been given a weak rope in the past and been hurt, you would probably distrust all ropes. You'd test even the best-looking one because it might seem too good to be true. You'd probably keep on testing it until it broke, even if you were testing it beyond reasonable expectations of its strength and well beyond the strength necessary to support you.

Once repeated testing has successfully broken one relationship, if you don't realise what you're doing, there's a risk you will test every relationship to breaking point.

'Come and get me. Prove that you love me by chasing after me, even though I'm pulling away and saying I don't want you. I shall refuse any advance you make towards me to test you and to show that I really meant it and it was not just a manipulation. Once I finally commit myself to you, I shall do it with a show of great reluctance to demonstrate that the relationship is now your doing and that you are responsible for anything that may go wrong. If you behave in any fashion that differs from my view of the way a devoted lover should, because I was reluctant in the first place, I will have an even greater right to be hurt and angry.'

Trapped in this cycle, the obvious conclusion is that relationships are too hard and it is easier to try living alone. Unfortunately this is obligatory aloneness and not freely chosen solitude, so it is therefore painful and requires a great deal of energy to maintain.

If vulnerable people find themselves faced by potential disapproval or failure, they are sometimes tempted to retreat into the safety of a child's role. By becoming sick or claiming exhaustion they are looking for acceptance or forgiveness as a lesser but safer creature. By abdicating from an adult role into the child-like vulnerability of sickness, they are hoping they won't have to face the expectations of adult levels of performance. This way they feel safer because they haven't so far to fall if they fail.

By making yourself vulnerable to reduce your vulnerability, you are also making it clear you are not trying to compete as an adult, challenging for adult territorial rights. Your survival brain figures this will inhibit attack as well as avoid rejection.

At work you can signal you are harassed, tired or your headache is so bad you can scarcely think straight, which sets up a fallback position if things go wrong. This is getting in first – delivering the message that others should understand the pressure you are under, excuse your mistakes and still like you if you don't do or achieve what they ask. If something does go wrong the failure is not really yours because it was caused by the excessive demands of unsympathetic people on an already vulnerable person. At the same time you are pleading not to be asked to do any more, to avoid the unpleasant possibility of saying 'no'.

Making the best use of available resources is an appropriate way to behave from a biological perspective, as most of the evolution of our brains occurred when food was scarce. Now we have such an abundance of food, a lean body is probably abnormal, but not all fatness is simply the result of a natural urge to eat everything in sight.

Some forms of obesity are a desperate grab for safety. A percentage of fat people actually could lose weight, and sometimes do, but only briefly. For these people fat offers a refuge from rejection: there is no point even trying to form a relationship because no one would want them while they are fat. Just like alcoholics, convinced they can stop drinking any time they want, some obese people know they could have a relationship any time they wanted, if only they got thin. It's just that they never do.

A sexual relationship is most likely to survive to become long-term if it's based on friendship as well as large amounts of lust. The recently infatuated will earnestly declare that they are not only lovers but also best friends, firmly convinced they are the first truly great lovers because of this seminal discovery.

Frightened people can exploit the notion of friendship between lovers in a subtle ploy for escaping rejection. This is usually invisible to both participants and tends to be played out in a relationship that may have been developing quite well. An insecure person may start with a genuine desire for an adult, sexual union, but as this becomes a real possibility all the dangers of need, trust and loss of control bring a panicky urge to step back from the brink, and so the relationship is converted into a friendship. A previously genuinely interested person is left frustrated and bewildered, unable to understand why or even how this has come about. The relationship generally fizzles out, but can occasionally go on for years this way because the real rules are never spelt out.

In another, more transparent, form of the same game, a man may declare he has too much respect for his girlfriend to make a sexual move towards her. It's possible he's being good and pure, but he might also be hiding behind a façade of nobility to escape his fear of inadequacy and his belief that he will inevitably be rejected if he gets too close and his weakness is discovered.

A degree of self-doubt and an unwillingness to trespass or stick your neck out too far is a healthy piece of self-preservation. Unfortunately, a low self-esteem sometimes generates an unhealthy level of anxiety about your right to say what you want to, or a mistaken belief that what you say must be correct for you to be acceptable as a person. This can result in a wide range of ineffective behaviours. People mumble to avoid full commitment to an idea, or they give too much detail, jumping from one theme to another in an effort to justify, explain and avoid every ambiguity and escape being misunderstood.

Self-doubt may simply push you to repeatedly say, 'You know', 'You see', or 'You know what I mean?', unconsciously looking for feedback and reassurance that it's all right for you to go on. Fear of saying the wrong thing sabotages fluency, because it is an almost impossible task to speak and check other people's reactions at the same time.

Happy people look for love, while unhappy people run away from rejection. Even if you lose, the pursuit of love is an exciting and rewarding experience if you can believe you are lovable, but it becomes an anxious torment if your self-esteem is poor and you expect rejection.

Once you enter defensive mode, whether you are chasing or running away, your chances of pain are dramatically increased by your own actions. You may like someone, but dare not trust him to like you. He might very easily be doing his best to tell you that he loves you, but unfortunately once you have panicked you are more likely to listen to your inner truth that says he will reject you than listen to his voice as he insists he won't. He may have genuinely intended to love you forever, until you made it just too hard.

Looking for power

Self-protective systems that people use to look for more love are similar to the techniques people use to avoid rejection. In the same way, there is only a limited difference between healthy power seeking and desperately avoiding helplessness. The difference is one of degree.

The same principles apply to all defence mechanisms. They spring from healthy roots; their problems only start when they become overgrown. Systems that evolved to consolidate and even to gain power become exaggerated, and instead of adding to their potency, they cause a loss of status as well as an increased chance of rejection.

Gentle and dignified assertiveness is the single most effective mechanism for gaining secure and durable power within a healthy relationship, but assertion can lose its way and stumble into aggression. Then the power of equality that comes with assertiveness gets confused with the power necessary to dominate. From aggression there are only a few steps to violence, which in a civilised society always means loss of respect and can lead to loss of freedom.

To some people, assertiveness looks too much like aggression for them to feel safe with it. They want their own way, but they don't want to risk rejection for seeming to be selfish, so they try to gain power by stealth, which means manipulation. They apply pressure with guilt or by subtle threat of rejection. People who use these systems can become powerfully controlling of anyone vulnerable to the loss of their love. The usual victims are their children or child-like partners. This is tyranny of the weak.

There are several good techniques for pursuing potency that can sabotage happiness if overdone. Working gives a sense of territorial control and is satisfying because it is creative and helps define you as an individual by defining your territory. It also tends to produce money, and money is definitely worth having for the freedom it can buy.

However, overdone, work can become territory to be conquered for its own sake, rather than a means to improve life. It can stop being rewarding creatively and become a compulsion. A workaholic has lost his sense that he can exist without his work and he is not relieved by it, but anxious or guilty if he stops. He loses much more of his life by excessive work than he earns in money to compensate. Compulsive working may be designed to win power by promotion and this may be a good thing, but it can also lead to unscrupulousness and greed, where no amount of power is enough power.

Education is an obvious way to improve a sense of potency and status. Expanding one's territory of knowledge is a path to feeling bigger and more in command of your world. Too much of a good thing makes a perpetual student hide from the real world of work and relationships behind his umpteenth post-doctoral thesis. Intellectual snobbery and pedantry are a display of power as protection against a feeling of weakness and can merely result in tiresomely precise grammar or quoting Cicero to a disinterested audience.

Physical fitness is highly desirable in that it is attractive to other people, adds to your chances of longevity and in the jungle means you have more power to beat up challengers. With increasing physical fitness, there is potentially an increase in sexual desirability and therefore a wider choice of mate, giving you a powerful biological and emotional edge. These advantages are so desirable that people can drive themselves to destruction in their pursuit. People who are chasing the security of maximum power and perfect love by compulsively building their bodies to the grotesque or trying to beautify themselves by dieting into oblivion are achieving self-destruction rather than power.

Persistence and determination are forces that hold us to a goal and are vital motivators for exploration and territorial conquest. Unfortunately they can evolve to rigidity, stubbornness and perfectionism in people whose self-worth is over-invested in winning, or whose self-esteem is insufficient to allow them to lose or fail.

A determined and persistent person may be proud; which is fine as a strong statement of individuality provided it is not diminished by an obligation always to be right. Identities too fragile to be anywhere but on top are in danger of holding too ferociously to what they see as the truth, even when there is powerful evidence to contradict them. This is not strength but stubbornness; a desperate grab at power to avoid humiliation.

Most people know that a degree of independence is an essential element of potency and self-love. Some imagine self-love means not needing other people's love or approval, with the unhappy delusion that this is independence and therefore power. Such independence players are tempted to overdo a good thing; exaggerated elegance or haughty and disdainful behaviour are attempts to show they have so much self-love that they have no need of anybody. An affectation of not caring is closely related to the strutting, preening arrogance of vanity, which is designed to declare a boundless confidence in personal desirability, signalling that someone is armed with such quantities of self-love that he doesn't need anybody else.

Acting in an arrogant or superior fashion is always an attempt to compensate for a feeling of inferiority. It's a grab for power to escape the helplessness of rejection and weakness. Given most arrogant people believe their own story most of the time, it's marginally successful as a defensive system, especially as they can occasionally convince other people they are as important as they pretend to be.

Under attack, ultimately everybody must fight to survive. If the attack is physical, a violent response may be necessary and appropriate. If the attack is verbal, no response at all may be best, but some unreasoned and persistent attacks require an aggressive, although never violent, response as a last option. To safely use such means of self-defence, it is absolutely essential to be sure you really are being attacked and that there is no other way you can possibly deal with it.

If you are quite certain you are being belittled or rejected, and all other systems have failed, maintaining a chilly but polite distance might be the best strategy, but it's easily overused. Vulnerable people may try to take power out of a threatening person's hands by ignoring him, because treating another as if he doesn't exist is like annihilating him; denying his very existence.

People who are nasty and cold for no apparent reason invariably have such a poor sense of self-worth that they expect no one to like them: they anticipate being attacked. They can't face the depth of their own self-dislike, so, in true paranoid reversal, they see their own feelings about themselves in others and try to deal with this by ignoring them or attacking, getting in first to avoid their own difficulties. They have decided they might as well be recognised as having the strength they feel anger gives them, rather than pathetically running after approval they believe they will never find. Habitual anger is simply guarding against belittlement or rejection by doing it first.

Because anger can feel like the route to power, some people pump themselves up looking for a fight. In the society of drinking males at the bottom end of the social scale, this can lead to an actual search for violence, but looking for a reason to be angry is not limited to drunks in a bar. We all do it to some degree, usually in the form of searching for a defect in someone. Unfortunately, trying to find a fault or weakness in another person to feel better in yourself is a very fragile defence: 'I may not be as clever as she is, but brains aren't everything and I bet she could never get a boyfriend.' By actively belittling someone you can only increase your stature relatively, never absolutely.

If you embark on an anxious search to find out why you feel bad, you might conclude other people are ignoring or rejecting you because they see you as having some fault or weakness. You might decide they are critical of you because you haven't got their education or as much money as they have. Once you have come to this decision, you have provided yourself with an excuse to be angry with everybody for rejecting you for such unreasonable reasons. This allows you to be angry, and at the same time permits you to sidestep recognising that the real problem is your believing other people think you are worthless unless you come equipped with high status. The money or the university degree that you lack and feel you shouldn't be judged for lacking is easy to see and easy to claim as an injustice. This logic allows you the potency of righteous anger, far preferable to the helplessness of feeling inadequate.

Because people need power almost as much as they need love, they easily get their priorities confused and sometimes behave as if they don't need love at all, while struggling to exaggerate their individual potency. They get a sort of power, but at great cost. Remember, both scoops of the sundae of self-esteem need to be of similar size as well as being generous servings.

Avoiding weakness

For obvious reasons, helplessness is terrifying to everybody. To be helpless is to be without power, which in the jungle or on the savannah means to lose your territory, your chances of reproduction and almost certainly your life.

In the world of emotional defence, fighting against helplessness is a rearguard action when you feel you have been overwhelmed. Just as running away from rejection is not as healthy a coping system as running after love, so avoiding powerlessness is probably even more desperate than grabbing for control.

Conservation of resources is natural and rational. The vigour with which you defend your possessions depends on how likely it is you might lose them and how much you need them. Meanness is a slightly pathetic way of hanging on to material possessions; it makes them symbols of what little you feel is left of your spirit. Meanness signals you feel easily diminished and depleted as a person, so all you can do is hang on to physical territory.

Deliberately seeking comfortable time alone without intrusion or the obligation to look after anyone else is healthy. Self-isolation is different. It's not chosen time out; again, it's a rearguard action, trying to define yourself by separateness, putting distance between you and others. Withdrawing or isolating yourself sometimes arises from a need to protect a fragile sense of self from being swamped and lost among other people. At other times it's a passive anger at the perceived insensitivity of fellow humans. Of course, most commonly, isolation is self-protection from rejection; a system for avoiding relationships in which there seems no possibility of anything other than a painful end.

Non-conformity can be a healthy expression of a secure identity when you feel good in yourself and if meeting a particular requirement would violate your values. Sometimes childlike disobedience is lent dignity with the label of nonconformity, when it is merely a concealed rebellion, too frightened to declare itself openly. Being late, overspending on your husband's credit card, or other covert forms of anger are last-ditch ways to protect against feeling like a nothing.

Passive anger in the form of stubbornness, pedantry and contrariness are also techniques for resuscitating a moribund dignity. A small flame of individuality flickers in situations where you fear too open a display of feelings would simply lead to your being snuffed out entirely. It is a system suited to survival in the army or a prison camp, but it can become a very alienating habit in more potentially amiable company.

Feeling powerless is a terrible feeling because nobody who feels powerless can ever feel safely loved. It's easy to see why most people will do almost anything to avoid it.

Avoiding everything

Everybody needs a break. No one can be mature and grown-up all the time. Quite reasonable people take time out from stressful jobs with headaches, menstrual pain or 'the flu', although the same problem doesn't always stop them going to a party.

It is possible to avoid thinking about something to avoid being so troubled by it, and this is not necessarily an unhealthy process. Pushing thoughts out of your mind can reduce the pain of an emotion. This is a perfectly reasonable manoeuvre if you have done everything that you can to fix a problem, or if the next move depends on forces over which you have no control. Then, if you can do it, pushing a problem aside is far better than anxiously and fruitlessly thinking about it, or boring and frustrating people with its endless public examination.

If it's not possible to just push something out of your thoughts, you may still be able to turn your mind to something else, based on the observation that it is very hard to think of two things at the same time. You can use distraction constructively to escape from physical and emotional pain. Working hard, immersing yourself in an activity or calling a friend are great ways to feel better, even if the problem hasn't gone away.

Even when a problem is inescapable, the rules for healthy self-management do not change:

> If you do things that are creative and help you respect yourself, or that bring you closer to other people, you are defending yourself well. If you do things that diminish you by making yourself child-like and undignified, or if you distance yourself from other people, you are not being intelligent in your self-care.

In other words, if it helps you to forget about the mortgage, going to bed at three o'clock in the afternoon to make love to an enthusiastic partner is good, but going to bed to sleep to escape is probably not in your interests.

Healthy distraction techniques still allow awareness if action is required. Distraction becomes counter-productive when it evolves to denying that a problem exists and needs attention, as opposed to simply delaying thinking about it because at the moment nothing can be done about it.

A child can pull the blanket over his head; then he can't see the tigers, so they aren't there. This is fine for kids, but its success as a defence depends heavily on there being no tigers around. Adults practising denial, as opposed to kids under blankets, are a different proposition, and they can be as endlessly frustrating to others as they are destructive to themselves. Yet again, these are people who are in danger of believing their own self-deception, so opportunities for healthy action are lost.

The alcoholic who can hardly stand yet tells you he doesn't drink, or the gambler whose life is falling apart but will tell you he's breaking even, is doing more than lying. Their system of denial is so powerful that they truly believe what they say and they are affronted if you challenge them. Denial is ultimately a hopeless system because it has no flexibility, and since it makes the problem cease to exist, by definition the problem can never be addressed.

Drugs are a more extreme escape route after distraction and denial, although of course they are all intimately related. Ingesting or injecting an uncertain quantity of an uncertain chemical requires some fairly heavy denial. The inhibitory effect of alcohol on the frontal lobes of your brain is liberating, and if you are using it for its mood-elevating effects in low doses, it is probably a relatively safe drug. If you are using alcohol to escape physical or emotional pain, it is every bit as bad as the rest.

Drugs, of course, can be lethal for the body as well as the mind and are therefore a pathway to the final escape of death. Suicide clearly has some position in everybody's option list, but it is a very small one and this is not the place to debate it.

It's worthwhile to note that madness is not a defence system. It is not biologically possible to be driven to or to choose madness. The only way to choose to become psychotic is by using excessive amounts of some mind-altering substances.

A common fear for those who suffer panic attacks is that they will lose control of their minds; but you simply can't make yourself mad, no matter how hard you try or how distressed you are. There is not a thin line between sanity and insanity, but a huge physiological gap.

In this chapter I have tried to offer an overview of the unproductive things we do under threat, drawing them together with some of the behaviours I have discussed earlier.

There is a legion of defensive techniques designed to grab at love and power or avoid rejection and weakness. All of them are much less intelligently self-interested than pursuing love and potency with acts of kindness and dignity.

We'd all be more comfortable if we could appreciate we will rarely be rejected or belittled for what we are, but the distorted ways in which we try to protect ourselves can make into a reality something that previously only existed in our fears.

Ideas

- Nobody is so secure that they don't need to protect their feelings.

- All defensive systems spring from healthy origins.

- Healthy and effective defence systems can be overplayed to become ineffective, and even destructive.

- The first instinct of secure people under threat is to pursue love and strength, while insecure people are more preoccupied with avoiding rejection and weakness.

- Your personality style will be determined by whether you are more a love seeker, more a rejection avoider, or whether you are predominantly a power seeker or a weakness avoider.

- Any move that brings you towards people is good for you. Anything that takes you away from other people is likely to be bad for you.

- Working, education, physical fitness, persistence and determination are healthy ways of pursuing power. They give an increased sense of territorial control, as well as making you feel more desirable.

- Some people choose to be angry because it helps them feel they are strong.

- Some would choose to be a bastard rather than a fool, based on the mistaken belief that no one loves a bastard and no one loves a fool, but at least a bastard has dignity.

- Habitual anger is simply guarding against belittlement or rejection by getting in first.

- Once you have done a quick scan of your conscience and genuinely find no adequate reason for someone to be in some way angry or dismissive of you, you can assume it is because he doesn't like himself.

- To have hopes of other people is fine, but expectations are risky.

- Not valuing yourself means not trusting other people to value you either.

- A person who signals a lack of self-love is a bottomless pit of need and scares everybody away.

- Manipulation – the application of pressure through guilt or a subtle threat of rejection – is tyranny of the weak.

- Searching for a fault or weakness in another person so as to feel better in yourself is a very fragile defence.

PART 3

~

Intelligent Love

The Qualities, Pitfalls and Management of
Different Types of Relationships

CHAPTER 17

⤳

Lovers and Friends

IN THE COURSE OF YOUR LIFE, through family, school, interests, or work, you'll meet thousands of people and relate to them with varying degrees of intensity. Most you will never get to know at all; some relationships will be brief, others merely convenient. Some will turn out to be close friends and a few will become true intimates.

From these encounters you will select a series of people, and perhaps ultimately the person, who will occupy your innermost orbit of intimacy. If you do, this person will be your sexual partner and hopefully someone whom you can continue to love when the physical attraction isn't the strongest force any more.

Loving, intimate relationships are central to our lives. Most of our songs are about love, we write about love, and we spend a great deal of time thinking about love. Irrespective of how individualistic we are, most of us want a loving relationship, so we have to have a system for selecting someone.

If it were true that everybody wants somebody to love, finding a partner shouldn't be so hard. Unfortunately, when you are very definitely available, everybody else seems to be paired off. Of course, this is not really the case, but because we tend to judge people by their ability to be in a relationship, nobody wants to advertise that they are alone. As a result, large numbers of people are looking for someone, but most are pretending that they aren't.

Once we do eventually find somebody our troubles are not over, because we then need to be convinced they are the right person. Unfortunately, it's very difficult to accurately judge someone's personality on first meeting and it's absolutely impossible to predict their reaction style. You have to wait until you see them under pressure.

You probably know instinctively how vulnerable your decision in choosing a possible partner can be, because you recognise that in your first meetings he or she will only be showing you their travel brochure. Of course, it's not that you are in a big rush to show them your bad sides either. Despite this, filled with hope, you will still probably launch into the highly uncertain process of falling in love.

Here is a series of ideas to make the process more understandable. If you know what you're doing, you have a little more control.

The glance test

Your choice of someone as a potential partner probably began with the 'glance' test, which assesses desirability in an instant. In this, you began your relationship with the same system as every other animal when it comes to choosing a mate; responding to what is essentially sex appeal. This works very well for animals that simply meet, display sexually and then mate with no programming for long-term pairing. It also works moderately well in the piano bar on a Saturday night, but is not necessarily a great system for an animal that wants to mate, but is also looking for a lifetime of love and companionship.

Duration of the relationship

We are obviously driven by the same forces as other animals. If the purpose of life is to reproduce, sexual activity is essential. As human beings we attempt to enrich our lives beyond mere copulation in the mating season and we search for love, support and intimacy in a long-term arrangement that we often formalise into marriage.

Lifetime pairing is extremely rare in the animal world and obviously is not natural to us, but that is no reason not to attempt monogamy, or monandry for that matter. Some of the best of humanity comes from the unnatural things we do, and loyalty in marriage is one of them. Our children are very vulnerable and need a lengthy period of nurturing and safety to grow up as happy, self-respecting adults. A child probably gets his best chance for this as part of a stable, faithful relationship between his biological parents. It's not the only way, of course, but it's potentially the easiest.

Growing a relationship

Once you have met someone who has passed the glance test, you appear to have passed his and he seems to be living up to most of the promises in his travel brochure, you are almost certainly in love. Now you want the relationship to progress.

A relationship advances through the growth of intimacy. This depends upon your willingness to be one step ahead. It also depends upon your partner's willingness to match your openness. If he plays by the rules, he should be willing to equal the revelations you make about yourself with details about his own needs, hopes and weaknesses. True intimacy requires each of you to show your underbelly, progressively revealing more information, potentially making yourself increasingly vulnerable.

A growing relationship advances in steps, each person offering something of himself, matching what has been offered and then raising the stakes a little. It does not mean a headlong rush into total self-exposure; rather a shared and parallel progression. Too great a rate of self-exposure will make you look over-eager and desperate; too little openness will make you seem cold, distant and disinterested. *You get to know someone by letting them get to know you.*

You can't afford to be distant, even if it is only because you are afraid you won't measure up. Equally, you can't afford to be seen to fall in love too quickly, before you've had time to gain any real knowledge of the individual. Do this and you look as if you are in love with the idea of being in a relationship, rather than in love with the particular person. This is a massive turn-off, because people want to feel they are exclusive and specially chosen for who they are, not what they can offer. The balance lies in being willing to raise the stakes of commitment, but pausing for a roughly equivalent response before moving on too far or too fast.

Searching for similarity

Similar people are attracted to each other. They instinctively know that there will be less conflict over territory. That opposites attract is a myth. A dominating man and a submissive woman may look different, but underneath they are both vulnerable children, dealing with their fears in different ways.

When we talk about the person we love, the most common theme is similarity: 'We have so much in common. We like the same things: music, art, literature, the beach ...'

We are really saying how wonderful it is to find there are so many areas where our satisfaction of needs will not be in conflict. We are not unreasonably concluding that we will not have to fight for our own way too often and so threaten love and intimacy. We are hoping that we'll listen to the same music, go sailing together and when one wants to go surfing, the other will either enthusiastically participate or at least sit happily on the beach.

The earliest stages of a love relationship are dominated by an urge to suppress personal differences, as people try to achieve a total unity with their lovers, reinforcing their oneness with their sameness.

In the first rush of love and lust, people figuratively and literally try to blend with one another. They unite their bodies in sex as often as possible and try to please each other totally by being willing to do anything. No sacrifice or effort is too great. A cup of tea while she stays in bed on a cold morning? Not a problem! We'll see any movie, eat any food and wear any clothes.

These behaviours are designed to be more lovable and strengthen the relationship by serving the merging process. Individuality happily takes a back seat, because there is no sense of being diminished, lost or submerged. On the contrary, lovers feel expanded by incorporating another like mind and body. Nobody feels bigger and more powerful than someone who is in love. A man who is in love and feels loved in return is potentially at his lowest level of aggression. This heady time is one of the rare occasions in which scoop of the sundae seems able to fully occupy the plate.

Commitment

If a relationship is not growing, it's dying. If you want the richness of an intense relationship to have a longer shelf life than just the first rush of lust and compromise, you must behave in a committed way. Somewhere along the line you need to judge when to signal a lifetime intention; the timing being decided by the other person's willingness to offer his own growing commitment. Given the background to pairing and marriage is reproduction, as a general rule signals of commitment need to involve some sort of reference to children.

If you do not publicly state and privately decide that your goal is a shared life, your relationship is likely to eventually sink under the weight of disappointment.

Choosing a suitable partner

Everybody can be a good partner, if both of you understand and follow the principles of *An Intelligent Life*. It's not necessary to start off with a good self-esteem to have a good relationship, although obviously it helps. You can use the same system that you use to build a good self-esteem to make a good relationship.

If you can conduct yourself intelligently with someone who passed your glance test and merged with you well, provided you are willing to make a commitment, it should be possible to have an intimate, enriching relationship for a very long time, and even for life.

If you did your best to behave with kindness and dignity from the very beginning of your relationship, you have already begun your selection process. If you conducted yourself with kindness, you were attractive to everybody. *If you also managed to maintain your adult dignity and equality and refused to compromise your core values, you increased your attractiveness to healthy people, but you would have scared away anybody who wanted to dominate you, make impossible demands or was irreversibly self-centred.*

If you have had a string of bad relationships and have been hurt, it doesn't mean that you are hopeless at picking people and everybody else can see things that you can't. It's not necessarily that you are more vulnerable than anybody else to choosing the wrong partner – everybody gets taken in by other people's travel brochures – it's more likely to mean you haven't got rid of bad relationships fast enough. Perhaps you were too nice, or you were too afraid of losing someone, so you forgot or dared not to make a stand on your equality and dignity. Then, like a gambler, you were too far committed and too afraid of losing everything to stop. Of course, if you had stood up for yourself you might have lost your partner earlier, which in retrospect might have been a good thing, but on the other hand he just might have been capable of moulding himself to meet your profile of adult self-respect. *Remember, you can change people, but only by changing yourself.*

The best partners are those who like themselves, or at least who live their lives intelligently, which ends up meaning the same thing. They will be warm, intimate, ardent, sexy and self-revealing. They will also be friendly and be a good friend to others as well as to you. There will be lots of people who like and respect them and if your partner is female, she will have intense relationships with a couple of girlfriends, to whom she will sometimes say more than she says to you. If your partner is a male, he will relate to other males intimately, warmly and not only in the setting of the pub.

Ideally a prospective partner will have had previously enjoyable, stable sexual relationships and if she hasn't because she's too young, she may need more experience before she is ready to be a long-term partner to anybody.

The most potentially suitable partner will be similar to you and the perfect partner would probably be a clone. Your relationship will have more strength if you have reasonably similar levels of intellect, education and – unfortunately – race and social class. The same sense of humour is a help, as is having the same level of ambition. A partner who does not have a clear commitment to fairness, equality and kindness, supported by genuine empathy, will be hard to live with in the long term.

It is essential you find someone with the same core values as yourself. If a would-be partner regularly violates your ethical values, your relationship can only continue if you squash your own spirit.

Your adult dignity demands that you live by your core values. By definition, an intimate partner becomes a piece of yourself. *If you couldn't live with yourself if you acted the way your partner does, you won't be able to live with him or her either.*

Your partner should be able to be comforted by your love when unhappy and have enough self-respect to tell you to go to hell when you are being impossible. If you have sufficient self-esteem to listen to criticism and take responsibility for any change you can see is justified, you have the makings of a wonderful, lifelong partnership.

Being a good partner

The best way to have a good relationship is to be a good partner yourself. If you are good to somebody who is in a relationship with you, you will bring out the best in them. At the same time, by behaving in a loving way you will automatically elevate your self-esteem. The profile you present to someone who values you will influence the way he conducts himself. If you behave like a self-respecting adult you maximise the chances the other person will feel and behave the same way. The only way to have an enduring and enriching relationship is as two equal adults.

Ideally, each of you will try to make the other feel good. You need to establish this as a tradition in the relationship as quickly as possible. Try to make her feel beautiful, clever, generous and sexy. If you're a woman, don't forget that men will do a lot for praise; you could do worse than reward anything that you genuinely feel is good with thanks and love.

If you tell your partner she is wonderful, you are not lifting her above you and making yourself small; on the contrary, by giving love and building her up, you rise with her. If you make her feel beautiful she is very unlikely to decide she's too good for you; she is far more likely to want to stay with you than if you fail to nourish her self-esteem.

You best serve your own interests by keeping your partner happy, meeting her security needs and at the same time encouraging her individual self-expression. If you don't care for her needs her anger, hurt or withdrawal will in some way threaten you, making you resentful, guilty or anxious. In short, if your partner isn't happy, you won't be either.

If you don't care how your partner feels, you are not being clever. Remember, your relationship with yourself, which is your self-esteem, is profoundly influenced by your relationships with others and the person with the greatest power to influence your self-esteem is the person who occupies your innermost orbit of intimacy.

You may be doing your very best for your partner, but it is important to be aware that he or she may not seem to recognise all your virtues and may not reward you at the rate you would like or feel you deserve. Don't be too quick to expect praise; hope for it, but don't expect it. Someone who has been a regular part of your life may be slow to recognise that you have changed, and even slower to adapt. If you have been chronically misbehaving and you change your way of life, it may take someone a little time to trust its reality before she takes the risk of being hurt again.

Love should be as free of strings as you can make it. As we've seen, it is strongest as an agreement between equals, which means two freely consenting adults. *Don't mistake possessiveness and jealousy for love*: if you squeeze a person too tightly, either you crush her vitality or she will flip out of your fingers.

To be a good partner, you must err on the side of generosity, being willing to give ground rather than demanding more. By choosing to please ahead of self-gratification, you have valued love and belonging a little more than individuality, which is the core of civilisation and the essence of love. Even if she would never have known the difference, give her the bigger piece of cake. Behaving in a loving and generous way is profoundly self-interested, because it makes you like yourself so much more, even if it is only your Observing Self who sees it.

You must remember to show love in a direct and unambiguous way. A sharp, clear statement of 'I love you' is the substance of commitment and needs to be said and said again. 'But she knows I love her ...' is not good enough. People cannot read minds; they can only read verbal and bodily language. You must repeatedly affirm a warm relationship between you. A smile, a pat, a kiss clearly state there is something alive and vigorous between you.

Spontaneity is a wonderful bird with beautiful plumage, but not often seen. Some people believe if you try to catch it you lose it forever, which may have some truth. Unfortunately, if you stand back and wait for spontaneity to appear, you may never even catch a glimpse. You can wait a long time for the joy of spontaneous love to sweep you into a show of affection. If you leave it too long, your unhappy and anxious partner may swamp you with demands that make the spontaneity of your anger the only spontaneity either of you get to see.

If an act of fondness can be truly offered without thought, clearly it is a joy for both. While admittedly less than ideal, there are times when an intellectual decision to behave in an affectionate way, even if it is not spontaneous, has a lot to offer. The pleasure for the receiver is just as great when it looks spontaneous as when it really is, and for the giver there is still a warm glow that is more than merely intellectual. *If you want to feel good, you must act well.* This is only making a case for simulated spontaneity, not simulated love.

Obviously, the most convenient person with whom to be desperately in love is your partner, especially if you share a history, friends, a mortgage and children. Therefore anything you do to

prime the pump of love is intelligently looking after your own interests. Make sure you offer a regular supply of premeditated, loving
gestures. Only you will know whether it is true spontaneity or not,
and it doesn't matter; it's the act, not its origin, that is effective. If
you are a male, it is probably worth adding that you might be wise to
make sure not all your affection involves the bedroom.

When people say you have to work on a marriage, they mean
you have to perform. You have to put energy and thought into a
partnership if you want to get the best for yourself from an equal and
self-respecting adult. This is not saying relationships are all hard
work, to be planned and choreographed, but expecting love to be
self-generating is not really wise.

Unfortunately love doesn't cure everything, even if it's streets
ahead of any other medicine. Your best efforts may not have much
effect on a badly damaged personality, and one day you may need to
leave. Until this awful moment, if in doubt, administer love.

Ideas

- It's very difficult to accurately judge someone's personality
  quickly and it's nearly impossible to predict his reaction style
  under pressure.

- Everybody's judgement of other people is potentially flawed,
  because everyone makes their decision before they have
  enough information to make the decision.

- Similar people with similar core values are attracted to each
  other, instinctively knowing that there will be less conflict
  over territory.

- Intimacy progressively reveals information that makes you
  vulnerable. You need to show your bad bits, or at the very
  least the bad bits you know you won't be able to hide for-

ever, without wanting forgiveness, reassurance or congratulations for being so honest.

- A relationship should advance in steps, each person offering something of himself, matching what has been offered to him and then raising the stakes a little with a further intimacy.

- If a relationship is not growing, it's dying. You must be willing to signal your commitment.

- The best partner will be someone who likes himself, or at least who lives by the principles of *An Intelligent Life*, which ends up meaning the same thing.

- The best way to have a good relationship is to be a good partner and to make your partner feel good.

- Show love in a direct and unambiguous way. People cannot read minds, they can only read verbal and bodily language.

- Make sure you offer a regular supply of premeditated, loving gestures.

- If in doubt, administer love.

CHAPTER 18

や

Problems and Pitfalls in Relationships

OUR RELATIONSHIPS ARE THE MOST IMPORTANT and valuable things in our lives, but they don't always come easily, especially if we're a bit uncertain about the rules. Unfortunately evolution isn't a perfect process. Nature doesn't care the least bit about our emotions or whether we're miserable, provided our unhappiness doesn't interfere too much with survival and reproduction. So it's no great surprise that things go wrong.

Our relationships are the makers and breakers of our emotions, but our emotions are possibly the shakiest part of our construction and if we don't take care, they can drive us into behaviour that can do great harm to our relationships, which obviously does further harm to our emotions. There's a horrible circularity in this, which justifies taking a closer look at some of the potential problems created by our relationships.

A positive response to the glance test has a very powerful effect. Once a few circuits close and our survival brain starts yelling lustfully, it's painfully easy to become caught up with someone totally unsuitable or, let's face it, to behave in a thoroughly unsuitable fashion ourselves. In love and in lust, it's your survival brain at work, driving your need for the safety of attachment and the joys of sex, which of course is a confidence trick, as we are pushed towards reproduction by our selfish genes. The problem lies in the differences between the short-term strategies of survival and reproduction and the much more complex, longer-term techniques for maintaining a loving and enduring attachment.

As any relationship advances, incompatibilities surface. Insubstantial beginnings will falter as individuality is reasserted after the delirious compromise of first love. This is not necessarily because there has been active deception, but because you have both been putting on your best face; a combination of the best of yourself, the best you feel a person of your age and sex should be, and your best judgement of what the other person wants.

As I've said, our travel brochures only show the best bits at first. After a longer visit the good bits remain, but there may be some ugly sights too, which you didn't read about before you bought your ticket.

Dreams of perfect love

This early window dressing obviously makes a major contribution to any disparity between your original image and the person who emerges after you have known him for a while. However, the other person is not the only one responsible for this altered image.

There is a natural human tendency to superimpose our own dream of the perfect partner on the person we see. That's why it is possible to fall in love with someone across a crowded room – you know nothing about him. While he may be as wonderful as your fantasies tell you, there's a real risk you'll write his travel brochure for him.

If there has been too much dreaming, not enough accurate observation and you were in love with an ideal, you will eventually have a powerful sense of betrayal. That's why people get so angry and behave so viciously during the break-up of a relationship.

Idealisation

An obsessive, child-like love believes love should see no faults. An immature love will try to see a partner as being perfect and will be outraged at any suggestion to the contrary. *Unfortunately, the same apparently blind love can explode into rage when expectations aren't met.*

In short, if a lover insists you're perfect, better by a thousand times than anyone he or she's ever met before and you find yourself on a pedestal, they are probably relating to you more as a child would relate to a parent than as an equal. A daily delivery of a dozen roses may prove to have even more thorns. You are being worshipped in the hope of making your love as perfect as possible to meet your partner's needs. You'll find yourself pushed to heights of performance and expectation from which you can only fall. You may have been seduced by what seemed to be a promise of unconditional love, but you will find that it only lasts until you break the conditions.

Hoping your partner will complete you

If your self-esteem expects you to be recognised for your good looks, brains and class before you feel good enough, there's a real risk that you'll expect the same high-level performance from your lover. If the gaps in your self-respect are too big and the self-image you want supported is too lofty, no one has a chance of being beautiful or clever enough to fulfil you.

Telling your wife: 'You're not the woman I married,' may well mean: 'You're not the fantasy I married and you're not supporting my fantasy of myself.'

Nothing a human being does has a single motive. We all have layers of agendas and needs. Amongst all the good reasons for choosing a partner, we are also hoping that he or she will add to our self-respect; not only give us love, but also become a part of us that will enhance our identity. The greater your expectation that your partner will enhance you personally, the more readily you will see yourself as being held back from perfect happiness. Your life would be so much better if you were not burdened by such a defective partner. Married to someone better, you would definitely be a movie star or a millionaire by now.

Panicking over the differences

Once a close relationship is established and the honeymoon of near-total compliance is over, the majority of people will try to re-establish their own personality profile. In even the best and most durable of relationships there is no hope of maintaining the original blissful unity, because the drive towards individual expression is too strong; eventually both of you have to renegotiate your individual territories. In one way or another this means saying: 'Will you permit me to have this difference? I understand that it was not quite written into the original contract, but I really need to do this to keep on feeling I am me.'

Even when you establish separateness as gently as possible, there's always going to be extra pain in the first few arguments over disputed territory. What's happened to this person whom you loved? Someone you trusted sufficiently to let into your innermost orbit of intimacy, someone who seemed to believe the same things you believed and think in the same way and who laughed at all your jokes? Now she seems as interested in spending an hour on the phone to a girlfriend as she is in hanging on your every word.

Whether love is going to survive and mature into an easy intimacy depends on how you handle your differences, because you're inevitably going to be disappointed with a partner you discover is not quite as you thought, or not as easily changed as you'd hoped.

As each of you re-establishes your individuality after the initial orgy of compromise, then the more robust your self-esteem, the greater the differences in your partner you will be able to tolerate. The more fragile your sense of self-worth, the more you are in danger of angrily demanding your partner be just like you. If you don't like yourself enough, discovering your partner has differences can easily feel as if he or she doesn't love you.

One solution to the dilemma of difference is to leave for ever. Unfortunately, ending a relationship means forgetting that once you did love this person. Even now, it may not be too late to look closely at your core values, making absolutely sure you're not treating peripheral values as being central, destroying your relationship for a principle without a point. If you focused on behaving with kindness and dignity, you might yet save what you have. If both of you see difference as rejection, then you will have a repeated clash of insecurities.

Falling back on the principles of *An Intelligent Life* won't make you like the differences any more than you did before, but you will like yourself better, your partner will like you better and you might find that the gap between you is not quite as wide as you thought.

'We found we had nothing in common' is generally terminal. He wanted one thing and she wanted another. The reality of the differences between them couldn't be avoided any more and the capacity to compromise in support of love has failed. The gain from pleasing could no longer override the urgency to assert individual choice.

Prediction and protection

In your search for love, you will meet many people who are utterly delightful, charming to their friends and acquaintances, warm and considerate. The vast majority of these people will be just as you see them. When you meet a potential partner with these characteristics, abandon your heart but hold on to a little of your head.

Always behave as if you take what you see and hear at face value. If you treat everyone with suspicion, you will be miserable. Just because people seem too good to be true, it doesn't mean that in the long term they will not be enough of what they seem to satisfy you. *It's much better to trust than to doubt, but your trust should be at an adult level of hope, not like a child's expectation of perfect love.*

You might feel you have found the perfect candidate to occupy your intimate world, but the inner orbit reserved for your adult sexual partner is much more testing than the outer orbits of more peripheral relationships. The demands, expectations and disappointments of genuine intimacy are very much greater than the casual ease of friendship or acquaintance.

People in your outer orbits can easily impress you. A smile, a joke, holding the door open for you or helping old ladies across the road are really endearing bits of behaviour, but murderers and child molesters can do this too. Travel brochures only show some of the truth.

'No man is proven to be good until he has had the opportunity to be bad.' *Sadly, the bad can be more accurately predictive than the good.* Random acts of mindless benevolence are unfortunately no guarantee of future performance, whereas just one act of mindless cruelty is highly predictive and will almost certainly be repeated. If he kicks a cat, beware; you've seen the tip of an iceberg big enough to sink you both.

Getting to know someone is getting to know how bad they can be, not how good. Never, ever believe people who behave horribly and then back away, claiming they didn't really mean it. They may not mean it now it's caught up with them, but they did mean it when they did it and they will mean it again one day. Unless he has just eaten a bad oyster, someone who spits in public will do it again and he probably has other delights in store.

Getting out

Falling into a relationship is easy; once someone has passed your glance test, you are on the slippery slope. Getting out of one, as everyone knows, is another matter.

When we leave relationships we don't want to get hurt and we usually don't want to be hurtful. Unfortunately, if you make these your absolute criteria you're stuck forever. If you have to leave, the best you can hope for is to hurt and be hurt as little as possible.

Being less hurt yourself

If the faults or differences in your lover are hard to tolerate now, they will only get worse with time. Although such advice is doomed to be ignored, if you are arguing repeatedly and there is no sign of mutual compromise, you would be wise to seriously reassess your partner and perhaps yourself as well. Do be careful not to have a baby in the utterly mistaken belief that it will strengthen the relationship.

It's possible to hang in a relationship forever, waiting for that lovely person you first met to come back. You may need to abandon some of your old talent for blaming yourself to excuse someone else's behaviour. If you're a bit scared of being alone, it's tempting and comfortable to use self-blame to avoid having to look too closely at your partner and feel forced to make a decision. *Don't forget that people who like to blame other people gravitate very happily to people who choose to blame themselves.*

Women in particular seem to have a potential to forget who they once were. A woman who was independent and self-respecting can find herself in a relationship with a dominating man and lose sight of the fact that she was once perfectly strong and quite able to survive by herself. If she forgets she was once able to be unattached and happy, she is helpless because then she doesn't dare use the only weapon available to civilised people, which is the withdrawal of love. That is, your only real power is to leave. *If you do not know and feel that ultimately you can leave, you have thrown away any power you might have had in the relationship.*

Don't forget, opposites do not attract. If you are needy and he likes it, he is needy too, even if he is currently enjoying the role of mega-masculine protector. If he is dominating you, it just means he has you bluffed; he is every bit as vulnerable as you are. Remember, unless he is being violent, there is no such thing as domination, only submission. Remember also, if he's been violent once, he's very likely to be violent again, even if he apologises and says he didn't mean it.

Obviously, none of these ideas can prevent your hurt once you're in a relationship that has to finish, but if you bear them in mind you might recognise what's happening and take control a little earlier.

Causing less hurt

Healthy people don't like to hurt other people. This is both because a sense of empathy causes us to feel somebody else's pain as if it were our own, and for the slightly less noble reason that we want other people to like us, even after we leave.

It is a mistake to believe you can let someone down gently by setting them up to want the relationship to end. A peculiarly male technique is to be increasingly unpleasant in the hope that she will break it off herself. The conscious plan is usually to make it easier for her, but in reality its prime motive is to force her into the final move and so avoid being seen as the bad guy.

If you have determined to leave someone, there is a far better strategy. If you treat her with kindness and do your very best to make her feel lovable, even if you can't make her feel loved, you can build her up and make her stronger. Rather than weakening her by undermining her self-esteem in the process of trying to get her to take responsibility for the breakup and push you away, by behaving in as kindly a fashion as you can, you leave her at her strongest to deal with the pain of being left. The only problem is that if you treat her well, you get the very best from her and then you may not want to leave after all.

Dealing with disappointment

Ultimately, there is no reliable way to pick a bad partner before you have been burnt a bit. The key concept is being burnt only a bit, not avoiding getting burnt at all. If you pull out of a relationship the moment you see any possibility of being hurt, you will never have anything that lasts very long. Grown-up people know the perfect partner doesn't exist. You need to give someone a reasonable try, as well as a few warnings and options to change. You must give him room to express his individuality, but if he doesn't seem capable of working out for himself where reasonable limits lie, you probably won't be able to teach him.

Adult love acknowledges differences and defects, which by definition you could not possibly like. Adult love is not blind. Acknowledging problems in a reasoned way means making a behavioural decision, which is a deliberate choice not to correct, punish or belittle, even if you are disappointed. This, in turn, requires you to first recognise and acknowledge to yourself your irritation at faults or your anxiety over differences. The next step is to resolve to stop punishing her and not to make them reasons for leaving or for setting her up to leave you. This is quite different from struggling to deny the reality of a problem in a snowstorm of self-deception, or indulging in the unctuous patronage of telling someone you love her for her faults.

In short, if a self-respecting person is in a relationship with you and decides she wants to stay, it does not mean that you are exactly as she would like you to be, but it does mean she has determined to accept the differences and more or less leave them alone.

Ideally, you would not try to change your lover, but not many people are so good, so blind or so self-effacing. With varying degrees of subtlety, as a relationship progresses most people will not simply re-establish their individuality around their partners; they will also try to remodel you a little. Fortunately, while they are trying to do some re-shaping, people also tend to mould their own style to match and complement the other. However, the fact remains that most people want to maintain their own personality profile and hope their partners will modify to fit them.

All relationships contain an element of competition, because no one is so secure that they can keep their loving completely free of coercion. That people try to change each other is not necessarily an illegitimate thing; the issue is more the means by which it is done. Secure people can afford to make some changes without feeling compromised, just as they can accept differences in their lover, but there must be a point where they will make a stand.

Paradoxically, the courage to risk rejection by standing up for yourself and, if necessary, directly asking someone to change something that is impossible for you to ignore is more likely to save the relationship than damage it. The vital element in your stand is that it must be made early, it must be clear, potentially negotiable at its margins and it must not be delivered in a belittling way. In the long term, both you and your partner will feel better if you behave assertively.

While we may not be biologically programmed to remain with the same partner for life, it is a goal well worth striving towards. To have any hope of achieving this, we have to recruit our very highest human capacities for empathy, tolerance and the ability to give up power and territory in favour of love. We have to override the natural but potentially pernicious influence of our survival brain as it demands its own way immediately or the gratification of a new sexual partner. We need to take a longer-term, intelligently self-interested view.

To manage the negative side of your relationship, you must start from the position that love has to be preserved and nurtured to be kept alive, especially on down days. You will need to appreciate that far from feeling blessed with the perfect partner, there will be times when you definitely do not like your lover very much at all. Then you need to organise a conversation inside your head, telling yourself that *difference doesn't annihilate relationships; the damage is done by frightened and angry behaviour in trying to eliminate them.*

It is quite possible to argue within rules that put a minimum strain on the relationship. It's also important to recognise very few arguments are resolved in a satisfactory way, but that doesn't mean they have to go on for ever. *Certainly, letting unfinished issues fester can cause difficulties, but so can the obsessive pursuit of resolution.*

Not all problems have solutions, and sometimes the art lies in finding the least bad solution. There will be times when it's best to sweep things under the carpet and avoid them if you can. Once a problem is under the carpet, while there's a risk the lump will trip you, it will usually flatten out with time, if you can only leave it alone.

By disagreeing with you, your partner is clearly misguided and probably stupid, but your dignity can and will survive even if you can never get her to recognise her failings or acknowledge your wisdom. Unless you have absolutely and definitely decided to leave, never roll out the big guns of rejection, hate, abuse or regret. If you over-invest in proving just how wrong someone is, your relationship may be worn away by your determination to be right.

Sex, love and commitment

After the initial five-times-a-day enthusiasm of a new sexual relationship, male sexual desire can run out quite quickly, especially if it isn't really fuelled by love. What looked like an intense and loving relationship just fades and dies, often to the total bewilderment of a female partner, who may beg to know what she has done wrong. She is confused because, as a female, she probably couldn't turn off so easily, or at least not unless she discovered her partner really had done something terribly wrong. In terms of her feminine logic, it therefore follows that she must have failed miserably or done something very bad. All she wants to do is fix things so that love can come back.

Women tend to have trouble understanding male sexuality. They tend to be slower to let go of love and once they have committed themselves sexually, they tend to feel much more involved than some male partners. For a woman, sex is more likely to be inseparable from love and mutuality, while for a man love is wonderful and so is sex, but they don't inevitably have to be so closely related.

Women are often confused, hurt and angered by attitudes that seem perfectly reasonable to men. She probably dreams of being loved by a man who will love her with a woman's tenderness. Instead, she may find herself loved by a man wanting a woman who will make love to him with the appetite of a man.

Her boyfriend truly wants to love her, but he may be as disappointed as he is disappointing. She isn't much interested in wearing provocative clothes and doesn't even think to pose sexily. To her, there's a good chance an exotic sexual position is doing it on the couch. He forgets female sexuality is fuelled much more by love and intimacy than it is by the less personal forces of eroticism. He probably doesn't stop to think that the women in erotic magazines hungrily yearning for sex have been posed and photographed to act out male fantasies. The model is probably wondering when she'll get the ironing done.

Male pursuit of sex is a strongly territorial behaviour as well as a search for love. Despite this, most single men are looking for a relationship, but while they are looking some of them may spend a lot of time in sexual conquest without any serious thought for the person inside the woman. This is difficult for a woman, who will be generally trying to nurture and grow a relationship.

Women often instinctively recognise the element of conquest in their partner's sexual behaviour and feel there is too much physical demand without enough emotional offering. She pulls away, or at least can't respond to his approaches, and he dismisses her as being passionless and lousy in bed. She feels unloved and her male partner, who is often poorer at expressing his emotions in words, feels easier showing his love through sexuality. The woman feels locked out of the relationship, even if she is pinned to the bed. The man feels deprived of both love and his manhood, which needs the reassurance of conquest and copulation, programmed into his survival brain millions of years ago.

An intelligently self-interested, single woman needs to know a bit about men. If you have been going out with someone for a long time and he is content to let the relationship stay as it is, making no move toward cohabitation or kids, the truth is likely to be that he doesn't want you, or at least, doesn't want you enough. It's sad, but you might be better off if you faced it now and took some action, because he's not going to.

Men are capable of parking themselves with you, waiting for a better spot. It's quite useless using your feminine logic that loves love so much. You're so nice to him and spoil him. You feed him when he drops in for sex and then goes to sleep in front of the television, but your loving kindness may not be able to make him love you enough to commit to you. If someone were so good and gentle and loving towards you, it would work on you, but you're a woman and more vulnerable to being a fool for love.

You may be a perfectly attractive, adequate woman and human being, but you simply haven't got what it takes for him. Despite the fact that he's overweight, his breath smells and he only lasts long enough for you to climax when he's drunk, he still wants a super-model.

You could take a charitable view and see him as being simply too scared to risk rejection or of losing his independence. Thinking like a woman, you may decide everything would be all right if he could only get over his commitment phobia. In reality, you are probably being much too charitable. Calling him commitment-phobic gives him a wonderful escape clause, lending dignity to someone too obsessive to decide, too gutless to move on or too insecure to have anything less than the perfect woman to fill the gaps in himself. 'I'm none of these things, I'm commitment-phobic.'

Please don't lose sight of the fact that this chapter is specifically about the negatives in relationships. Men are not awful and all women are not vulnerable little flowers just waiting to be loved. I am describing elements of human behaviour, not humanity itself. Most people are kind and want love, but males and females have biologically programmed reproductive reasons for taking a different approach to sex.

Sex always has the potential to be a problem as there is very little chance that you will both want the same things, in the same way, at the same time. Don't try to coerce someone into something they don't want. Your satisfaction will be brief and you'll pay the price of your lover's distance and hurt. If you are struggling with different levels of desire, don't forget that acting in a loving way has strongly aphrodisiacal qualities for both sexes.

It's not always the man wanting more sex than the woman. After the initial rush of enthusiasm, his interest in sex can wane dramatically, especially if he is stressed at work or financially pressured. In other words, he may be preoccupied by territorial issues but his partner may interpret his reduced passion as no longer loving her so much. She may then pursue him for her own erotic needs, or it might be that the sexual pressure she applies is simply a hunger for greater closeness.

Sometimes a man hopes his wife will make him want sex more, expecting her to somehow give him the feeling he had when they first were lovers. This can't be made to happen, but there is a danger that he will blame his wife for his own biology and seek a new partner, with whom he inevitably enjoys a renewed vigour, but only for a while. Provided your relationship is sexy, sexual and sexualised, it doesn't matter how often you make love.

Once you are in a relationship, you are no longer in complete control of your life. *Loving somebody always makes you vulnerable, but vulnerability and the chance of pain are many times better than never taking a risk.* The ability to maintain an enduring, intimate and respectful adult relationship is one of the highest measures of your skill as a human being.

Ideas

- The greater your expectation that your partner will enhance you personally, the more readily you will see yourself as being held back from perfect happiness.

- The more robust your self-esteem, the greater the differences in your partner that you will be able to tolerate. Grown-up people know the perfect partner doesn't exist.

- It's better to risk hurt than to take no risk, and better to trust than to doubt, but your trust should be at an adult level of hope, not a child's level of expectation.

- Getting to know someone is getting to know how bad they can be, not how good.

- People who like to blame other people gravitate to people who choose to blame themselves.

- If you decide that you cannot exist without your relationship and forget that you were once able to be single, self-respecting and happy, you have thrown away your power. Difference doesn't annihilate relationships; the real damage is done by frightened and angry behaviour trying to annihilate the differences.

- Obsessively pursuing an issue towards a resolution or understanding that isn't going to happen can do more damage than the original difficulty.

- Provided your relationship is sexy, sexual and sexualised, it doesn't matter how often you make love.

- Despite all the problems and difficulties, relationships are still the best things we have. To be a rewarding, long-term, intimate partner is the ultimate measure of your skill as a human being.

CHAPTER 19

✌

Parents and Children

WHEN YOU WERE LITTLE your parents were everything. They were safety and the source of all truth and wisdom. You lived in a world they created and existence beyond your family was a hazy concept.

If you were unhappy and had been capable of even considering leaving home, the idea would have been overwhelming because you hadn't had time to develop any real sense of a separate identity. You also had a profound need for your parents' love.

As you matured, you gained more sense of yourself and a greater understanding of the world beyond the front door. Once you reached adolescence your need to please your parents and your desire for their approval was not so strong, but your freedom was far from complete. Happy or not, you were probably obliged to behave rebelliously to reassure yourself of your independence.

Your parents were the people most likely to have raised you when you were small, but you had no choice but to become attached to whoever brought you up. Your attachment or bonding to your parents became hardwired into your brain, leaving you with powerful and irreversible feelings about them. The most powerful element of those emotions was love, whatever your parents were like as people.

As an adult, even if your feelings towards your parents could never be described as love, you are unlikely to be neutral about them. Your parents, or the images of them you carry in your head, continue to hold power for the rest of your life. Evolution programmed you to become attached to them, but failed to provide a program for uninstalling them later.

As human beings we describe strong attachment as love. For survival in the jungle you had to stick close to your mother, actively maintaining and competing for her attention. Reaching your adult years doesn't guarantee you leave all your infant feelings behind, but paradoxically, the warmer and more loving your parents, the less likely you are to keep needing them. If you felt safely loved when you were a child, as a grown-up you will be more able to leave them and less likely to think or worry about them. The security of their love liberated you from both the obligation to come back to please them and the need to repeatedly check they are still there.

Healthy children are safe to test loving parents to see how much independence they can take. They will demand they have their own way, be ungrateful for what they get and loudly resentful that they don't get more. They have tantrums and yell how much they hate their parents, but in reality they'd be terrified if they had complete control or the ability to hurt the people whom they really want to be strong. In happy children this is not anxious, compulsive testing, because they do not have a fear of being left. They're simply pitching for more freedom, preferably warmed by parental blessing.

Plenty of unambiguous love from your parents when you were young has the potential to put large deposits of self-love in your human credit bank. This gives you much to draw on when you are mistreated, belittled or rejected in your adult life.

Frequently, the less loving and less available parents are, the more strongly bonded a child becomes to them. This powerful hold is not a calm and easy love, but an *anxious attachment*. Anxiously attached children often become anxiously attaching adults, unable to leave their parents and terrified of displeasing them; the same unsatisfied need sometimes driving them to cling with limpet-like determination to their lovers and friends.

Growing up is a series of tasks. A loved child who becomes an adult can finish the job of maturing from dependent childhood to adult independence relatively easily, forming a loving but more detached relationship with his or her parents. There is a sense of completeness, coming from a job well done that doesn't need to be thought about any more.

With the death of parents, less loved adults have missed their last chance to win the love they wanted all their lives. Grieving for them is likely to be more prolonged and incomplete because of disappointment, anger and fear mixed with the sadness.

If your children take you for granted, use your house as a cheap hotel, fall over backwards to help their friends, but begrudge washing a dish at home, you're witnessing the outcome of one of three possibilities:

1. Your children may be so strongly genetically programmed to be lazy and unloving that no style of parenting could have ever changed the course of their lives. This is the least likely.

2. You may not have dared set reasonable limits because your self-esteem wasn't sufficient to believe your children would still love you if you didn't please them totally. This sets them up to treat you with contempt; angry that you weren't strong enough to be the protective parent they wanted. Sometimes this lack of limits can have the opposite effect, pushing children into the role of a parent, holding them with a guilty bond of good behaviour.

3. Your children are paying testimony to the quality of parenting you gave them. They are so confident of your love that there's

no need to anxiously guard it and please you. On the surface they seem to value their friends much more than they value you, but this is because they are less secure with them and so have a greater need to please them. If this third option is the case and it is the most likely, you might reasonably hope one day your children will mature beyond their selfishness.

Your children are at your mercy. If you handle them with clumsy fingers you can leave indelible marks. At the stage of their lives when they are most able to be shaped as people they have no real capacity to effectively resist you. By the time they can do something it's not too late, but it is harder to rewrite the effects of a training that has already set them in a particular direction of thinking and feeling.

Whether we want to or not, taking away love is our instinctive technique for control and punishment. When you are angry with someone, the message delivered is clear and unambiguous: 'You will lose my love if you don't do as I say.'

Delivered too often and enforced too rigorously, especially if there is not sufficient evidence of love in between arguments, the message received by your child may be equally clear: 'You can have my love, or you can have your individuality, but you cannot have both. Take your pick.'

Overly controlling parenting tends to have one of two effects, following the general observation that extremes often breed extremes:

1. Too much domination can produce children with excessively deferential, respectful, even obsequious personalities. Grown up, they can spend their adult lives in tense and resentful relationships, servants to symbolic parents they feel they can never please. If they rebel at all it will be in passive silence, stubbornness or martyrdom, with occasional outbursts of blind rage.

Their rage is blind because they are terrified. To overcome their fear of showing any independence and losing a fragile love, they close their eyes and rush in before thinking why.

2. At the other end of the spectrum, repressive parenting can generate an obligatory rebel; someone unable to tolerate even the most benign authority. The child in the adult sees anyone with power as a representative parent, trespassing on his territory and belittling him. These people can become unbending, antagonistic, ferociously independent individuals, who cannot or will not compromise and are therefore hard to live with. For them, love has to take a back seat to self-expression.

A sense of anger, rejection and belittlement is inevitably part of the response to being dominated, and these emotions make people rigid and less able to change. *By putting love before discipline, you give your child the best chance to establish his or her own self-discipline, which, by definition, cannot be imposed by you.* Your love allows your child to develop his or her own sense of individuality and worth. In addition to making their lives happier, you can also make your own a lot easier. A good self-esteem greatly increases your child's capacity to resist pressure to use drugs, steal cars or say 'yes' to sex when it might be wiser to say 'no'.

If your children felt love from you before they felt your control, you have given them greater freedom to see each new person as a new experience and not as a recycled parent. Their good experience of you allows them to look back with comfort and gives them the capacity to clearly separate the emotions of the past from those of today.

Childhoods spent with limit-setting but primarily loving parents are more likely to breed adults who defend their individuality strongly, but not any more vigorously than necessary. It also allows them to set their individuality to the circumstances. They are free to defer to a respected person or, if good sense demands it, grovel to a dangerous one. They have strong principles, but are not martyrs.

Don't give a rebel a cause

If you are a parent and you have your own best interests at heart, you will treat love as more important than discipline. You'll have more freedom and expend less emotional energy because it's time-consuming and exhausting to be an eternally angry policeman. By putting love before discipline as a principle, you get more room to move, allowing you to safely misinterpret a situation and be unjust and bad-tempered with your child, as we all inevitably do. If this occurs every now and then in a setting where you have made your child feel safely loved, you are much less likely to set up the nev-erending cycle of rebellion leading to punishment, leading to fur-ther rebellion. You free your child to see bosses, authorities and policemen as being as good or bad as they really are. If you put love first, you are less likely to be obliged to waste your hard-earned sav-ings on bail or termination of pregnancies.

If you have enough self-respect to apologise and acknowledge you were wrong or unfair when you realise you have been too tough or you have misunderstood your children, you can not only clean the slate, you can actually strengthen your relationship. You also provide the model for self-respecting apology your child needs to see, freeing him to apologise to you or, more importantly, to other people when he is wrong.

If you can't put love before control, you increase the chances of having a child who feels unloved by you – the most important and powerful person in the world. A delinquent is simply living a role that feeling unloved and unloveable dictates. An identity of defect or badness is nobody's first choice, but some sort of identity is better than none. Believing you are bad is slightly superior to a sense of helplessness, trying to reach a parent whose approval can never be won. It's all too easy for your child to find support for delinquent behaviour from other kids, many of whom may have felt they are not good enough for their parents either. If they are all bad together, at least there is a sense of belonging.

You can bet you do love your kids and you can bet you want the best for them, but it's painfully easy to become trapped in the cycle of anger that provokes rebellion and more anger. This is unnecessary. Sometimes uncertainty about the best way to manage problem behaviour, combined with insecurity about your own dignity, can force you to take a stand on points of principle with no room for retreat. If you could learn to respect yourself a bit more, you would be liberated to let them get away with things and secure enough for you to be wrong, back off or apologise.

Easy to say, but how do you get to feel better about yourself in the heat of an argument, when your children are infuriating you as only they can do?

In an intelligent life, you start with your behaviour. If you want to feel good, you must act well. When you find the crumpled clothes littering the floor, or the job your son was supposed to do still undone and you feel your anger rising, start with the conversation in your head. Say to yourself: 'I'm furious, but I'll have more power if I'm gentle. If I attack him I'll feel better right now, but I'll push him into rebellion and then I'll feel angrier and worse. Soft words and a soft voice are not weak, they're powerful! I want to change him, not break him. I'll feel better and like myself more if I do this gently.'

It's easy to be loving with great dignity. Don't wait to feel good about yourself, get your behaviour right first and the Gang of Three – thoughts, actions and the responses of other people, in this case your kids and maybe your approving spouse – will start to drag your feelings into line.

If you have overdone your anger or misjudged your child, don't try to justify your mistake by blaming him for something else. Even if he is still in the wrong, apologise for being too angry and don't take it away with a 'but ...' It's highly unlikely that your child will fall into your arms because he's still hurting and angry with you, but you are changing a pattern with a longer-term goal in mind. Try it, and see how much bigger you feel.

If you completely blow it, try again next time. If you have adolescent children, the next time they make you angry won't be far off. There's lots of opportunity for practice.

Mummy dearest

Even if their parents are demonstrably unfair or unloving, at the age when children's attitudes and self-image are being formed, they do not have the capacity to decide the problem lies with their parents. They have no choice in needing their parents' love, so finding themselves bonded to people who are not particularly loving or loveable, children are likely to start seeing the world in a sadly distorted way, although they may never put the feeling into words. It is probably a defensive understanding at an instinctive level, as a brutalised dog would have of the people to whom it is attached: 'My parents are the world and this is what the world is like. They are perfect. Therefore, as they don't seem to love me, it can only mean that I am bad. I am at fault, so I must either correct the fault or make up for it by endlessly acknowledging my badness. Then I might be able to earn their love.'

The ultimate threat to a child is to be separated from his or her parents; either to lose them physically or to feel at risk of their rejection. In the millennia when your brain was evolving its survival strategies, to lose your parents meant inevitable death. In an angry and rejecting household, even in the presence of such a potentially overwhelming threat, a child still has to live and grow. Given that the child does not die, emotional survival requires a system of beliefs to make sense of the world as it appears to be and techniques to protect against rejection and therefore death.

Paradoxically, a child's assertion that he is bad is made in self-defence. If he says to himself 'I am bad,' he's in fact trying to feel better, believing this makes the world potentially more manageable, because if he can find and change the badness inside himself, he will be able to please his parents. An adult fishing for approval with humility and apparently critical self-understanding gains a sense of short-term safety, but it has been traded for the chance to act as a grown-up with an automatic and easy self-respect. A child who finds himself in an environment that tells him to dislike himself can make it a habit as an adult. Children need love – and so do grown-ups.

Ideas

- Your attachment or bonding to your parents is hardwired into your brain as a child, leaving you with a profound need for their love.

- Your parents, or the images of them you carry in your head, continue to hold power for the rest of your life. They are the major players amongst the people of your Observing Self.

- If your children feel your love before they feel your anger or your control, you are liberating them to see each new person as a new experience and not as a recycled parent.

- A childhood spent with limit-setting but primarily loving parents is more likely to breed an adult who defends his individuality strongly, but no more vigorously than necessary.

- If your children take you for granted, it's most likely because you have been a good parent, so they don't have to be careful with you.

- The less love and security children feel with their parents, the more tightly they will hang on. This is called anxious attachment and can continue as a style in adult life.

- If a parent is too angry and too disapproving, the child will receive the message: 'You may have my love or you may have your individuality, but you can't have both.'

- If you can find enough self-respect to apologise and acknowledge you were wrong or unfair with your children, you can strengthen the relationship with them and show them how they too could apologise to you when they are wrong, although it certainly won't happen in this particular fight.

- When children conclude they are bad, it is a decision made in self-defence. It makes the world more manageable for them because they believe that all they have to do is identify their own faults, correct them, and then they will be loveable and loved.

- Your love feeds your children's self-esteem and greatly increases their capacity to resist destructive peer pressure.

- If you can put love before control, you give your child the opportunity to feel loved and safe with you, the most important and powerful person in the world.

CHAPTER 20

꒦ꕥ

Your Parents

PARENTS ARE NOT RESPONSIBLE for every neurosis, every misde-
meanour and all the self-doubt of their children. There is a powerful genetic shaping of personality for which parents are no more to
blame than they are for the speed and endurance of a sperm or the
receptiveness of an ovum. There are some genetic programs for personality that no environmental factor or the best parents in the
world can override.

Fortunately, most inherited personality factors are not absolutes
but potentials, and these can be moulded and modified, even if they
can't be removed. Whatever programming sits on children's chro-
mosomes, good parenting optimises adaptability and feeds the self-
respect of offspring. Some kids will need more limit-setting than
others, while some need more reassurance, but if your parents
defaulted to love rather than to angry control, they maximised your
chances of a good outcome, even if your genetic programming was a
bit dodgy in places.

Unfortunately, or perhaps fortunately, neither you nor your parents probably ever thought about you in terms of your DNA. Most
genetic shaping of personality makes it easy for parents to treat their
children as the most loveable creatures ever to tread the earth. On

the other hand, it's possible for you to have been programmed to be more than usually demanding, miserable and resentful. To your parents you may have been a profoundly difficult child whose behaviour made them very angry, while in your eyes they were too tough and didn't even try to understand you.

It's possible your parents weren't really all that bad, just trying to do their imperfect best. You can bet a lousy mother didn't want to be a deficient parent. It might have been she was a hopeless transmitter of love, but it's also possible your antennae weren't well tuned to receive her messages. Your mother might have had to survive your endless, angry insistence that your sister was getting a better deal than you. She might have done her best to be fair and love you equally, despite your behaviour. If you decide to confront her with her cruelty and neglect, don't be too surprised if she is not especially receptive.

Paradoxically, it could be helpful to find evidence that your own innate reaction style may have played a part in the unfortunate mess. I'm not suggesting martyred self-blame, but looking for the sense of power and control that comes with genuinely taking responsibility.

Then again, you may be perfectly correct in deciding your parents were the root cause of your unhappiness. This recognition may be vital to understanding the forces that shaped you and to helping you decide what to do. It might be perfectly reasonable to see your parents as having a duty to fix things for you, but what people ought to do and what they will do are not always the same. For this reason, it's important not to take blaming other people beyond the academic level of useful self-understanding.

If you conclude somebody else caused your problems and therefore it is that person's duty to do something about it, you undermine your motivation to change and risk becoming a helpless hostage to your hurt and anger. You are also in danger of devoting large amounts of time and energy to punishing your parents for being bad, or trying to make them good through guilt. Neither manoeuvre will produce much satisfaction.

You can spend your life looking for perfect love to fix you, but if you do, you will become angry and hurt because you will always be let down. Once you are an adult, no one, not even your parents, can legitimately offer you the care of a true parent–child relationship. If you start to signal your despair you'll make people feel guilty; if you try to punish them for failing to match your expectations you'll make them angry; if you appeal to them by playing the good and obliging child they'll treat you as a burden to be avoided.

Love can be hard to find

If you didn't enjoy your childhood you should be trying to live in the present as a self-respecting adult. The last thing you want to do is keep reliving a childhood you hated, but there is a powerful and normal human desire to try to correct wrongs by confronting the guilty person.

Unfortunately, if you confront someone it usually makes them anxious or angry, putting them in a rigidly defensive mode and very rarely into a reflective state of mind. More unfortunately still, even if there is no doubt your parents were cruel and neglecting, no bad person thinks he is bad.

The very characteristics that allowed your parents to treat you badly when you were a child will make them highly unlikely to accept responsibility now you are an adult. Almost everyone can justify their actions, at least to their own satisfaction. If what they did was just too bad to deny, they will probably still claim that they are in the right because the end justified the means at the time: 'Look at you. You're doing fine. What are you complaining about? You don't understand what it was like for us and how difficult you were. Your life was a picnic compared to ours when we were kids.'

To suggest somebody might have been a bad parent is a profound threat and is more likely to provoke anger than insight.

Even if your parents don't get angry or deny what they did or didn't do, their blank stares, patronage or display of being hurt will leave you impotently angry or effectively shut you up with guilt. Because a sincere acknowledgement of their failings is so hard to get, it's risky to put too many of the eggs of your happiness in the basket of their understanding.

There are, of course, parents who will listen and will concede their responsibility, but as a broad principle anyone who is secure enough to admit his defects is likely to have been secure enough to freely give love in the first place and therefore not need confronting.

Despite these obstacles, it is absolutely worth trying to heal the problems between you and your parents by open discussion. I have seen people confront their parents and receive an unreserved apology with dramatic emotional results, because validation and reconciliation in the present can go a long way towards limiting trauma from the past. If only you could develop a new feeling of closeness to your parents, which an obviously genuine apology from them would offer, you could be at least partially liberated from the self-perpetuating difficulties of disappointed anger or anxious clinging.

If you feel damaged by your childhood and you have tried to reach your parents but failed, a few ideas are worth considering. These might help to modify your attitude towards your disappointing parents and hence your feelings about yourself.

A great number of people believe their parents didn't love them, or at least not enough, or that they loved a sibling more. In the early stages of treatment, I usually encourage them to recognise and feel their anger, but there is more to do.

Exploring the past and looking more closely at their parents, mostly by recall, occasionally in family interviews, it so often becomes clear their parents did love them. As I've said, it is very rare to come across someone who didn't love or at least didn't want to love his child.

I have heard stories of appalling parental behaviour, but I have not always been convinced the events were acts of conscious, deliberate cruelty. Fear, ignorance, depression, sexual deviation, obsessively misguided principle or sheer inability to cope, perhaps, but pure malice in a parent towards his biological child doesn't occur all that often. I must admit children of other unions don't always fare so well, but most people love and care for children, even if they are only theirs by default as stepchildren.

Less than perfect

As they grow older, children who continue to live with a parental message of disapproval often become convinced they really are defective or bad. It is usually easy to see that the parent was fragile him- or herself, doubting their own loveableness and so seeing every act of individuality or non-conformity in their child as a rejection. Frightened suppression of a child's differences can very effectively obscure genuine love.

The sensitivity and vulnerability you feel from your childhood could be, at least in part, due to an inherited programming for anxiety, perfectionism or depression. Your father may have carried the same genes, causing him to be utterly miserable with himself. Perhaps he slipped too easily into anger, responding to his own fear of being out of control. When you misbehaved you became a focus for his depressive ill-humour, which might have made him hate himself more, but he lacked the courage to swallow his pride. Hard as it may be to believe, it doesn't necessarily mean he didn't love you, rather that his lack of self-love was so great that the power of an aggressive outburst at his child felt like the only strength he had.

If you are willing to consider this as a possible truth it doesn't take away the pain you suffered as a child, but you might be able to re-examine your hurt and anger in the light of a different understanding. This is worth doing because understanding gives a sense of control. Remember, a generation ago there was nothing like the psychological information available today. Parenting was really flying blind back then; your parents were totally dependent on the model offered by their own parents, which often wasn't all that great.

If you linger too long trying to fix the injustices of your past, it's a little like sitting an exam and spending all your time on the first question. It might be better to recognise you are genuinely cheated and disappointed, that your childhood was a horrible experience and to acknowledge you will never be able to make it totally right. You can choose to face this squarely, but you can ease some of your hurt by conceding the failures of your parents may have been weakness rather than malice.

Of course, you were only a child and they should have known, but then your parents were only imperfect people.

If you have understood your own potential contribution to past difficulties, recognised the failings of your parents and tried talking to them but you feel no different, you may need to re-consider the role you are currently adopting with them.

If you are taking the position of a hurt and needy child, your liberation from this will depend totally upon extracting a confession, an apology and a resolution. This is risky because, as I have proposed, often they won't even listen. If your goal is their complete understanding and reconciliation, you are probably setting yourself up for more pain. It is definitely worth trying a couple of times, but

once a pattern of confrontation and denial is established, it is virtu-
ally impossible to break.

Switching roles

You can also find yourself playing the role of parent to your parents,
dutifully looking after them as they get older and more demanding.
People caught in this role become increasingly angry and frustrated;
the child in them is still trying to get the approval and recognition
they missed when they were young; the adult is feeling utterly
trapped. Sometimes the hurt and fury can be so great that it can
drive people to verbally and even physically abuse their parents,
while they repeatedly return and cling to them.

Once you are an adult, playing child or parent to your parents
won't make you feel better. In your relationship with disappointing
parents, ideally you would assume the role of an equal adult. Unfortunately, to feel equal with your parents is harder than with anyone
else. They have such power to make you feel like a kid that the ideal
of equality may be impossible.

In practice, your best available option might be to try position-
ing yourself at a metaphorically higher level: playing a parent role
towards your parents, but with a difference.

The critical element in managing your feelings is to give up
trying to reach your parents to get the response you have wanted all
your life. Because you have their picture printed on your brain, if
you keep trying to reach them it will always be as if you are reaching
up from below, as you did when you were a vulnerable child. If you
can bring yourself to give up trying to get what you want from them,
you may be in a better position to stop making the same pointless
sacrifices or enduring the same level of frustration.

It is tragically common to see a woman looking after her parents while she neglects her own family, particularly her husband. She chases her parents' love and approval until eventually her husband gets so angry over her emotional neglect he refuses to have anything to do with them. This makes her doubly anxious, as she loses her husband's approval and feels blamed by her parents for his behaviour. The more distressed she becomes, the more she clings to her parents in an endless cycle of behaviour, driven by her anxious attachment.

If you were able to mentally place yourself above your parents, you could look on them from the more powerful position that comes with greater understanding of their weaknesses and needs. If you could stop trying to get what you needed, wanted and deserved as a child, but will never get as an adult, it might be possible to stop chasing them or punishing them, even if you can neither forgive nor forget.

If you were to consider acting – please note, I said acting – as if you have forgiven them, abandoning the helplessness of a child-victim for the more powerful position of a forgiver, you might begin to liberate yourself from endlessly replaying your childhood unhappiness with your unreachable parents.

Taking a parental role with deficient parents should not be done in the hope they will be pleased with you and love you after all. On the contrary, it is designed to put you above them in the kindly role that gives you greater power, looking on them with a degree of pity for the unhappiness that made them act the way they did. If you take advantage of the fact that the most powerful role for a human being is to be the giver of love, you will not feel quite so much the hurt and resentful child. *It is essential you are not baiting a hook with care and forgiveness, still fishing for the response you have always wanted. This approach can only change you, not them.*

The impossible dream

A successful psychotherapy which began by encouraging anger, may end by helping someone return, in a different role, to their parents. With greater understanding of their parents' human needs and fears, it's possible to see that behind their weakness there's a chance they wanted to show love, but it was lost as they struggled against the pressures of their own misery. They simply didn't love themselves.

This system may fail you because one of the many biological tides you will not be able to swim against is the inbuilt desire for your parents' love. The need for the security of their love is so huge that cheated of this, even the most elegant philosophic, psychological and behavioural gymnastics may not get you past your hurt and anger. Ultimately, you may be better off hating them and having little contact with them than endlessly trying to get the love you never had and will probably never get.

However, before you accept this as final, you would be wise to make sure there is absolutely no possibility of reconciliation and if this isn't possible that equally there is no chance that you could see them from the position of greater strength that comes with understanding. Even pity for their fear or their self-indulgent weakness is better for you. Hating them or distancing yourself from them may be superior to impotent anger or desperate searching, but it is a less liberating option.

In whatever way you choose to respond, part of being a grown-up is accepting that you are ultimately alone. Your parents may have truly been the cause of your pain, but you will not be happy until you take final responsibility for your own comfort, choosing to live as a self-respecting adult and not trying to fix an unfixable past.

Ideas

- Parents are not responsible for every emotional problem in their children. Genetic programming plays a large part in personality style.

- To suggest somebody might have been a bad parent is a profound threat and is more likely to provoke anger than insight.

- The very personality characteristics that made parents treat you badly when you were a child will make them less likely to accept responsibility now you are an adult.

- It is extremely rare to come across someone who doesn't love or at least want to love his child. Thus, hard as it may be to believe, mistreatment from a parent does not necessarily mean he or she didn't love you, more often it points to a profound lack of self-love on their part.

- Try at least once to get your parents to understand your position, because if they can accept it and apologise, the validation of your feelings can go along way towards changing the effects of past trauma on your present feelings.

- You might ease some of your hurt by conceding the failures of your parents may have been through weakness and fear, rather than malice.

- You may never be able to forgive or forget, but by playing a powerful, caring role with your parents, you will feel much better than endlessly trying to punish or please them.

- If you do take a protective role toward parents because you can see were weak, not inherently bad, don't do it in the hope that you will change them. This approach can only change you, not them.

- Ultimately, and sadly, you may never be able to reach your parents. If you can never find a way to view them from a different position you're probably better off distancing yourself from them, but if you are anxiously attached to them you will find this terribly hard.

CHAPTER 21

Your Children

IF YOU HAD A MISERABLE CHILDHOOD, your self-esteem is likely to be vulnerable. To do something about it you'll need a system for dealing with past pain. Confronting your parents, pitying them, parenting them, or even hating them may help, but as techniques they are unpredictable.

Trying to give your children a happy life is a powerful approach to overriding the ill-effect of your own bad experiences. This is a much more reliable system for lifting some of the burden than confronting or caring for your parents. For a start, it is much more under your direct control, and secondly, you and your children have a common motive in loving each other.

The reward that comes with being the best parent you can be is self-evident, but I propose the self-interested value in loving and caring for your children goes beyond the obvious pleasure. The value to you is obvious in light of the forces of evolution that have shaped us.

The purpose of life is to make more life. Biological fitness is measured by an animal's success in raising young who can then raise their own healthy offspring. Therefore, the fitter your children, the more biologically successful you are. Happy children are more likely to become happy adults because they will tend to have better relationships. From the very beginning, a kindly, dignified manner increases your reproductive opportunities because it is attractive to a potential sexual partner. This is especially so in a world beyond the jungle, where brute strength won't necessarily get you a mate.

Going with the flow

Behaviour that goes against your evolutionary programming doesn't work very well. Communism could never work because people are territorial and want to preserve and enlarge their own patch. Capitalism works because it is theoretically territorial without violence. Christianity is particularly successful because it supports individuality but also places a huge emphasis on love. In the same way it is natural and makes good evolutionary sense for you to want the best for your children. You will be less comfortable if your behaviour makes you less biologically fit; that is, your actions reduce the chance of having successful children. If you neglect or abuse your role as a parent, your own inner discomfort will automatically push you towards wastefully expending more energy in self-justification, denial, anger or alcohol. These are the defensive behaviours of an alienated mind.

By building your children's trust and love, you are swimming with the evolutionary current. You make it easier to build a much more loving world for yourself and then live in it, ensuring your adult life is not an endless rerun of your childhood unhappiness. As an adult you have much more control than you did when you were a kid; you just need to recognise it and put it into action.

Treat your partner the way you wish your parents had treated each other and your children the way you wish you had been cared for yourself. If you do this most of the time, you are a long way towards liberating yourself from the past. It's not written in stone that you have to pass on the bad stuff, but if you do, it is highly likely to come back to you in the form of your own children's distressed behaviour and less obviously, but just as potently, in wordless, prodding discomfort from your survival brain, aroused by your potential biological failure.

If your childhood wasn't too good, to be happy in your adult life, your past and your present need to be made as separate as possible. You can best ensure this by setting up a family in which you act with love and healthy self-assertion. Ideally you would have had your parents as models of kindness and dignity, but unfortunately if you are struggling to free yourself from past unhappiness you may not have had this privilege.

If your childhood was painful because of your unhappy experiences, you must be constantly aware that you are in real danger of repeating with your partner and your children the things your parents did to each other and to you.

If you do react badly to something your family does and you see the looks on their faces, try to remember how you felt when it happened to you. *The greatest strength is the ability to acknowledge weakness.* Back down, apologise, tell your partner how you feel. There's huge dignity in this. Search for the courage to say what happened to you and how painful it was. *Don't ask for forgiveness; try to explain but not justify; then give love to get love.*

If you are a parent of an adult family and one of your children is accusing you of something you know is not true, please pause a moment before you angrily deny it or question her memory or sanity. Remember, it is true to her. Ask her why she sees it that way and whether you both might examine an event she recalls as particularly painful. Try to work out why you see it so differently.

Remember the rules for surviving criticism: don't just leap in and deny; at the very least try considering what is being said. Your child, young or adult, would always prefer to get close to you, not to destroy you. The anger of attack you receive from a critical child is just as much in anticipation of your being unwilling to listen as it is because of her view of the past.

If you attempt to make sense of her anger, validating anything that you can possibly agree with and apologising if you can see you should, you could do more good in a few moments than you might ever do again in your life.

This is looking after yourself in an intelligent way, because you will get vast amounts for yourself from a reconciled and loving relationship with your child.

If you suffered as a child yourself, openness about your pain is a valid approach to your adult partner, but always made as a statement of facts and never as a plea for forgiveness or as pressure for extra concessions. Trying to explain wrongdoing in the light of your own past suffering may be justified, but it won't get you nearly as much love as taking responsibility will do.

On the other hand, it is very rarely and probably never appropriate to be too open with your children about your sadness or your unhappy past. If you put your burden on your children, even a very young child will respond to your need for understanding and too easily slip into the role of being your pseudo-parent. In trying to protect you, a child can become afraid of hurting you, denying himself the freedom to test you and to be naughty without guilt.

With your children, just give love. Pretend not to be hurt when they cut you down with contempt or go against you on principle. Try to hide your vulnerability and anger. Young children will very rapidly give you love in return and by playing the role of a strong, loving and self-respecting parent, you will be doing the very best you can to free yourself from the past. Even your adolescent might become a little less difficult if he finds you can be loving without automatically getting angry.

Back room boys

I am sad to say – and I would love to be wrong – but I suspect mothers are more important in the delivery of love and care to young children than are fathers. Irrespective of how loving you may be as a father, young children will more often turn to their mothers for comfort. Children are biologically programmed to see mothers as the ultimate caregivers, so when a mother fails there is often much more pain and anger than when a father does. This is absolutely and categorically not to say a father can't be a sole parent and raise children perfectly well, but he will need to think and behave more like a mother than a woman alone needs to be like a father.

One of a father's roles is to recognise the primary importance of mothers to young children and give his wife loving and practical support so that she can get on with mothering.

A man also needs to suppress the competitive urge and even anger provoked by seeing the exclusiveness and intensity of feeling between his wife and children. A father needs to avoid becoming another child, caught in hostile sibling rivalry with his own offspring.

Men often underestimate the power and importance of their love. Even if it were true that the mother is the deliverer of original and basic love, quite frequently older children grow to value the less available love of their fathers more than the nourishing but more predictably present care from their mothers. A man should appreciate and enjoy this power and use it as power should always be used to earn respect: tenderly and gently.

Give them space to grow

Your children are genetically programmed to become irreversibly bonded to you, and even rude, sullen, disobedient teenagers want and need your love. Offer it early, offer it frequently and offer it in a form that they can recognise and respond to. Allow them to keep their dignity, even if that means tolerating the grunting unresponsiveness dictated by their years. Don't visit your own disappointing experiences on them.

Of course, no parent is so rational as to always criticise the behaviour and not the person, nor so secure as to not get hurt and angry and then withdraw and reject. The fact that as a parent you are less than perfect – vulnerable, frail, uncertain and sometimes inconsistent – probably doesn't matter, providing that through it all, in between your worst moments, you demonstrate your love in an enduring and unambiguous way, so your child ultimately feels safe.

There is a world worth aiming for; a world where you will be happiest and your kids, who are your genetic investment, will be able to make the best of themselves, too. A healthy family structure is achievable because you don't have to do it perfectly for it to be perfectly all right.

There is a natural drive towards growth and biological success; that is, to be as effective a creature as possible. All you need to give your kids is an environment that is *good enough* and then their basic animal programming will oblige them to make the best of whatever their individual genetic potential will allow. If your children have faults or go wrong in their lives, it's not inevitably your fault, but you must still try really hard to get it right as often as possible. The chances of things working out well are much higher than the risks of disaster.

It is possible to broadly define the style of parental love that offers children their best chance of a robust self-esteem. From their earliest years children need to feel loved infinitely and irrationally; loved without limit, loved simply for existing, and in a way not contingent upon beauty, performance or obeying the rules. Punishment should entail as little withdrawal of love as possible, and should never be belittling. *Tell your child he's naughty, but don't tell him he's stupid.*

Whatever children do, reflected in their mother's and father's behaviour there should be the message that ultimately they are good enough; that it is not possible to be bad enough to be permanently rejected. Not speaking to a child for lengthy periods when he or she has sinned is a viciously destructive punishment and a cruel instrument of control.

However badly they behave, and no matter how much they deserve and get punishment, there should always be the message of an infinity of love beyond the anger. Nothing a child can do should be able to push him off the edge of his world of safety. If he discovers as a child that he has the power to bring about his own rejection, he is likely to repeatedly test his adult relationships, trying to anticipate and guard against the effects of his own sense of badness.

As a parent you need to present firm, openly stated and generally consistent limits. Privately you should be willing to back away in the interests of love, rather than maintaining them in the service of perfection or what you believe is necessary for your dignity or authority. Few things could be less dignified than an adult screaming at a child over an issue that is a principle rather than a necessity.

A family should be the island of security to which a child can return after a bruising by a difficult world outside. It shouldn't be a place of discipline and fear before being a safe harbour of flexibility and kindness.

You should smile at your child when you see him, rather than scowling and making it quite clear you haven't forgotten the last crime. He hasn't forgotten either, he just hopes you still love him. By smiling you don't approve of the misbehaviour, but you do approve of him, helping him feel more secure and like himself better, which might free him to make his own decision to change.

Children need to get into trouble and to see the stern side of their parents. This allows them to develop emotional muscle, but they need to develop their emotional muscle in a setting of manageable anxiety, not overwhelming fear, which will break and not strengthen them.

Children need to be able to respect their parents for their wisdom and knowledge, but more importantly still to respect their parents' strength to be wrong, to fail, or not to know. They need the example of a loved and powerful figure absorbing the blows of failure, smiling through pain and apologising, taking possession of and responsibility for errors. Possibly a child should also see a parent sometimes accept blame when he or she doesn't deserve it, perhaps taking responsibility for failing to tell the child what to do, rather than just blaming the child for not knowing.

If you have done everything right, or as close to right as reasonably might be asked of you as a parent, it's less likely but still possible that your children will behave terribly. Even an ideal family cannot guarantee emotional stability in children; they still have their genes and the influences of friends and society to manage. If you have done your best and with a good heart, at least you needn't carry too big a burden of guilt. There is also a high chance that the love someone had as a child will give him a foundation for a more mature personality, even if it develops at a rate of his choosing, not yours. In your own childhood, you may have been a victim. If you want to rise above being a victim and make sure no more are created, give love to your family now.

Ideas

- Giving your kids a good childhood is a great technique for overriding your own bad experiences.

- By building your children's trust and love you can build a much more loving world for yourself, and then you can all live in it.

- To liberate yourself from the past, treat your partner the way you wish your parents had treated each other, and treat your children the way you wish you had been cared for yourself.

- If your parenting is being criticised by one of your children, remember she would rather get close to you than destroy you.

- By refusing to listen, you can force your children to settle for hurting you, but they would much rather love you.

- One of a father's tasks is to recognise the primary importance of mothers to young children and so give your wife loving and practical support so she can get on with mothering.

- A father needs to avoid becoming another child, caught in hostile sibling rivalry with his own offspring, jealously competing for his partner's attention.

- Men often underestimate the power and importance of their love to their children, especially when they feel eclipsed by the child's bond to his mother.

- When you are in pain, give love to your children and pretend to be strong. Share your confidences with your partner, but not too many with your children or they will start looking after you, which is not good for a young child.

- Appropriate punishment is an important part of children's emotional development, but they should always receive a clear message that it is not possible to be bad enough to be permanently rejected.

- A family should be an island of security away from the difficult world outside.

- A healthy family structure is achievable, because you don't have to do it perfectly for it to be perfectly all right.

PART 4

About Us

The Things We Do and the Way We Are

In sooth I know not why I am so sad:
It wearies me; you say it wearies you;
But how I caught it, found it, or came by it,
What stuff 'tis made of, wherof it is born,
I am yet to learn:
And such a want-wit sadness makes of me,
That I have much ado to know myself.

Antonio in *The Merchant of Venice*, Act I, Scene I,
William Shakespeare

Antonio knew well enough that he didn't feel good, but he had no idea why. Shakespeare knew why because he created Antonio, putting words in his hero's mouth, drawn from his extraordinary grasp of human nature. Antonio was trying to understand himself: he knew instinctively that understanding the origin of his feelings would give him some sense of control.

Life is easier if you have a grasp of the emotional forces that drive you and the people to whom you relate. But, as Antonio found, it's hard enough to fully understand your own motives, especially if you are distressed, let alone be confident of others' shifting, individual agendas. In spite of this, you can realistically ask yourself to understand the underlying needs that drive us all. Recognising that very few things we do have a single motivation or meaning, and seeing the way we complicate and sometimes sabotage our lives, it's also possible to start seeing how to do something about it.

The best layered plans

Most of us try to be strong rather than weak and kind rather than cruel, but at the same time everybody is trying to look after their own best interests. If we can't handle the potential conflicts amongst our motives with skill, we can do some remarkably self-defeating things.

This section of the book, *About Us*, introduces a list of the things people do every day. It has my customary emphasis on the negative, based on the belief that bad things need attention, while the good can generally be left to look after themselves. As you work your way through these ideas, I hope you will appreciate people's intentions are usually good, even if their application is sometimes a disaster.

Identifying the various layers of meaning and need in the things people do is not an exercise in cynicism, nor is it an exposure of the 'real' meaning behind your actions. It is simply using a greater depth of knowledge to reduce the likelihood of blind miscalculation and to increase your chances of feeling good about yourself.

Let me try to illustrate this. When you help an old lady across the road, you are doing it for a number of reasons:

1. You are a truly kind person who cares about old ladies.

2. Your mother, your father and the headmaster resident in your head as your Observing Self are telling you that good people help old ladies.

3. You might be performing a little bit for an audience: showing passers-by what a kind person you are.

    When you finally get the lady to the other side and she tells you that you look scruffy rather than thanking you, there is likely to be an immediate recognition:

4. As well as being a truly kind person who cares about old ladies,

somewhere in there you were performing your kindly act to get a quick dose of love in the form of gratitude.

None of these motivations alone is the real reason for your good deed, nor are they equal reasons, and some may not be present at all. But they, and probably a few I haven't thought of, are all possible.

If you are equipped and willing to recognise these layers, while still stung by her black ingratitude, you are in a better position to laugh at yourself, but still help the next old lady across the road. On the other hand, if you believe your only motive was to be good and kind, you are in danger of misunderstanding where your anger comes from when your old lady doesn't respond to you as you expected.

If your self-esteem is not as robust as you deserve, but you can understand your motives, you are at less risk of jumping to negative conclusions about yourself, your life and old ladies in general. By understanding your potential for less obviously noble motives, you are less likely to fall into the trap laid by yet another layer of meaning:

5. You might be compulsively helping people so as to make yourself into a person good enough to get the love you missed as a child; in this case from symbols of mothers in the form of little old ladies.

If you don't understand what's happening, there's a real risk of endless replays of your search for reward from a good parent. Because you won't find what you are looking for, you might turn to angrily denying yourself the pleasure and self-respect that comes from helping people, even if you don't get all the love you'd like in return.

After this dissection of motives, I hope I haven't made you too self-conscious to help little old ladies in future. As with everything in this book, some of the feelings and behaviours I describe may seem exaggerated and some will have no relevance to you, but in clinical practice I've seen all this and more. Life has also taught me there is very little difference, if any, between the people who consult a psychiatrist and those who don't.

I hope you can find some useable tools among these ideas.

Acting irrationally
Action
Agendas
Anger, aggression and violence
Anxiety
Anxious attachment
Apology
Arrogance
Asking, hinting and manipulating
Being yourself
Boasting
Buying love
Certainty
Changing people
Cliff of rejection
Clinging and neediness
Competition
Complaining, nagging and whining
Compliments
Confession
Confidence and self-confidence
Conscience
Control
Conversations in our heads
Criticism of other people
Criticism of yourself

Cruelty

Decisions

Deference, humility and modesty

Dependency

Dignity

Distrust

Domination and submission

Expectations

Fear of success

Forgiveness

Generosity

Gratitude and thanks

Guilt

Honesty and Lies

Hurt

Identity of defect

Independence

Inferiority

Intimacy

Jealousy

Loneliness

Love

Manners

Mind-reading

Naturalness

Niceness

Orbits of intimacy

Panic attacks

Paranoia

Pedantry

Perfectionism and high standards

Phobias

Pleasing people

Possessiveness

Power games

Procrastination

Punishment

Rebellion

Rejection

Reliving the past

Respect

Right and wrong

Roles

Security and insecurity

Self-consciousness

Showing feelings

Shyness

Standards

Status and worth

Strength and stubbornness

Stress

Success

Sulking

Support

Taking responsibility

Taking things personally

Tantrums

Testing

Trauma

Trust and unconditional love

Truth

Victim and victimised

Winning and losing

Worrying

Acting irrationally

Nobody acts irrationally in the light of their own truth. The way some people behave may look foolish and self-destructive, however, it makes perfect sense to them. Sometimes when people lash out with anger, hide in fear or give up in despair, no one else can understand why. It may look irrational, but it is perfectly logical to them. They are responding to tigers they can see very clearly. It's just that no one else can.

Action

If you want to feel good you must act well. If you feel bad and act badly don't be surprised if you feel worse. Bad actions are actions that make you less loveable or less dignified. If something goes wrong, fix it. If you can't fix it, strengthen yourself by strengthening your relationships. You can do that most easily and most quickly by acting with as much kindness and dignity as possible, remembering to establish your dignity with gentle self assertion.

You have very little direct control over your emotions. The way you act towards other people decides how you feel about yourself. If nothing is going right, act as well as you can within your role. Be a great friend, boss, spouse and, above all, be a great parent. By making other people feel good about themselves and about you, you can make yourself feel good.

Agendas

Nobody can ever be confident he understands another person's agendas. You may be right in your interpretation of the more obvious motivations, but there can always be layers beneath that you do not see. It is really important to remember the only mind to which you have access is your own, so in ambiguous situations your judge-ments of other people's agendas and the contents of their minds are at best suspect and often plain wrong. *If you read minds, you are in great danger of reading from your own text.*

The biggest problems between people flow more often from misinterpretation and misunderstanding than from insult or delib-erate malice. Beyond their basic needs, it is a totally unrealistic expectation to believe you should be able to accurately work out other people's agendas when it is hard enough to know your own. 'I'm very sensitive to atmosphere and an excellent judge of other people' is usually another way of saying: 'I have a mild case of para-noia.'

It doesn't matter that you can never hope to reliably under-stand and predict the precise agendas and subtexts of any individual in a particular situation. It doesn't matter because everybody with whom you have to deal has the same basic needs for love and indi-viduality.

If your behaviour responds to the basics, the fine print tends to sort itself out. If you stick to the basics of recognising everyone's need for love and individuality, you will have all the predictive power you will ever need and you will be better placed to accurately judge a positive or negative response to the way you are behaving. You have to shape your behaviour in a way that is universally right, not try to tailor yourself to exactly fit each new person you meet.

Anger, aggression and violence

Anger has evolved primarily as a motivation for territorial defence, so the events most likely to make you angry will be trespass, viola-tion, injustice or put-down, whether real, imagined or exaggerated.

We all get angry when we feel belittled. Some people get angry when they feel rejected. Anger in response to rejection has two potential meanings: either you are regarding a friend or lover as your possession and it's a territorial rage, or you feel so vulnerable that your survival brain has convinced you that if you are alone you will die. Then your anger is at someone who you feel will kill you by leaving you.

A few points are worth noting:

1. If your love can turn to hate when someone leaves you, you have to question how generously you were loving in the first place.

2. The less you like yourself, the more you're at risk of deliberately pumping up your anger to blot out the helplessness of anxiety and despair. Using anger as an antidote is a way of getting in first and follows the flawed premise: 'Better to be a bastard than a fool. No one loves a bastard, no one loves a fool, but at least a bastard can enjoy the illusion of power that comes with aggression.'

3. If you're angry over something, it's worthwhile having a brief look at yourself because you might find that some of your anger is with yourself. You might be angry because you sense you have set yourself up to feel small, deciding you've been weak, too generous or you haven't stood up for yourself. If you hear yourself protesting that you've been used, could it be that you simply haven't received the love and appreciation you feel you have earned with all your goodness?

4. These observations are equally true in reverse. Anybody who is angry with you without good reason is doing it because he feels bad about himself. If a quick scan of your conscience shows you have done nothing wrong, someone being nasty is getting in before you can reject him or show up the weakness he fears in himself. He is trying to say: 'I'm so strong, I don't need anybody.'

Lots of things in life will make you angry, and this should be the motivating force to make you do something about a problem. If your anger is consuming and you can see no direct solution, you would be wise to ask yourself the question: 'Am I angry because I feel put down and powerless, or is it because I feel rejected?'

If you look behind the complexities of any negative feeling, be it anxiety, sadness or anger, you will always find the origin is in loss of belonging or loss of territory. If you can appreciate this, you have more control because you then have the option to follow the simple guidelines of this book.

Anxiety

Anxiety is nature's early-warning signal. You get anxious when you think there might be a tiger around, even before you see him. Anxiety has evolved to be an intensely unpleasant, intrusive discomfort; something so bad that you try to get away from the feeling itself, rather than wait until the tiger has you by your throat.

Anxiety is the original survival tool and you still need it. If your survival brain tells you there's danger about, don't ask it to relax. Any rational animal would choose to be alert and anxious if there's something around that can kill him.

If you want to reduce your anxiety, understanding the forces that are making you anxious has to be the first step towards managing the emotion. If your survival brain anticipates a rejection or a put-down, it will yell at you to escape before you are killed. If you have no established system for understanding and dealing with the sense of danger, you have no hope of controlling the anxiety. Once you understand why your anxiety is unnecessary and can plan rational action, your relaxation therapy or meditation will work much more effectively. Peacefully chanting your mantra is a lot easier once you appreciate there isn't a tiger behind you.

Understanding gives a sense of control.

Anxious attachment

This is a phenomenon in children who have not had enough love. Parents are supposed to represent safety and sanctuary, but sometimes they are absent physically or emotionally, or more rarely they are actively cruel. A child does not have the ability to say that his parents are no good and to run away, because where would he go? A child's solution is to cling more tightly to the very people who hurt and scare him, yet are his only source of safety. The more they let him down, the more he clings.

Anxious attachment can live on into adulthood, when theoretically you should be free of your parents. Unfortunately, the urge to cling in a child-like way to someone who is hurting you doesn't always disappear with age. If you didn't get enough safe loving as a child, each new relationship can acquire a parent–child quality and each new partner starts off as the good parent you never had, only to later become much more like the miserable, untrustworthy one you actually did suffer.

The phenomenon of anxious attachment allows many cruel and dominating men to keep their partners long after they should have been left. It also explains why brutalised and sexually molested children tell no one for years.

When a crushed partner finally leaves or a molested child tells of their treatment, they are often overwhelmed by guilt, or at least guilty fear. They feel they have betrayed and lost a parent and their awful feelings are only made worse by people telling them how angry they should be. When you are a kid, it's just too scary to be angry with a parent who is dangerous, but is all you've got.

Apology

To apologise is to make yourself small. It's a ritual lowering of yourself, a bow, an obeisance, a symbolic way of making someone else bigger by reducing yourself. If you have done something wrong, you take responsibility with apology. Apology is a way of paying somebody back and is totally appropriate and dignified when you have truly done wrong.

Unfortunately, vulnerable people sometimes use an excess of apology to buy love and they do this by offering up their adult dignity as a sacrifice. If you say you're sorry when you've done nothing wrong, you're making yourself small, abdicating from the role of a potentially challenging, equal adult. You're trying to secure what you hope is the more certain acceptance of being wonderfully nice and polite, but you're doing it in the role of a child.

If I tread on your toe and say: 'I'm sorry,' it means: I'm sorry I trod on your toe and I hope it doesn't hurt too much. If I say: 'I'm sorry, I'm sorry, oh my God, I'm so sorry, I'll never forgive myself,' I'm actually saying I don't give a damn about your toe, but I'm really worried you won't like me, so please reassure me that you do and I'll pay for the reassurance by making myself absolutely tiny, which, of course, means you wouldn't punish me, would you?

Arrogance

Some people are arrogant because they genuinely believe they are better than most. They may be right, but only if better is measured by status or having the power to take more territory.

If you do actually believe you are the best – although not many people really do believe it, including the most arrogant – good sense would suggest you keep your personal satisfaction to yourself. You could pay a high price for your strutting and preening.

In the jungle, the top ape gets the territory and the girls. In human society you can often get away with being arrogant because the ape is still very close to the surface in both sexes. A sports car, an expensive suit and a lot of self aggrandisement can have distinctly aphrodisiacal qualities. Models are taught to act as if they are haughty and unattainable. Sometimes it will work, but generally loud signalling as to how powerful you are is not always going to find you the best long-term partner or the truest friends.

Arrogance and snobbishness are mostly efforts at emotional self-protection. This is based on the recognition that people who obviously like themselves get more liking from others. Everybody knows this instinctively, but some people try to show they have such an abundance of self-love they don't really need anybody.

Asking, hinting and manipulating

Directly asking for something as one equal adult to another, with neither expectation nor unnecessary apology, is dignified, intelligent behaviour.

Manipulation is asking in a loaded way that makes other people feel small, guilty, or responsible if they refuse. Hinting is a form of manipulation in which you don't take full possession of your request. Just because you don't ask directly doesn't mean you don't really want what you are edging towards, merely that you are afraid of disapproval for asking and trying to protect yourself. By half-concealing your request, you avoid the responsibility of asking for too much. If refusal or disapproval looms, you are freer to step back and deny it was ever in your mind. Manipulation is simply a bid for control while trying to avoid any risk of rejection.

People hate being manipulated because you take away their freedom to say 'no' and they feel controlled and trespassed upon. You may get what you want, but you risk losing respect, which may be a very high price to pay.

Being yourself

'Just be yourself', often teamed with similarly helpful suggestions such as 'relax' or 'don't worry', may seem good advice, but most of us don't actually know who we are, so how to go about being whoever we are can be a bit of a mystery.

Obviously this kindly advice comes from someone on your side, who is trying to say: 'You're a really competent, nice person and people will like you, so you don't have to make an extra effort to be super-nice or especially clever.' Often the person is also saying: 'I can see you feel vulnerable and you have a bit of a habit of overdoing it, so don't blow it by trying too hard.'

So, what are the rules? Simple. They're always the same:

- *Try to act with kindness and dignity.*
- *Treat everybody as if you believe they like you.*

It's really important you appreciate asking you to treat people as if they like you is not instructing you to believe it, merely suggesting you act as if you believe it. We are all at our most attractive with people we know and trust to like us. Behaving towards someone whom you don't know, as if there were no reason on Earth why he wouldn't like you, frees you to be suitably open and friendly, kind and dignified and therefore attractive to him and to yourself. I must emphasise this is not saying you act as if you really, really like somebody you've just met or couldn't possibly know (which can be seriously tacky, even if you feel it is just showing how warm you are), it's simply acting as if you have assumed someone will like you well enough, not that you are new best friends already.

Were you able to broadly follow this principle, you might find life so pleasant you won't need to bother working out who you are. Having said that, you may recall in Chapter 4 I proposed the closest you will ever come to knowing who you are is to clearly decide upon your core values. By defining the ethics and principles you hold most dear, you define yourself most clearly.

Boasting

Boasting is claiming more territory than you really own, or more love than is really yours. Boasting, like lying, is addictive. It's the junkie's choice: short-term gain but long-term pain.

Buying love

In reality, we never do something for nothing. Everything we do has multiple layers of motivation and even the most noble acts are not always entirely selfless.

It doesn't diminish goodness to understand it, because *what you do is what you are*, and if you choose to be good and kind, that is you and that is enough. Buying love is good and we all do it. It's the way we do it that matters. Buying love is only a problem if you give too much to get it and then you are resentful if you don't get the payback you feel you have earned. Don't destroy generosity by calling in your debts; let others pay you back in their own time and manner. If you are not paid back as you deserve, hide your resentment and recognise that feeling used sometimes means what you gave was not a gift but a pre-payment: 'I did it out of the kindness of my heart. I wasn't asking for anything, just a little bit of thanks.'

Gratitude is a long way from nothing. Gratitude is a little bit of potted love and we prize it very highly. We all buy love because we all value love more than anything else. Just don't do it too obviously.

Certainty

The need for certainty is death to decision making. If you wait to be certain you'll never do anything, if you could be certain as to what you should do, there would be no decision to make. Obsessional anxiety is based on the need for certainty, or at least on the fear of a lack of it. The anxiety that generates indecision is not so much a need to be right as a terror of the consequences of being wrong.

Trying to satisfy too many competing agendas, trying to please too many people and trying to be absolutely certain of what is right all at the same time can mean nothing gets done. People who are always late often fit into this category. They can't leave without doing all the ironing or they can't stop talking to the last person until they're confident he's happy and understands them completely. Then they're late for the next person, so they have to give him extra time to compensate for the feeling that they aren't liked so much because they were late.

Changing people

You're not supposed to want to change people, but everybody tries to. You're also not supposed to get caught doing it. People don't like you trying to change them because it's trespassing, and anger and aggression are the first responses to violations of territory.

Changing people is obviously very difficult and the results of trying are unpredictable and can blow up in your face. The most potentially rewarding approach to changing another person requires changing yourself. The only people you can reasonably hope to change are people who are in some sort of relationship with you and who place value on that relationship. If people want to relate to you they will tend to modify the profile of their style to match yours.

If you behave like a child, you set the other person up to behave like a dominating parent. If you behave in a dominating way yourself and the relationship survives, you'll be left with a needy child.

The easiest and most satisfying way to change someone is to act like a kindly, dignified adult. The personality profile that best matches your behaviour is, not surprisingly, also that of a dignified and kindly adult. This is the only effective and lasting way to change somebody and it can work because adults feel best when they behave like adults.

People won't always manage to act like grown-ups, but given the right circumstances, they'll often choose to make a change in the direction of adult equality. By behaving with kindness and dignity you set other people up to act in the same way, which is twice blessed – it makes both parties feel good. As in any animal, rewarded behaviour increases in frequency. Show someone a reliable way to feel good about himself and you may have changed him.

You can also sometimes produce a change in another person by making psychologically accurate comments to them. If you point out the love-seeking, rejection-avoiding, power-seeking or weakness-avoiding elements of others' conduct, they may hear you. Even if you are heard, very few people can change on the spot, but sometimes changes occur downstream, perhaps without the person ever quite realising. Interpretation is risky, because it can be seen as patronising, but your alternatives are doing nothing, or trying abuse or tears, which never work more than briefly.

Cliff of rejection

Just as we all want love, we are all terrified of rejection. The poorer your self-esteem, the closer you feel to the edge of a cliff.

Someone with a good self-esteem feels miles away from the edge, secure with his deposit of human credit. An insecure person feels himself hanging on to his acceptability like a cartoon character teetering on the edge of the crumbling cliff.

If he feels himself backed into this position, an insecure person can be stubborn and quite unable to apologise, or excessively apologetic and obliging. He senses the pressure of just one more defect, which could push him backwards over the cliff to the annihilation of rejection. When a vulnerable person gets angry in an argument or refuses to concede the possibility of being wrong, he is not just defending a point, he's defending his life. If he becomes obsequious, he's begging for his life.

Clinging and neediness

Clinging to the edge of the cliff is really clinging to people. Your ancestors would have died if they were rejected; their babies died if they were unloved. Clingy people are people who have a poor self-esteem and expect to be rejected. Neediness is the survival brain's response to a threat of death, and needy people are acting as if survival depends on keeping love at any cost. Loss of dignity means nothing in the face of their fear.

Clingy behaviour is sometimes called attention-seeking behaviour, but it's really attention-needing behaviour.

Competition

We all compete because we value territory almost as much as we value love. Competition is simply the word for non-violent, territorial struggle.

Healthy competition becomes divisive when too much rests on the outcome, either in reality or in the eyes of the participants. In the jungle you have to win. There's only room for one at the top and if you don't dominate, you lose. In the jungle the only status is strength and the winner takes all: he gets the harem and the best piece of ground.

For human beings competition is potentially a bit easier. Even if it doesn't quite work out this way, theoretically there is one girl for every guy and most of us can establish our own patch somewhere. If you think we're a violent species now, picture the bloodshed if there could only be one winner.

In human society, there is room for lots of winners. One man can be the best football player, another the best chess player, while another might settle for being well-read. You can be the conquering hero in a computer game. By definition, most of us will never be the best at anything, but if we live intelligently we can be content with being good enough. Each of us has the potential to be happy with our lot and so be happy with ourselves.

Being happy with being good enough is one of the most peaceful and comforting decisions you can make. It doesn't mean mediocrity; it means doing your best and liking yourself when the outcome isn't perfect.

Complaining, nagging and whining

We all want to be heard, because if no one takes any notice of us, it's as if we don't exist. If I speak to you but you do not acknowledge my presence I'll feel angry and I'll become more insistent that you hear me. I may even become aggressive and shout. If that doesn't work, I'll keep on trying until something I say or do does finally make you hear me.

Complaining, nagging and whining is our view of what other people do when they try to get us to listen to them. When we say something over and over again, trying to get someone to see the obvious sense, fairness and logic of our argument, we may think we are doing no more than trying to make a point, but we are also demanding validation of our existence.

A nagging wife is someone who doesn't feel she has been heard.

Compliments

A compliment is a gift of love. Never refuse a compliment, because it is too precious to waste and it is rude to refuse a gift. Even if you don't believe the truth of a compliment, thank whoever gave it for his kindness in saying what he did. You may be afraid you are being mocked, or that accepting the compliment adds vanity to your list of imagined faults, but refusing a compliment looks like fishing – or false modesty at best and insulting at worst. However, if you are anxious about accepting a compliment, you can always safely say: 'Thank you, that's really kind of you to say so!'

You are not saying you actually believe you are pretty or clever, you are simply being polite to the person who has said such nice things. If you accept the grid concept in Chapter 15, you are looking after yourself at the same time.

Compliments are wonderful if you have the courage to believe them, but a misery if you don't. Try telling a girl with an eating disorder how pretty she is and see what sort of a reception you get. Refusing a compliment doesn't mean you don't want it, on the contrary it simply means you dare not believe what you would love to believe.

You can never know for sure whether a compliment is really meant and the more you doubt yourself, the more trouble you will have believing it. Unfortunately, if you look fragile and full of doubt, you increase the chance of a compliment being no more than a well-meant remark to make you feel better. On the other hand, if you look as if you like yourself, you liberate people to be more honest with you. They can see you are robust enough to be told that the colour really doesn't suit you or that they liked your hair better the way it was before. If you look as if you respect yourself you can trust people more to say what they mean and your intimacy and equality with them will automatically increase.

Confession

Confessing is a good thing to do, but it can be done for very bad reasons.

When confession is done in a healthy way, it's designed to reinforce your decision not to do the wrong thing again. Unfortunately, it can sometimes be manipulative. Confession can be used to offload a burden of guilt, manoeuvring for forgiveness. After he chopped down the cherry tree you can bet that when George Washington owned up he was secretly hoping that the virtue of his confession would eclipse the offence.

Confession can also be used to draw a line under your crime. Once you have confessed and you have been heard, there is a silent demand that no further punishment is allowed and the topic must not be raised again. Having acknowledged his infidelity, an unfaithful partner sometimes seems to feel he has the right to be affronted if his wife keeps returning to her hurt and anger over it.

Confession at its worst can be a self-indulgent shedding of responsibility, merely serving as a substitute for corrective action.

Confidence and self-confidence

Confidence is knowing you can do something; self-confidence is knowing you'll be fine if you can't.

If you always have to be confident in order to act, you won't do much. If you're self-confident, provided you know that no one will get hurt, you can try anything. Self-confidence is the ability to be wrong and still like yourself.

Conscience

Your conscience is a voice in your head, your internal policeman. The voice started life as the voice of your parents, teachers and society. When you were a child the values you followed were external – they clearly came from powerful parents and parent-like figures. Before a conscience is properly developed, guilt means being afraid of getting caught.

As you grew older your ethics became your own. As an adult you can reasonably hope your conscience will stop you doing something before rather than after the fact. However, as a healthy and normally imperfect person, you will still occasionally do things that go against your conscience. If you are an animal lover and you kick a cat, whether someone sees you or not, you have violated your moral values and you experience *true guilt*.

If your self-esteem is poor it is possible to be troubled by your conscience more than you deserve, especially if your particular way of feeling secure is to be self-effacing and a bit too much of a giver. This may mean that you feel guilty about acts that please you and do not violate your ethics, but you fear will displease other people. You may become distressed over acts that do no worse than put your feelings and rights at the same level as those of other people. Then your conscience may trouble you with *guilty fear*, which is the fear of rejection, rather than true guilt.

Control

We all want to be in control. We would like to have control of our own feelings and actions, and given the chance most of us wouldn't mind being able to control other people, at least a little bit. Control is simply the ability to command your own territory.

Control only becomes a problem when it becomes obsessive. Obsessive self-control is a child's terror of doing the wrong thing or making a mistake and getting into trouble. Happy people are free to make mistakes and so do not need to manage themselves so closely.

In an intimate relationship, if your partner obsessively controls you, he is trying to stop you being different because if you are, it's as if you don't care about him. Your different version of truth violates and threatens his territory of truth and in his eyes, if you really loved him you'd change to be the person he wants you to be.

Sometimes excessive control means something else. Everyone identifies with their partner. Your partner sees you as part of himself, so if you behave in a way he doesn't approve, it's as if he is acting like this himself and he fears he will be blamed, belittled or rejected for your actions. Controlling you becomes an act of self-protection. The same thing can happen at work. A controlling boss is insecure and in his mind, if you don't do the right thing he will get into trouble. Sometimes this is solved by never delegating, so you're never given any decent work to do. At other times it means unreasonable fury at small mistakes. The greater his anger, the more certain you can be that your boss feels like a child afraid of getting into trouble, not simply a man who wants a job well done.

Conversations in our heads

We all have conversations in our heads; occasionally out loud to ourselves, constantly as thoughts.

An Intelligent Life attempts to give you a structure for your conversations to allow you to talk to yourself when you feel bad, acknowledging you cannot control your feelings directly and allowing you to plan behaviour that could make you feel better. If you live intelligently, when you feel bad emotionally the conversation would go roughly as follows:

'I feel disgusting! There are only two possible reasons. It must be because either I feel I have lost love, or I feel weak and belittled, or maybe both.'

'If I can take action and do something about my sense of rejection, or my feeling of powerlessness and I can do it with kindness and dignity, I should do it now.'

'If there is nothing immediate I can do about the problem, I must look to my relationships and try to be as loving as possible with as much dignity as possible.'

'This won't solve the problem, but I'll feel as good as I possibly can, given what's gone wrong.'

Although it may seem paradoxical, a particularly good way of approaching the hurt and angry conversations that come with the feeling of being a victim, is to search honestly for any contribution you have made to the difficulty. As a victim you are powerless, while genuine self criticism gives you power if you can see where you might have been wrong and played a part in your own downfall.

Criticism of other people

Some people richly deserve criticism, preferably to their faces. Most of us can only find the courage to criticise behind people's backs; generally when we are trying to recruit others to our cause. We may find the sense of tribal unity that comes with having a common enemy, but if we are hoping to turn somebody new against our enemy we risk being seen as pathetic and manipulative. On the other side of the coin, if you want to avoid office politics, never allow yourself to be recruited. Once you have been seduced into joining a criticism, you'll find yourself under endless pressure to stand by your word.

Publicly criticising your partner never works. You will always lose your dignity, and sometimes your friends.

Criticism of yourself

Self-criticism has a series of motives and may be driven by either true guilt or guilty fear. If you truly believe you have violated your own core values, the conversation is more likely to be confined to your head, as it is largely between you and your conscience.

The louder and more public your self-blame, the more likely it is to be driven by guilty fear. If your major concern is the disapproval of other people, you are much more likely to feel the need to publicly lacerate yourself to prove how guilty and contrite you are.

Here is a list of most of the motives for self-criticism or punishment – private or public.

1. Punishing yourself because you genuinely believe you should be punished.

2. Punishing yourself to reduce the chances of doing the same thing again.

3. Being humble to make yourself more loveable, trying to make up for the disapproval of having done something wrong.

4. Preventing people from thinking you are so bad you don't care.

5. Reducing other people's expectations of you by lowering yourself to a more child-like state.

6. Getting in first, applying your own punishment at a level that you can control, rather than waiting for other people to decide how to punish you.

7. Gaining credit through confession.

8. Gaining credit by showing your depth of self-understanding: 'You can see I'm not such a fool that I don't know I'm a fool.'

9. Taking blame and responsibility to get a sort of control.

The good thing about genuinely accepting responsibility for a problem is that if it's your fault, you can do something about it. On the other hand, if it's not your fault but other people seem to think it is, you're a misunderstood victim.

Genuine self-blame is quite different from resentful or wounded self-blame, which is self-blame with another motive: it signals angry defeat but has nothing to do with accepting one was wrong.

'Fine, so I'm stupid! I always do the wrong thing' is fairly unconvincing. You know the same issue is to be fought again and probably soon. The person who says this certainly doesn't want you to believe he is stupid or wrong; it's just that for the moment he can see he isn't going to win, he wants to regroup and while he does, he wouldn't mind if you were a bit guilty as well.

Cruelty

Cruelty is a failure of empathy, which is the ability to feel somebody else's pain as if it were your own.

Our perception of what is cruel depends on who and what lies within our sense of ourselves and ours. A hunter would be outraged if anyone hurt his dog, and some of the people who cheer as an animal is tortured to death in a bullring might describe themselves as animal lovers.

We are all capable of cruelty. When the Titanic sank the lifeboats were full and there were people in the water. As the lifeboats sank deeper under the weight of people, some of those aboard stamped on the fingers of those still trying to climb in. Their fear of death overrode the core values of kindness that you can guarantee most of them had. When we face rejection or belittlement and our survival brains tell us it will kill us, we can stamp on metaphorical fingers too. Nobody is irrational according to their own truth. It may not help much, but the boot that descends on your fingers is much more likely to be driven by fear than by malice.

Our capacity for empathy, like guilt and healthy self-doubt, is one of the invaluable forces that make the human species distinct. The kinder you are, the further your empathy extends. We can extend the borders of empathy beyond our family, our nation and even our species to include other animals, trees or even the planet itself. Unfortunately, the price of our empathy is suffering for the creatures or objects we include as ours, even if the reward of empathy is ultimately greater love and intimacy.

Decisions

To make a decision is to act when you cannot be certain of the out-come. If you don't act you haven't made a decision, you're just thinking about it. If you can be certain, it is not really a decision, merely a choice.

Most decisions are behavioural decisions; that is, you commit your behaviour entirely to one course of action, even if it is not fully decided in your head.

If making the wrong decision will prove lethal, you may decide never to decide. Most decisions are not life-and-death issues, but vulnerable people may treat them that way, in fact worrying more about being rejected for making the wrong decision than over the actual issue itself.

Many decisions have a scary and a safe option. With the safe option, at any one moment nothing much changes, so it is always tempting; just leave the plaster there and hope it will fall off. The scary option means ripping off the plaster; horrid anticipation of

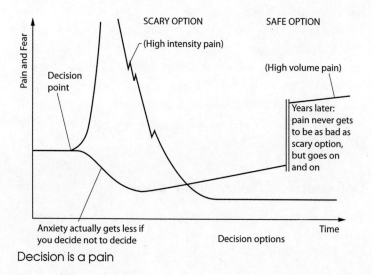

Decision is a pain

pain and it often really hurts, but you sense it's a good idea. The best possible example is the fear of committing yourself to a new relationship, when, in common with everybody else, you can't be sure it will last forever. The process can easily be illustrated (see page 257).

Scary option high intensity, but less total pain
Safe option   high volume, but less intense pain

If you look at the scary option, you'll see this means risking anxiety or pain so intense that it almost goes off the page, but then it settles back down. This spike could be the anxiety when you commit yourself or the pain when you have committed yourself and the relationship ends. You might be really unlucky and you could have two peaks of horribleness; the fear of commitment and then the pain of rejection. Putting it that way, the safe option of not trusting and not taking the risk looks pretty good. The critical difference is how you measure pain. If you are absolutely sure you will die if you are rejected, don't risk the intensity of anxiety and possible pain of the relationship ending, so never commit yourself. On the other hand, if you avoid intensity of pain, you have to face volume. If you consider the line of the safe option, it goes on forever, gradually rising over the years. Never committing and never feeling the intensity of the scary option, but the area under the safe line is much, much greater as the years pass. This area, the so-called area under the curve, represents the total amount of pain you will suffer. Safe, but alone and a much greater volume of pain than the scary option.

Deference, humility and modesty

These are ways of signalling you are less important than another person or that you're not claiming equality. They are ways of buying love – paying with your power – but that doesn't make them bad.

Deference can be a mark of respect if it's done as a self-respecting adult, comfortably acknowledging that your status is less than that of somebody else. It becomes obsequious or sycophantic when it is used to signal a much greater gap than really exists, exaggerating your inequality in status and even denying your equality as a worthy adult.

Humility and modesty are the antithesis of vanity. They are virtuous and earn love but, as ever, a good thing can be overplayed. Excessive humility or false modesty is overpayment for love. Overly humble people risk dismissal and rejection for their undignified, tacky behaviour rather than the acceptance they hoped to secure.

Dependency

To be dependent is wonderful. To need somebody else to complete your happiness is the healthiest and most secure human state. Comfortable dependency lies in an enduring and intimate relationship between two equal adults. Both are enriched and secured by the relationship, but remain confident they could survive by themselves. Healthy dependency liberates you to acknowledge that you feel your best with someone whom you love and feel less complete when you are without him or her.

It is perfectly reasonable to depend upon another person to make you feel your best when you already feel good, or better when you feel bad. Clearly, in my view, we find our self-esteem in our relationships, but this doesn't mean just one relationship. If you have every bit of your self-worth invested in one friend or in your lover, you lose your independence and become dependent in a way that can be alienating. Dependency becomes a problem when you are asking someone to supply too much of your identity; it becomes the desperate neediness of a child, clinging to a parent he doesn't trust. Then the comfortable warmth of dependency is replaced by anxiety, anger and sadness. An anxiously dependent adult becomes a burden and dependency becomes an epithet, not a pleasure.

Dignity

Dignity is the well-preserved territory of your spirit. It is no more than the gentle assertiveness of a self-respecting adult.

Distrust

There are some people whom you would be most unwise to trust; for whom your distrust is merely healthy self-protection. Distrust becomes a problem when you are expecting too much of someone.

A jealous lover who checks your diary and mobile phone, or wants to know about your past boyfriends, is terrified you will leave him because he doesn't trust you to think he's good enough. If he respected himself he would know that if you were unfaithful there might still be room for negotiation and if he loses you he won't die. He does not understand that even in the strongest adult relationships trust can never be absolute; not like a child with a good parent.

It's probably worth adding that if he liked himself better his behaviour towards you might have been better, giving you more room to move. He would have less reason to distrust you because he would have given you less reason to move on.

Domination and submission

Healthy people want power with others, not over them, but if forced to choose one or the other, they'd naturally rather be on top than underneath. Nobody wants to be the underdog, although some people will choose to submit for safety rather than take the risk of challenging as an equal.

In the jungle, brawn will almost always beat brain. If there is a risk of physical violence, submission may be the best choice. In the absence of violence, there is no such thing as domination, only submission. In an argument that is restricted to words, someone can only beat you if you give in. If you choose to hold your ground, acting with kindness and dignity, you will never lose. You may not win, but you'll never lose.

Expectations

In human relationships it's reasonable to hope, but never to expect.

If you expect another person to behave in a particular way, you set yourself up to be angry, anxious or sad. You may behave impeccably and follow all the rules, yet still be treated appallingly. Certainly, by behaving well you maximise your chances of being treated well in return, but it's no guarantee. You may have been the best, the most loving and the sexiest wife in the world, but there's no absolute certainty it will keep your husband out of other beds.

This is not a formula for constant suspicion or distrust; on the contrary, by taking this attitude you increase your chances of getting what you want. If you expect something of somebody, there is a danger that your manner will carry an edge of anger, treating it as a territorial right. Other people tend to be sensitive to expectation and anger and they may feel trespassed upon, controlled and manipulated. This has the potential to push them into frustrating your expectations on principle, as they try to reassure themselves of their own independence.

Fear of success

There is no such thing as a fear of success: everybody wants success because everybody wants status. People with a poor self-esteem who succeed sometimes feel like a fraud. This makes them afraid because they are afraid of discovery. They feel once they have succeeded, people's expectations of them are higher and there is further to fall. Obviously, if you don't deserve your place on the pedestal, it's only a matter of time before you're pushed off.

A fear of success is really a fear of failure.

Forgiveness

To forgive is not to forget, unless the crime you have forgiven was utterly trivial or you have Alzheimer's disease.

Forgiving is a circular process. If you have to forgive someone, it means that you still blame him.

Forgiving is a behavioural decision. Whatever the conversation you are having in your head about what has happened, you have decided to remove criticism and blame from your behaviour and, if remotely possible, stifle the angry thoughts as they enter your head. It doesn't mean you have forgotten, and it certainly doesn't mean you think what he did was right; you have simply decided to give up your right to punish.

This might be seen as a cynical dismissal of forgiveness, but it is merely intended as an aid to understanding the process. I suspect that all good and worthy human behaviour has layers of motivation, just as bad behaviour has its levels of meaning, but this is not the point. If you can see another reason behind doing something good and then belittle the worthiness of the act for not being the real reason, you are making a mistake. If you can forgive, irrespective of the subtexts of forgiveness, it is good for you and good for the person you forgive, and that should be enough.

Generosity

Generosity is giving more than would be expected of you. It is intelligently self-interested to be generous, because other people will like you and so will you.

For your generosity to be a true gift, there should be no expectation of payback, but even the healthiest people feel affronted if they don't get some of the payment they hope for. Something as trivial as letting someone into the line of traffic but getting no wave of acknowledgement produces a small twinge of irritation. The mark of good sense is not letting your desire for payback become too visible.

Generosity can be overdone as a form of buying love, when it's obvious the cost of your generosity is greater than you can reasonably afford or that there is a hook buried in the bait. Then your generosity can be a burden and people will withdraw from you because they don't like the feeling of guilty obligation. Overdo your generosity and you can be trapped in a cycle of hurt and anger, giving so much yet not getting your money's worth in return.

Gratitude and thanks

Gratitude and thanks are the glue that holds relationships together. They are small packets of love. By being grateful and thanking people we can deliver instant, highly valued payment for services rendered. Without this agreed barter, society could not function.

Guilt

Guilt is a particularly valuable human emotion. Guilt helps keep us civilised because it is such a horrible feeling, we generally do our best to avoid it. You will be told guilt is a waste of time and that is true of *guilty fear*, but not of the *true guilt* you experience when you violate or fortunately even think about violating your own moral values.

True guilt is a sort of moral anxiety; a disturbing discourse between you and the voice of your own ethics.

Guilty fear grips you when you are afraid someone won't like you for what you have done, springing from a feeling you should treat other people's wishes as if they are more important than your rights. Then guilt is really a fear of disapproval and rejection masquerading as true guilt. Guilty fear wastes a great deal of emotion and thinking time.

If you suffer from guilty fear, you probably secretly know that there is nothing wrong with what you have done, but your fear, pretending to be your conscience, still gives you a hard time. You have to apologise repeatedly because if you didn't, you would be claiming you were equal, your acts reasonable and you would lose the safety of being a contrite child.

If your self-esteem is reasonably robust, your version of guilty fear is shame. If the bank's computer makes a mistake and deposits a large sum of money in your name, only the potential discomfort at being caught might stop you quietly withdrawing the lot. After all, it's only the bank and it easily falls outside the orbit of your conscience. Shame is guilt when you are caught.

When you are feeling guilty, ask yourself whether you are solely worried about the hurt you have caused another, or whether some of your guilt might be mostly a focus on how you are being seen.

While true guilt is a good and necessary emotion, trying to make other people feel guilty is quite a different matter. If their inner policemen didn't make them feel guilty enough to stop them hurting you in the first place, you almost certainly won't be able to get them to feel truly guilty, or at least not guilty enough for long enough to make them change. If you do get close to reaching them, they will merely get angry to avoid the feeling.

Honesty and lies

Telling a lie can be a good and necessary act. You might easily be living a model life if you lie to protect someone else's feelings, treating love and care as being more central to your core values than even honesty itself. If you lie to protect yourself or to make yourself seem more powerful or more loveable, it's like boasting; the drug addict's choice: short-term gain but paying a heavy price later.

Without a basic commitment to honesty it's clearly impossible to have a truly intimate relationship, but even honesty must have its limits. The naïve ask their lovers to tell them the moment they think about being unfaithful, insisting that above all they must have honesty within their relationship. Unfortunately, you can rely on most people to be honest over almost everything except infidelity. In much the same way, if you are foolish enough to ask your partner about past lovers, remember you may really be asking for reassurance as to your exclusivity, not a painful truth, so just hope that she won't be honest enough to tell you.

Honesty can be seriously abused. To avoid weakness, insecure people can treat honesty as more crucial to their identity than kindness. They unleash scathing honesty, telling people without reserve or sensitivity what they think. These are people who have forgotten the sundae of self-esteem: they are proudly and intensely individualistic, clearly marking out their personal boundaries, but nobody likes them much.

Hurt

We all feel hurt when we are rejected or belittled, especially if we don't feel we deserve it. Hurt is a mixture of anxiety and sadness, with more than just a little anger lurking in the wings. Vulnerable people are hurt more easily and frequently. As a result they are in danger of being angry more often because they see themselves as being unfairly treated more often, which may well be true because their behaviour invites it.

Sometimes you will be genuinely, justifiably terribly hurt.

When you first discover your partner has been unfaithful, you will have a rush of pain that can feel bigger than anything you could ever survive. You will move between fury and blinding despair, nearly paralysed by the degree of your hurt and struggling to work, talk or think of anything else. Your pain will come in waves as you repeatedly run through anguished conversations in your head or create pictures of your partner with another person. Naturally this won't just go on in your head; you will lash out in anger and just as quickly slip into weeping despair or overwhelming anxiety. For days, weeks or possibly months, you will return to the scenes and chatter of your thoughts, which will drive you into more outbursts of rage, recrimination and tears.

Horrible as it is, you will keep going over every detail because part of you wants to. All humans can feel as if our thoughts are real and as we endlessly replay a scene in our head, we are trying to change the reality. Unhelpful but well-meaning people will tell you time will heal everything and, irritating as they are, they are sort of right. You cannot maintain the same level of emotion indefinitely; it's not that you'll go mad if you do, it's just that your brain runs out of emotional steam. Eventually the time will come when you are ready to make the decision to stay or go. For quite a while you have probably been acting as if you are doing both, which contributes to the miserable confusion in your head. A disaster becomes a tragedy if you don't make a firm decision, design your behaviour around that decision and then act.

If you decide to stay, it's like forgiveness; you have to give up your right to punish. Your partner doesn't deserve it and shouldn't get away scot-free. No matter how hard you try to stick by your decision, you'll back-slide, giving in to the need to make sure he knows just how wronged and hurt you are.

Unfortunately, if you are going to survive emotionally, at some point you must abandon the temptation to repeatedly force home the magnitude of his crime and the degree of your pain. What has happened obviously can't be undone and it will stay in your memory forever, but its intrusiveness will be largely decided by how often you revisit the crime scene in your head.

At the risk of stating the dead obvious, the less you think about it, the less you will suffer. When you find yourself back on the topic again, you have to tell yourself something like 'Don't go there' and keep on pushing yourself away from the thought, even although you feel forced to return, like a tongue to a sore tooth. You have no hope of doing this at first, but when enough time has passed for you to decide on staying, you may be ready to try managing your feelings. The moment you realise you have started down the path of torment, launch into saying to yourself over and over, 'don't go there, don't go there, don't go there.' The sooner you start chanting in your head each time you realise you are having the awful thoughts, the more effective you will be in turning yourself away. If you are saying the words out loud in your head, you can't think the same thoughts and you can move towards another subject. Then back come the horrors, so back to 'Don't go there.' The more you do this, the less frequently your behaviour will slip into outbursts of recrimination or signalling your despair. With some control over your thoughts and behaviour, allowing you to re-approach your partner in a more loving way, you can hope your emotions will start to move into line.

If all your behaviour doesn't finally become directed into staying or going, you will simply make your life a monument to how wronged you've been. Clearly you have every right to do this, but it won't make your partner any more determined not to betray you again or any more guilty over his crime.

Identity of defect

A poor self-esteem, a lack of self-respect or an inferiority complex are all terms for the same thing. They mean not liking yourself enough, expecting other people not to like you very much either, and so suffering more than necessary from the three negative emotions: anxiety, anger and sadness.

Because your self-esteem is you looking at yourself as if you were another person, if your self-esteem is poor, at some point early in your life you have looked at yourself and decided that you saw something deficient, defective or bad. This view of yourself has become built into your sense of identity. However, your identity is the territory of your spirit and in common with all territory, you are programmed to defend it vigorously. You may not like the feeling that this is your identity and you may long to change your sense of yourself, but you are obliged to protect it because it is who you are. To let go of your identity, however disappointing it is, would be to lose yourself.

Once you have made the original mistake of believing there was something wrong with you, over the years of your life you will probably have accumulated evidence that somehow you are defective. You have built your identity on a mistaken self-opinion, but it's like a house of cards. To think differently about yourself or to dare believe a compliment would be to pull out the bottom card so your entire identity collapses. It's easier to keep on believing that you are deficient.

Once you have decided you are deficient, you have an identity of defect. This is some inner emptiness or even badness; some unspecified fault in your personality. You probably don't clearly know what it is, and instead have conclusively but illogically decided everything that is wrong with you is because you are too fat, too poor or too dumb. If you make this decision, you can end up with an eating disorder or as an obsessive worker, but most people aren't satisfied with such simple solutions. They continue to feel that there is something vaguely wrong that is not properly defined, but defective and definitely a problem.

Once you have made up your mind that you have an in-built defect, even though you can't see it, there is the fear other people might be able to see what you can't. This means there is always the potential for discovery, but if you don't know what's really wrong, how can you ever hope to hide it? Unfortunately the solution for some people is to live behind a defensive wall, so nobody can see anything much of them at all.

Independence

Independence should be the opposite of dependency, but it's not. True independence is the ability to be comfortably dependent and not frightened by needing other people.

Ferocious independence shouldn't be confused with genuine security. Secure independence allows someone to enjoy solitude, endure being alone but still suffer with loneliness. Ferociously independent people are often hungry for intimacy but afraid they are not good enough, so they get in first and usually angrily, to prove they really don't need the people they are afraid will reject them.

Inferiority

A sense of inferiority has many layers. No reasonable person likes himself without question. If you believe, with every bone in your body, that you are truly inferior, you are probably suffering from a severe depressive illness and you should seek medical treatment.

Most people who feel inferior are not totally convinced. I believe this is absolutely central to understanding poor self-esteem or a sense of inferiority. People who declare they have a poor self-esteem are, by definition, acknowledging that they do not rate themselves as highly as they feel they really deserve. If someone says

'I have a poor self-esteem,' he is in fact saying 'I don't believe I'm as good as I know I really am.' It is as if there is a surface layer of necessary deference and doubt, beneath which there is still a flickering flame of self-belief. His public face is one of humility and anxious self questioning, but his quick anger if he's criticised betrays something else. If he truly believed his own self-criticism, surely he shouldn't resent criticism from someone else who is merely observing the obvious fact of his low worth? This anger tells him his poor self-esteem is a cloud sitting on top of him and not truly and wholly his own sense of who he is. It is a feeling of obligation to act the role in which he believes others see him in order to hold their approval. To avoid the confusion or dissonance of two incompatible beliefs, he's forced to both act and try to believe he's not good enough.

In practice, he part believes his self-doubt but he resents it profoundly and it will often show. He is putting himself down in an attempt to protect himself against rejection, but in common with all poor defensive systems, the defence becomes the danger.

One of the many self-imposed difficulties of a sense of inferiority is the potential to believe people are looking down on you. There is a risk you will see them as looking down from the same height above you, as you feel you are looking up to them from below. In short, it's easy to believe someone thinks he's better than you are. Because most people with a sense of inferiority don't fully believe they are inferior themselves, but they are fairly convinced others see them as less, this sense of a slope or gradient between them and you is a fertile source of anger.

In reality, people of high status who also enjoy high self-respect do not want to look down on other people. Apart from the fact they probably don't feel superior in the first place, to feel you have beaten someone who is inferior makes your success much less than to have beaten a potential equal. In turn, all someone who feels he has less status has to do is act as if he still views himself as an equal and worthy adult, which means acknowledging the loss without hurt or angry signalling. Beaten soundly at tennis and then accusing your opponent of cheating is a disaster, but offering to buy him a beer and cheerily threatening to break his leg before the next game and you're a star. It's possible to be a failure at things, but a sensation as a person.

Intimacy

In distant relationships, it's relatively easy to keep only the good side of you visible by being on your best behaviour for the moment and saying little about yourself. You can let your guard down later. In an intimate relationship you should try your hardest to never let down the guard on your behaviour, while you strive to be as unguarded as possible over your inner feelings and vulnerabilities.

Jealousy

We are all biologically programmed to feel jealousy. If somebody has more of what we want we have the potential to covet his possessions, achievements or attributes. The material end of jealousy is envy, which is simply the resentment of an animal eyeing someone else's patch, mixed with a feeling of inadequacy to do anything about it.

Jealousy generally refers to our urge to possess another person and our fear of losing them. Jealousy always contains anger and the potential for aggression; the responses of any animal whose territory is threatened. Sexual jealousy is the most violent and the worst form of jealousy, and its origins probably lie in the harsh world of survival of the fittest.

If life has a purpose, it is probably to reproduce. A pregnant woman always knows she is the mother, but her partner can never be sure he is the father, which may explain why sexual jealousy is much more common in men. If a man allows himself to be cuckolded he is a biological failure. Male jealousy is largely driven by the angry territoriality of sex; one random copulation by his partner and if he stays with her, he risks diverting his resources to someone else's child.

Female jealousy tends to be more the jealousy of love and women tend to be more tolerant of sexual transgression than their partners, although this by no means makes their jealousy less intense. Female jealousy has a much bigger fear component. If your sexual partner takes his love elsewhere there is an ancestral fear of being abandoned without food or protection, helplessly suckling even more helpless children.

Sometimes jealousy is totally justified, supported by clear observation of fact. Then the most secure person can really suffer.

Frequently jealousy is unjustified, built on no more substance than anguished and angry suspicion. Then it is an exaggerated response to self-doubt: 'I don't like me, so you wouldn't like me, so you must like somebody else.' When jealousy is more self-doubt than reality, both parties suffer horribly. As a general rule, the more unjustified someone's belief in his partner's infidelity, the more he will persecute the innocent object of his suspicion and the more tortured the mind of the accuser. Sometimes jealousy has the potential for such intensity that it becomes delusional, especially in alcoholic men who have been unfaithful themselves or whose sexual powers are fading.

Whether your jealousy is justified or based on self-doubt, the approach is the same. Here is a list of rules to follow. Whether your partner is really unfaithful or only in your fearful imaginings, the pain may not go, but at the very least you can practise damage control, preserving your dignity and not losing someone you shouldn't have to lose.

1. First, you must confront your feelings in your own internal con-

versations. You must not fester on half-asked questions, but ask yourself directly: 'Am I or am I not totally convinced that my lover is being unfaithful?'

2. Next, ask yourself if you really must act immediately. The instinct is to leave or attack and not be made a fool for a minute longer, especially if you think other people knew you were wronged before you did. Think hard before you attack or leave because to do so on reflex might not be in your best interests.

3. Question yourself as to whether this is truly the end of the world. Could your dignity survive this? Could you go on, admittedly with a different level of trust? Remind yourself that unfortunately sexual fidelity is highly unnatural. Desirable and worth striving for, but still unnatural.

4. Is this his only transgression? If the answer is that it is not, this is but one of many, you can be sure there will be more, even if he is bleeding from the eyeballs to show how sorry he is. Maybe this is the time to go.

5. If you decide to stay, don't forget the principles of forgiveness. It doesn't mean you have forgotten or that you feel the crime is small, merely that you have chosen not to exercise your right to punish.

6. Hide your jealousy if you possibly can. The more visible your jealousy the weaker and less desirable you become.

7. If now is the time to confront him, do it. Say it, don't signal it. Tell him immediately how you feel. Hurt and angry body language just makes you easier to leave.

8. Avoid attacking if you can. Tell him how you feel, but not how you think he should feel. The more you blame, the less sense and the more defence you will get. The less you demand an apology or try to make him guilty, the better you will be able to assess the genuineness of his contrition and the likelihood of

his doing it again.

9. If you have decided to stay or not yet decided to leave, don't stand guard over your partner to ensure he or she goes nowhere and can have no space.

10. Never try to talk, bully, beg or shame someone into loving you. No one in the history of mankind has succeeded and you won't either.

11. Now is the time to act with kindness and dignity.

12. The more you can look as if you like yourself, the more desirable you are. Don't forget that to look self-confident is the sexiest thing you can do.

13. Create a life of some substance for yourself. Learn things, make things, strengthen your friendships.

14. Remember, self-confident people still get hurt, sad or angry. They practise assertive self-definition, but they can limit their attacks and they don't make other people responsible for their lives.

15. Never forget that to cling or attack, trying to weaken and so get power, is eventually death to your spirit and death to your partner's if he tolerates it. No matter how guilty he should be, eventually you'll make him angry. Then you'll be angry at his anger, because you will feel he has no right to be angry. Only you have the right to be angry, which may be true, but it won't win you any love.

16. Never forget that unconditional love doesn't exist between healthy adults. So you won't ever get it, but nor will anyone else.

17. Never forget that if you are an adult who loses an adult partner you will be miserable but you'll survive, even if it doesn't feel that way at the time. If you feel like an abandoned child inside,

you'll still survive but you have a lot of work ahead of you.

18. Finally, if it is you who has been unfaithful and your partner confronts you, please don't tell her she's mad. It is as damaging to your honour as it is destructive of her spirit. Confess with dignity, not for forgiveness. You will also need to decide what you are going to do and do it.

Loneliness

Loneliness is one of the worst feelings in the world. When your ancestors were lonely they were afraid, because to be a lone animal was to die. If your alone-ness is brief and you have warm relationships in the background, it can be delicious solitude. But if it lasts too long you become anxious and restless, and if you can see no end to your loneliness, you might become depressed.

Love

Love is the core of a life well lived. Having territory is good; having love is better; having both is best. You can live without territory with difficulty but you can't possibly live without love.

Love is almost all you need.

Manners

The basic principle behind good manners is to trespass as little as possible on other people. Our manners are a way of making others less aware of our bodily functions by throwing a thin skin of civilisation over our animal desires, fears and functions. Good manners give us guidelines in situations of uncertainty, maximising the chances of both feeling and being comfortably acceptable. It's not being mindlessly conformist to avoid treading on someone else's belief about what is right. If that person's views so violate your ethics, then insult him and get out of his space, otherwise, learn to suffer fools silently.

Mind-reading

We all read minds and sometimes we get it right. The more anxious we are the more we will feel we need certainty and so try to figure out other people's agendas. Unfortunately, the more anxious we are the more likely we are to read other people's minds in terms of our own fears and, naturally, to discover in our interpretation of another's behaviour the negative and critical thoughts we have about ourselves.

Mind-reading works the other way too. Vulnerable people sometimes expect others to read their minds, which puts them in danger of setting up tests of love: 'If you really loved me, you would know how I feel.'

It might not be unreasonable to hope to be understood, but unfortunately the other person might not realise he is on trial and may fail the test. Failing the test could mean he doesn't love you, but it could also mean he's not very good at tests or mind-reading.

Naturalness

Natural is not necessarily good. Syphilis and uranium are natural, but not especially wonderful things. Nature really is 'red in tooth and claw' and if we were honest, we'd probably rather live in the suburbs than in the jungle.

To be sick and die is natural, so are parasites, and to be dirty, cold and hungry – all things to be avoided if possible.

Civilised behaviour is a thin, artificial veneer over the more natural selfish territoriality of the animal within. Other animals don't queue. The best of humanity is unnatural.

If you have the disease of depression, you have a naturally acquired biochemical deficiency. Your unhappiness is almost certainly because of a low level of particular neurotransmitters that occurs in depressive illness. Antidepressant medication will not give you an unnatural high, but it will present you with a conundrum: antidepressants are unnatural but they can liberate you to be as you would naturally be if you weren't depressed. Without the artificial wonder of medicine, particularly antibiotics and antidepressants, the natural life of some of us is all too likely to be 'poor, nasty, brutish and short'.

Niceness

To be nice is to be good and sweet and gentle and kind. It is very much the behaviour of love. It is also possible to be too nice, which means unbalancing the sundae of self-esteem. Giving too much love without asserting your individuality is like a great, big dollop of ice cream dripping on somebody else's table.

Being nice is not enough and can be much too much.

Orbits of intimacy

You are the centre of the universe and other people exist in concentric orbits around you, like planets around the sun.

Your innermost orbit of adult intimacy is reserved for your adult, sexual partner. The ideal occupant of your closest orbit is your best friend with whom you also have sex. If your relationship with someone is warm and intense but not sexual, you are either best friends or loving siblings. You may be very close to that person, but he or she can only really be in your second orbit.

As a young child your parents can and should occupy your first orbit of intimacy, but the first orbit of a child is different from that of an adult, because there should never be sex in a child's life. As an adult, a parent probably shouldn't even be in your second orbit; both you and your mother should have moved on.

The more distant the orbit from you, the more people can easily occupy it. Having more than one lover at a time is exhausting. Three or four best friends are probably all you can manage, but beyond that you can have dozens of friendly acquaintances and hundreds of business associations.

The closer the orbit to you, the greater the demands of the relationship and the harder a person in that orbit will be to please or impress, but the more value you will get from pleasing her.

It's much harder to be a hero to your wife than it is to impress your secretary. The more you do for someone in an outer orbit, the more instant reward you will find, but cheaply earned love is less valuable in the long run. When you tell your secretary your wife doesn't understand you, in reality you're telling her that she does. If you can be an enduringly loving and faithful partner and a great parent, unfortunately it's not as exciting as a series of relationships with new and deeply impressed girlfriends, but don't marry any of

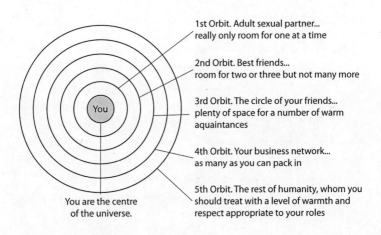

1st Orbit. Adult sexual partner...
really only room for one at a time

2nd Orbit. Best friends...
room for two or three but not many more

3rd Orbit. The circle of your friends...
plenty of space for a number of warm
aquaintances

4th Orbit. Your business network...
as many as you can pack in

5th Orbit. The rest of humanity, whom you
should treat with a level of warmth and
respect appropriate to your roles

You
You are the centre
of the universe.

them, otherwise they will soon understand you only too well.

We have a natural desire to fill our orbits and the closer the orbit the greater the urge to put someone into it. If you haven't a lover you are very likely to be on the look-out for one. This doesn't mean that you cannot survive without your inner orbit being occupied, simply that you are likely to be a bit more restless and have to put more work into being happy.

As always, your sundae of self-esteem needs to be balanced. You can deal with less love most efficiently by searching for more love. If you haven't a lover, you can feel good but with more effort by expanding the individualistic end of your sundae by exploring passions, interests and causes, as well as filling the love scoop of your sundae as best you can with wonderful friendships.

Panic attacks

Panic most commonly comes out of the blue with no obvious trigger; just a feeling of fear and spinning out of control. Panic is probably the way an animal feels when it finds itself too close to a tiger. As human beings we can grow tigers in our heads and then panic. If you suffer panic attacks you can panic when you think you will look different or make a fool of yourself in public. Some deal with this by not going shopping, never catching trains or avoiding even leaving the house. You can panic by deciding you could lose control; terrified that you might suddenly grab a knife and stab someone, fall or jump off a high building or turn the wheel of your car into the oncoming traffic. It's very common to panic at the thought of blurting out some obscenity or acting aggressively or even violently.

People feeling panic often think they are sick. They label their fear of heights as vertigo or become convinced they are choking when anxious air-hunger stops them getting a satisfyingly deep breath. You might decide you're mad, convinced you will lose control of your mind or that the horrible sensation of panic means you're about to collapse, your heart will stop or you'll have a fit.

The origin of panic, as with any anxiety, is always the fear of death. Doing something unacceptable causes a fear of rejection by the herd; a guarantee of death to your ancestors. If you suffer agoraphobia you can feel everybody is ready to look, laugh and criticise, forgetting human beings generally prefer to help.

The feared things never happen. No one who doesn't want to die ever jumps on impulse. The woman who is terrified she will hurt her baby never does. There is not another person inside you who can take over and make you do the very opposite to what you want to do. The urge to jump, to hurt or to act weirdly is not a measure of your desire to die or an inner evil that wants to hurt, these feelings are a fear of loss of control that never happens. Panic is the fear you will do something which terrifies you and is the very opposite of what you want to do or will do. To someone who is having a panic attack, each one feels different. The fact that you didn't choke during your last fifty attacks of air-hunger means nothing during number fifty-one. This one is different. This one will kill you.

Panic attacks can be effectively treated with medication, but they do better with explanation and behavioural therapy.

Paranoia

Paranoia simply means attributing your own feelings to other people. If you like yourself and you think other people like you too, you're not paranoid, just happy. Unfortunately, paranoid people are never happy and always see in other people criticism, rejection or hostility towards themselves. They then respond to this perception, their hostile behaviour earns them the label 'paranoid' and sadly this can make a feeling into a fact. Paranoid people are less likable because they tend to act on their belief they are not liked, accusing and blaming rather than hiding, as do people who respond to the same feeling with agoraphobia.

Pedantry

Pedantry is excessive territoriality. It is insisting your truth prevail and that other truths must give way to yours. Pedantry is an over-large scoop at the individualistic end of the sundae of self-esteem. People with plenty of self-respect are less likely to be pedants, even when they can see you are wrong. They like themselves anyway, so they don't have to aggressively prove they're right and bright, even if they are.

Perfectionism and high standards

Perfectionists are never trying to be perfect and never believe they are perfect. If they liked themselves more, they wouldn't try so hard. A perfectionist is someone with a poor self-esteem who is unhappy being himself as he is. He believes he can't afford to have anything related to him be messy, dirty, disordered or imperfect. He feels backed to the edge of the cliff of rejection, where one more fault could push him into oblivion. To the perfectionist, not perfect equals bad.

Perfectionists always have high standards, which they will insist are their own standards that they are merely trying to live up to. Obviously this is partly true, but they also have a harshly critical Observing Self telling them they must be much better to be any good at all. They are not trying to be perfect; they are obsessively trying to be good enough.

Perfectionists can have great trouble making decisions because they fear the consequences of making a mistake much more than is necessary. *They are not striving towards the carrot of success, they are running away from the stick of failure.* A perfectionist is responding as a child would to a critical parent; he is terrified of rejection and punishment for doing the wrong thing. In a perfectionist's background there may be a mother or father who could never be pleased, or he may have been passed the genes for obsessiveness, which the kindest parenting could not overcome. In my experience, it's usually both background and genes. A perfectionistic parent can be very difficult, demanding and often angry. His child then inherits the high self-demand trait and lives in fear of never pleasing his parent.

Perfectionists ferociously guard the territory of what they know to be right and correct. Men tend to be more territorial than women, and aggression and violence are the behaviours of territorial defence. It can be dangerous and hard being the messy, individualistic child of a perfectionistic parent, who forgets to put love before territory. Perfectionists are much more prone to depression than any other personality style. A perfectionist trapped by depression may force control on his child – the only person over whom he has any power.

Phobias

Phobias appear in some people because their survival system is overresponsive. The rational fears behind the vast majority of phobias are easy to recognise. Dogs were wolves, cats were tigers and the unknown and the dark can hold any danger. A crowd or even a small social gathering is a hostile herd to which you don't belong. Babies are scared of heights and strangers. In a small space you are trapped with no possibility of escape. People die in thunderstorms and loud noises make everyone jump. Strangers can be dangerous even to grown-ups.

In a phobia, your survival brain yells too soon and too loudly, seeing much more danger than really exists. It's not being stupid, because it is responding perfectly rationally to its own truth.

Pleasing people

Healthy people want to please other people. We all care passionately what other people think about us. Obviously we are most concerned about the opinion of people whose approval we most want and, equally obviously, there are some whom you hold in such low esteem that you'd be worried if they did like you – though such people are an exception.

Feeling equal, lovable and intimate takes the anxiety out of our need to please, but wisdom suggests that no relationship is so secure that we can forget the need to be pleasing. If you do have a relationship in which you feel no need to please, either you've utterly crushed your partner or she's just about to close the door behind you and walk out of your life.

Wanting to please other people originates from our need to keep our place in the herd. Now our need to please makes the best of us, increasing our sensitivity to other people and sharpening our desire to give love and to care about the feelings of others.

Possessiveness

Possessiveness is frightened, angry clinging. Possessiveness is provoked by a poor sense of self-worth and therefore an expectation of rejection. Some possessive people will punish someone in anticipation of their leaving, while others become more clingy, showing the vulnerability of their anxiety and sadness, which is designed to hold someone with a sense of obligation or guilt.

Power games

We all play for power, it is simply the way that we do it that matters. Healthy, self-respecting people jockey for position and would obviously prefer to win rather than lose, but they are not willing to belittle others in their desire to feel powerful.

Some insecure people try to dominate and gain control, primarily to get away from their fear of weakness. Power games imply manipulation rather than overt challenge. A power game is based on trying to belittle someone else so as to look big by contrast, rather than gaining stature through healthy competition with an equal. The game often consists of putting someone down in a way that is not quite obvious and can always be disowned: 'I was only joking.'

Sure he was.

Procrastination

Procrastination can be laziness, when the desire to get something done is not as tempting as the ease of inertia.

Mostly procrastination isn't laziness, but fear of taking on something and failing. Procrastination is often part of the pattern of a perfectionist, who fears rejection for not doing well more than he values completion. People who procrastinate usually don't like themselves enough and so don't trust they have a sufficient deposit of worth in their human credit bank to draw on if they are wrong or don't do something perfectly. Naturally they put it off, waiting for greater certainty before they start, meanwhile filled with guilt because they're convinced they're lazy. Self-doubting people are anxious to please perfectly, so they don't commit or they start too many things and rarely finish them, or only under the pressure of the last minute. Lazy people think it's somebody else's responsibility and it isn't important anyway.

Punishment

We all punish people because in reality or fantasy we all experience rejection or suffer some form of belittlement or rejection.

Healthy people know that between adults the only punishment

available to civilised people is to withdraw their love. They also know that it should be done gradually, with explanation and with progressively increasing disapproval and distance each time the same or a related sin is committed. They also know never to take love away from children. Children would rather have a controlled smack than be not spoken to.

Healthy punishment is applied gently, circumspectly and as a last resort. It is done in an effort to change another adult who won't listen when you tell him and whose internal policeman is failing to control him. Ultimately, if you are being irreversibly compromised you must be able to finish a relationship by taking your love away forever. If you are taking away your love to punish someone, you are still hoping to change them and to restore the relationship, because punishment always contains a desire to change someone.

Healthy people also know how far to take a punishment. However angry they are, they try not to forget that the relationship should be treated as more important than the crime, until they reach a point where their self-respect cannot tolerate any more.

Rebellion

Rebellion occurs when you just can't take any more. It means you have been trespassed upon, belittled and your territory has been diminished beyond the price you are willing to pay for peace or love. It means if you don't fight back you will feel that you will cease to exist.

Repressive parenting can cause rebellion in children, just as a repressive dictatorship does in adults. Unfortunately for a repressed child, rebellion can become an automatic, hair-trigger response to any authority, naturally inviting repression from even the best-intentioned regime. Again unfortunately, even the best loved adolescent may rebel ferociously; desperately uncertain he can preserve his identity in the presence of adults whose power he resents more than he recognises he needs their love.

Rejection

Rejection once meant death, either killed by the tribe that rejected you or eaten by a tiger if you were pushed out and alone. Now it just feels like death and we often run our lives as if rejection or disapproval could be lethal.

Nobody can ever get used to rejection, because love and belonging are primary necessities for life. You can never hope to lose your sensitivity to rejection, any more than you could get used to going without food, water, shelter or oxygen. If you are in sales, you'll always hate having to make cold calls. If you want to ask somebody wonderful to come out with you, only mindless arrogance can come between you and a feeling of fear.

You can avoid rejection by never asking for a kiss, but you'll kiss your life goodbye. The intelligent way to deal with rejection is to live with kindness and dignity as much as you can, which is quite a good way of avoiding rejection in the first place, but you must take risks. At least if you apply the knowledge I hope you have found in *An Intelligent Life*, you'll know why you feel so scared. Remember when you're so anxious you feel you're going to die, you aren't imagining it; your survival brain is working overtime. Tell yourself this is a million-year-old feeling. That will help a little, but nothing will really fix it till you take a chance. The feeling won't kill you, it just feels that way.

Reliving the past

If you have survived a childhood in which your parents didn't give you enough love or respect, it's harder to like yourself. A past without enough secure love will literally make changes in your brain that will never go away completely. However, it's not written in stone that they have to spoil your life forever. *The pain of the past does its damage by influencing the way you manage your relationships in the present.*

If you treat your present as if it is sure to be as disappointing as your childhood, it's as if you are driving down a street using your memory of the traffic half an hour ago. You need to plan your responses to the present with more thought than would be necessary if the past had been kinder. It's not fair that you should have to put more effort and it may well be somebody else's fault, but despite this, you'll have to work harder. Obviously, I'm hoping *An Intelligent Life* offers you some rational rules for getting on with it.

To live in the present you need to run your life with kindness, dignity and hope, without expecting or trusting blindly that others will follow the same rules, even when you do the right thing. You are safe in assuming most people will try to to treat you well most of the time, but other agendas can divert even the best of people. If you treat people well, maximising the quality of your present relationships, you will feel the best about yourself that you possibly can. Then an unhappy past has its least influence on you, even if your brain continues to alert you unnecessarily at times.

Respect

It's not hard to like people, but people whom you respect have an additional quality. Respected people are lovable, but also have an obvious strength. Power is an essential ingredient of respect, but you cannot have respect without liking. You can fear someone powerful whom you don't like, but you can't respect him. Fear and respect are incompatible.

A person worthy of respect has power but doesn't exercise it. If he does use his power, he does so with kindness and wisdom, accepting his high status but never behaving as if he believes this gives him greater worth. Such a person may in fact have the power to control you or take what is not his, but his ethical system would never allow him to do so.

Respect is the feeling you have for someone with power whom you like. Bosses and employers can get away with controlling by fear and may even be successful, but it's a vulnerable system, inviting cheating, revenge and defection. The most effective bosses take great care to preserve the dignity and self-respect of those below them. This makes willing workers, who are pleased to do extra and much more likely to take responsibility for the overall good running of the company.

Right and wrong

Any clown can be right, any idiot can succeed. The art of living intelligently is being wrong, failing and dealing with your mistakes in a way that lets you still like yourself, even if you hate what's gone wrong.

Being wrong isn't stupid, it's being aggressively wrong that's stupid. If you can be wrong gently, you are just wrong, not stupid. You can be aggressively right and very stupid. If you are certain you are right, why would you have to give truth extra force by backing it up with aggression? The truth can stand unsupported.

Roles

Each of us has a role to play. Our roles are mostly decided by age, sex and kinship. After that our jobs and other forms of status help define the way we should conduct ourselves.

Behaving in a role-appropriate way is not conformity but comfort. If you know how to belong, you can contentedly experiment with your individuality. If you can't, or won't, live within your role, some of your individuality will be no more than isolation or compulsively proving your difference.

If you are a parent, stick to that role. If you decide to be a socialite, a great lover or master of the business universe before you play parent, you deny your evolutionary and social role and will probably pay a price in your children's distressed or angry behaviour.

If you are a manager, don't spend too much time being one of the boys. If you are a junior employee, act like one; wait your turn to play the part of manager. A man of sixty dressing like a teenager is not behaving in a role-appropriate fashion. He would probably be happier if he earned respect by acting as a father figure, rather than as a figure of fun.

Your role with your sexual partner is as an equal adult. There is no other role that is consistent with an enduring and satisfying relationship. A husband who plays the role of a controlling parent to a woman who plays wife as a little girl will find himself with a resentful burden, unless she grows up and leaves.

Security and insecurity

You are secure when you believe you are lovable and strong enough; insecurity comes when you don't think you can measure up.

If you feel insecure, you experience three negative emotions – anxiety, anger and sadness – more often and more intensely. It's also likely that you experience them unnecessarily, at least unnecessarily until you start treating other people as if they are as prejudiced against you as you are prejudiced against yourself. Then your hurt or angry behaviour can turn your fears to reality.

Secure people still feel anxious, angry and sad, but they generally experience these feelings in settings where most people would agree they were merited. Even more importantly, the behaviour of secure people does not alienate others. Secure people know that just because they have a right to be angry, it doesn't give them the right to smash things or have a tantrum. In other words, secure people practise damage control. *They feel bad but they act well.* This means their bad feelings are limited to the original problem and not made worse by their subsequent behaviour.

Self-consciousness

The higher your self-esteem, the less self-aware you will be. Why would a person who truly believes herself to be good-looking bother to glance at her reflection in a shop window? Repeatedly returning to the mirror is not vanity but uncertainty.

It is necessary to be conscious of yourself in situations of uncertainty. Then you are monitoring your own appearance and behaviour, ready to make adjustments to ensure your acceptability. You flexed your biceps when your girlfriend first put her hand on your arm, but after a few months you may feel safe enough not to bother.

If you understand the rules of *An Intelligent Life* you have familiar guidelines for managing new people in different situations. If you apply the rules, you can be less self-conscious because you know that while you may not end up as best friends, you are very unlikely to be rejected or put down.

Showing feelings

Showing your feelings is like opening the curtains on a window to allow people to see you half-naked. If you like yourself, you are not all that afraid of what will be seen and so you feel safe enough to let people look in.

Naturally, nobody is so sure of themselves that they keep nothing in reserve, because we all carry some degree of vulnerability. To tell someone you love her is to hand her a knife and present your unprotected breast – it can feel as if you are giving up control, putting your emotional survival in someone else's hands. Equally, because anger and sadness are seen as negatives, you need to have a reasonable sense of your own human credit before risking your reserves by putting your feelings on display.

The happiest, healthiest people love to show love. They don't expect to be rejected, so they enjoy the giving and don't feel too vulnerable because they believe their love is worth having. Secure people are also willing to show their fear, anger and sadness, although in a more reserved way. The reserve is necessary because displaying your vulnerability does carry the risk of being seen as manipulative, unless you are very careful to show it in a dignified, adult way. If you let people see your distress, it should be as a self-defining statement and not a plea for help or forgiveness. If you overdo your public display of negative feelings, don't try to justify it by claiming you are just being yourself or that you're avoiding bottling things up; you are looking for justification or trying to enlist support. An apology might be more intelligently self interested.

Because extremes breed extremes, a poor self-esteem may produce either an excessive guarding of feelings or an excessive display of them. One person with a poor self-regard may never say anything, so his love, like his pain, goes unnoticed and unknown. By contrast, another equally insecure person may be effusively generous in his displays of love and dramatic in his show of pain. Excessive demonstrations of love spring from the simple logic that everyone wants love, so if you give lots of love, others will surely love you more. Overdoing sincerity has the same foundation. On the other hand, no show of love at all is usually guarding against being too hurt by the anticipated rejection. A version of getting in first.

Shyness

Shyness is the feeling you get with people you don't know and don't trust to accept you. It's an uncomfortable sense that in some way you aren't good enough for them to see you as belonging. Shyness is anxiety in the face of anticipated rejection and illustrates the way our herding shapes our emotions. If you think about it, being anxious with people you don't know doesn't make sense, because strangers don't know you any better than you know them, so how could they have any idea of your defects, weaknesses or past crimes? You really ought to be shy with the people who do know you, because they have seen how bad you really can be.

Naturally, it doesn't work that way, because shyness is an instinctive signal from your survival brain. You don't feel shy with friends because they appear to have accepted you with your faults and deficiencies. It's the sense of belonging or not belonging to the tribe that counts and has nothing to do with the reality of you as an individual.

Standards

Not everybody has your standards and they may not treat you in the way you feel you deserve. If you behaved towards them the way they seem to be treating you, it would mean you didn't like them or didn't care.

You are not living intelligently if you don't act in keeping with your view of the way things should be done – that is, keeping up your standards. However, expecting to get the same in return because you have behaved well has potential problems. Other people may have different standards, or may place different emphases on standards. Ultimately they may be as good and kind a person as you, but respond differently to the way you see as being ideal.

It's important to understand that if people don't appear to be playing according to your rules, their behaviour may not have the same meaning as yours would if you did things that way. If you promised to call on Tuesday but didn't, you might be sending a loud, clear message. But when he doesn't call it might simply mean he forgot. Certainly his not calling may mean exactly what you think. As always, you can't lose if you remember the grid of options in Chapter 15 and apply them when you feel under threat. *Treat people as if you believe they are on your side: when there is no physical danger, it's always better to mistake a hostile gesture as friendly and do nothing, than to react to a friendly gesture as if it were hostile.*

Status and worth

Whether we like it or not there is a hierarchy amongst people and one day you will be outclassed. You will meet someone who enjoys a higher status than you, who is perhaps genuinely better-looking, cleverer, richer or better educated than you are. To keep on liking yourself when this happens, you need to know the difference between status and worth.

The difference between status and worth is hugely important. Status and worth are related, but just like cost and value, they are not exactly the same.

You may never have status, but you can live without it. Worth is something everyone can have and you need it desperately. Without status you can be poor but happy. Without worth you can still be rich, but it's a lot harder to be happy.

You can get your status by hard work, but you can also get it by good luck or by accident of birth. To get worth you don't have to do any work, you don't have to be lucky and you don't even need to be clever or good-looking. All you have to do is live intelligently and then your kindness and dignity will earn all the worth you could ever want.

If you try to compete when you are outclassed, at best you will look arrogant, at worst a fool. Your willingness to show genuine admiration for someone else's achievement makes your own lack of

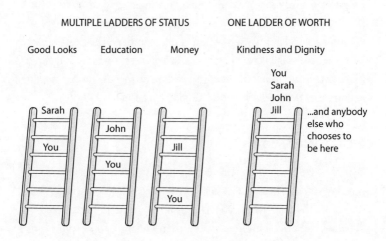

MULTIPLE LADDERS OF STATUS   ONE LADDER OF WORTH

Good Looks   Education   Money   Kindness and Dignity

You
Sarah
John

Sarah   Jill   ...and anybody
                                              else who
        John   chooses to
You   be here

                John
        You   Jill

                You   You

achievement much less significant. At first glance, status wins because everyone loves a winner, but after that, worth slowly catches up and takes an unbeatable lead.

Never forget that human worth is measured by kindness and dignity. The option to be kind and dignified is available to everyone. If you can behave this way you can stand on the top of the ladder of human worth and be equal to everybody and anybody, even if you're a bit close for comfort to the lower rungs of some status ladders.

Would it be better to be rich, beautiful and educated? Of course it would and if you can get the status and still act as a person of high worth, you are a major human success; an absolute triumph. Unfortunately, most of us will never achieve the status we'd like. Sometimes the rich and the beautiful are easy to resent, but we will be the ones to suffer if we lose sight of worth in a jealous and desperate struggle for status.

Strength and stubbornness

A strong person is someone willing to assert his or her individuality at the risk of disapproval, but who still considers the feelings of others. Someone who balances his sundae of self-esteem effectively is strong. Our idea of a weak person is someone who will give in at the least sign of disagreement, but it is possible to confuse stubbornness with strength. Paradoxically, stubbornness is a fear of weakness. Stubborn people mistake the dignity of giving in when you can see you might be wrong, with the weakness of giving up your position to buy love and approval, despite believing you are right.

Stress

You are put under stress when more than the usual pressures or demands are placed upon you. You will become distressed if you can't or don't believe you can meet the expectations of your environment. The more you feel you can lose if you fail, the more stressed you will become.

Once the stress of an event takes you beyond your sense of your own limit of coping, your behaviour will become less and less effective. Your limbic system – that region of your brain that drives survival behaviour – can't distinguish between urban problems and tigers; it sees things in terms of life or death, fighting, running or freezing. As your conscious brain becomes convinced you will not be able to solve a problem, pressure from your survival brain to punch, run or give up in despair increases progressively. Your panic-stricken survival behaviour can sabotage your ability to deal with an issue, making you look irrational to other people, even if your actions make perfect sense to your emotional perception. The magnitude of the problem then seems to grow until you can become submerged by anxiety, anger or despair to the exclusion of any further useful problem-solving action. Your behaviour can then become alienating, adding real threats to imagined ones.

The greatest stress often comes from an individual's excessive expectations of himself, which *he believes are what other people demand of him*. This sort of stress is tinged with anger, because it's easy to decide it's not fair to be put under so much pressure and be angry with others for their non-existent demands.

Our bodies are beautifully adapted to dealing with brief periods of intense danger, fear and action. Adrenalin serves us very well in emergencies, but unfortunately evolution has let us down a bit when it comes to chronic stress. Human beings can create tigers in their heads and then spend years trying to deal with them, or we can be forced to work in horrible jobs. When a threat goes on endlessly and with no escape, adrenalin ceases to be the primary hormone for adaption and we start to produce an excess of cortisol as part of a highly compromised system for coping with long-term pressure. Cortisol is the hormone of chronic adaption, but a high level for long periods eats at our stomachs and gives us ulcers and alters the way our body handles salt, pushing up our blood pressure. Chronic stress is bad for us and we need to know how to change our behaviour and expectations in an intelligent way. Chronic feelings of hostility are the most stressful and cause the greatest damage to your own body, particularly in the form of heart and blood vessel disease.

Success

To succeed is to conquer. You succeed when you hold more territory than you did before. Succeed skilfully and you get the power of knowledge, money or property, as well as the respect of people who like you as much as before or maybe even more. Succeed at unfair cost to other people and you will still have people liking you, because everybody likes to hang with status, but they will tend to be toadies or opportunists.

Success is wonderful nourishment for your self-esteem. It can fill you to the brim, but it's really only a top-up. If you are running half-empty, success can't fill the tank. You need your fill of loving and equal relationships before success can give you any lasting sense of completion.

Sulking

Sulking is manipulative. When you sulk, you are saying: 'I'm hurt and angry. I have stopped arguing but I still think I'm right and you're wrong. I know if I show my anger directly I'll get even further behind. Instead, I'm going to try to control the situation by withdrawing my love and to make you feel especially bad, I'm also going to show you how much you've hurt me.'

Everyone knows what's going on, but people are surprisingly nice and they'll often come to get you, provided you don't push them too far.

Support

Support may be material or physical, but mostly when we talk about support we mean emotional support. The principles of support are important to understand.

People need support when things are going badly. Being positive with somebody in difficulty is rarely helpful. By assuring someone he will be fine, telling him how much he has got going as a person, or advising him to be positive, you demonstrate conclusively that you have no idea how he is feeling. All you do is add alienation to his pain.

The essence of supporting someone lies in your ability to tolerate being helpless. It requires considerable self-respect to be effectively supportive, because often there is nothing material you can do. To support someone requires you to act as if you believe your presence and your love is worth having and is sufficient.

Resist the temptation to reassure. Abandon being positive and be satisfied with your attempt to find words to describe your empathic pain. You are being truly supportive by demonstrating that you see a situation through the same eyes, because then you help someone who is suffering feel less alone.

'That's horrible. You must feel awful. I'm sure I would feel absolutely terrible if that happened to me' is a thousand times more helpful than: 'Don't worry. I'm sure it will get better. Be positive and look on the bright side.'

If you can fix the problem for somebody, do it. If you can show him how he can fix it, that's even better. If you can't fix it and he can't fix it, showing him that he is not alone and has your sympathy is pretty good.

Taking responsibility

Effective, self-respecting people take responsibility. When they are wrong and they recognise it, they admit it. They are willing to accept blame, but slow to blame other people. When there is doubt and they offer an opinion, they own it and any negative consequences. They don't just do their job; they make sure the whole system works.

Taking responsibility means looking beyond your own obvious territory; not with a view to conquest, but rather because you recognise you do not function solely as an individual. You are a part of a whole; whether it is a family, a club, a corporation or even a nation.

Effective people know that charity begins at home, but also extends beyond. By taking a broader responsibility, you ultimately do a better job of looking after yourself.

Taking things personally

This means being oversensitive. You may see rejection or belittlement when none was meant, but even this need not be a problem until you start to act on your perception. Attempts to fix or reverse the problem are usually fuelled by anger, making a bad situation worse.

The solution lies in using thoughtfully chosen behaviour to manage your feelings. Remember the Gang of Three and the grid of possible responses to criticism and the outcomes? *If you treat people as if you believe they like you, even if you don't quite believe it, you'll never go wrong.* You won't lose friends, you won't make enemies and you keep your dignity with anyone who might already be your enemy. Make a habit of it and you'll start to feel more in control, and then you'll take things less personally.

Tantrums

Children have tantrums. A tantrum is no more than loud, verbal aggression, designed to intimidate and impose the territory of your truth. They rarely work with parents, still less with other adults.

Managing a tantrum in an adult follows the same rules for effective tantrum management in a child. Ignoring it will make it worse, because the purpose of a tantrum is to communicate something that doesn't seem to have been heard. If you can, and it's very hard because tantrums are so unlovable, you stay with the person, not giving in, not agreeing and not trying to shut him up. You just wait, gently offering your own position firmly and clearly, trying not to have a tantrum yourself. The quickest way to stop the tantrum is to give him what he wants, but reward undesirable behaviour in any animal and it increases in frequency. Not a good long-term strategy.

Testing

No one can resist testing others; we all do it now and then. It's not the fact that you do it that is the problem, it's how much importance you place on the result of the test.

'If he really loved me, he would have bought me flowers.' Unfortunately he didn't buy you flowers, so you've got a problem. More unfortunately still, if you are a chronic tester you are more likely to be chronically insecure in your relationships. Insecure people are more likely to have tantrums when people fail their tests, making their relationships even more insecure and launching a new round of testing.

Trauma

An event becomes a trauma when it threatens to overwhelm your usual coping systems. Then you are stressed to the point of profound distress.

Different people faced by the same threat can emerge very differently. Someone who takes up a challenge in a situation of danger can actually emerge with a heightened self-esteem, while someone who is overwhelmed can suffer a post-traumatic stress disorder for many years. It will come as no great surprise to learn that people who successfully manage a traumatic situation are most likely to be those who take a lead by showing strength through taking responsibility and who help others with their kindness. Having said this, expose anyone to enough trauma and he can be crushed.

Trust and unconditional love

Unconditional love between adults does not exist. If your parents did not love you unconditionally, you missed your only chance for such love. The most loyal and loving partner will not love you unconditionally. Someone who truly loves you will give you lots of room to move and to transgress, but ultimately if you do not stick even vaguely to the rules she is likely to leave. If your relationship survives you will spend your life either in bitter argument or with a weak and broken character.

Looking for unconditional love is lethal to self-respect and to relationships. You will be endlessly testing and endlessly disappointed. To look for unconditional love is to look for the trust that a child should find in a good parent, putting you in danger of trying to turn a partner into a parent. Worse still, you may actually find someone who is willing to try playing the role of your parent, which you will soon learn to resent profoundly.

You can trust a healthy person to love you at a role-appropriate level, but that will never be unconditional.

Truth

Objectivity is a myth. Everything is subjective because the world is viewed through the eyes of the subject, who always has his own agendas to satisfy. Your truth is your territory. What you believe to be true becomes a piece of you and there is always a danger you will defend it more aggressively than is wise or necessary. That's why it is a good idea to work out what you regard as your core values, your real truths, so you can place anything else on the periphery. Then you can waste less energy and have fewer fights over truths that shouldn't matter.

There's no problem if you think you're right about something, just don't go to war over it unless it's a core value.

Victim and victimised

Although healthy people want to like each other and would rather be kind than cruel, it can still be a rough world out there. Through the course of your life there will be times when you are genuinely a victim, innocent of everything other than of being in the wrong place at the wrong time. Then you have to take action if you can, or simply stick to behaving with kindness and dignity if you can't. Whatever you do, you're still going to feel bad. It's only a question of how bad, which is decided by the nature of the original problem and by the way you react to it.

People who take things too personally are constantly seeing themselves as victims and tend to claim the rights and privileges of someone who has been wronged. As victims, they feel they deserve greater latitude and should be allowed to behave in angry, helpless or self-indulgent ways without being corrected. In reality, everyone has to agree you are a victim before you will get such freedom, and even then you will need to stay within the limits of time and behaviour that your culture says are permitted to a victim.

Winning and losing

If your self-esteem is poor there is likely to be a lot of winning and losing in your life. A poor self-esteem often means you are more competitive and you have a more intense sense of hierarchy than someone with a healthy self-respect. To an insecure person, strength and lovableness are heavily dependent on winning. Secure people obviously like to win as well, but know they will survive if they don't. A good self-respect allows you to understand that not winning is not the same as losing.

If you shape your behaviour using an intelligent model you may not win, but you rarely lose, because real loss only comes when you make yourself unworthy by behaving in an unkind or belittling way.

Worrying

Worrying is simply anxious planning. If you have a problem and you suddenly think of the answer, you'll stop worrying. Worrying can acquire a value of its own, as if by worrying you are actually doing something to fix the problem. Worriers can be afraid to stop worrying because to stop would feel like taking their eye off the ball. If you want to control your worrying, you need to either work out its cause and fix it or convince yourself that at this moment there's absolutely nothing you can do. In a situation where there is truly nothing you can do, the decision that you are helpless and therefore ought to give up, at least for the present, can be calming. If you can't stop worrying at this point, then don't try to stop worrying because you actually don't want to take the risk of stopping. It's horrible at the time, but past experience says it will eventually pass, even when the worst does happen.

If your six-year-old child is late home, you'll worry and won't try to stop until she's safe, but make sure worrying is not a substitute for action. If your husband hasn't rung you and you're afraid something awful has happened to him, make sure it really is his welfare and not your own anxiety you are worrying about before you take action. Calling the police to find him when he is late home from a drink is a great punishment but a bit risky as a means to strengthen the relationship.

Who am I?

In Chapter 4, I suggested the closest you will ever come to knowing your self is to know your core values. I proposed these are the principles, ethics and morals that constitute your spiritual or emotional territory; principles that if you were to violate them you would never be able to truly forgive yourself. I have repeatedly made the point that it is behaviour that decides our feelings. You may have strong urges to break your own rules, but until you commit the murder you may have thought about and even planned, you are not a murderer. *What you do is what you are.* You are what others can see or could have seen. No one reads minds; we read verbal and bodily signals. Your judgement of your worth is the way you treat others, because when you are judging yourself, you are judging the way others will feel about you. It is you looking at you, as if you were another person and others only see your actions. You know all about you; you very well know your sense of weakness, anger or fear. You can have those things inside you, but if no one sees them surface in your behaviour, they are not you. If you can act with kindness and dignity, especially when things go wrong, that is who you are, and who you are is good.

Epilogue

IN ONE SMALL BOOK I've jumped from the evolution of our ancestors to the future of our children. I have tried to show that we are part of a natural order in which once only the fittest survived and that the forces of evolution have shaped and continue to shape our emotions.

To stay alive our bodies obviously need food, water, shelter and oxygen. The concepts of *An Intelligent Life* are derived from my proposal that our emotional life has also been shaped by the less tangible essentials of survival: belonging to a herd and the power to hold our own territory. With secure belonging comes warmth, peace and love, while pride, dignity and a sense of creativity spring from what was once the ability to hold some territory and perhaps conquer more.

Unfortunately, the same forces that push us towards survival behaviours can also prod us viciously when we miss out. Our ancestors undoubtedly suffered the fear of death if they faced rejection, and a terrible fury if their hunting and mating grounds were invaded. You can be certain that if they failed in their efforts to get back to the tribe, or if their anger didn't fuel the strength to fight successfully for territory, they slipped into their version of despair, abandoning themselves to certain death.

As an adult member of a civilised society in the twenty-first century, you should not die if you are rejected or belittled, but in common with everybody else, you have a problem. The region of your brain I choose to call your survival brain – that part of your cerebrum copied from your ape ancestors over thousands of generations – has absolutely no idea of the context in which you live. The possibility of forgetting what you are supposed to say in front of an audience, or even thinking about asking someone attractive to have dinner with you, can trigger the same emotion as your ancestor would have felt if his tribe rejected him and left him to the tigers. Having someone take your parking place or steal your ideas can provoke the same murderous fury as your ancestor felt when another ape moved into his patch or looked lustfully at your hairy, knuckle-dragging ancestral mother.

Life really is quite simple. Every single waking act that does not look after your physical survival is devoted in one way or another to acquiring as much love and belonging as possible, while simultaneously securing a robust sense of individuality, control and power by effectively marking out your territory. Your self-esteem is determined by how clearly defined as an individual you feel and how loved you feel for being that individual. Do this skilfully and you have a well-balanced sundae of self-esteem. It's no accident that kindness and dignity are the only real measures of human worth, because these are the behaviours of love and power, belonging and territory.

All our emotional problems are variations on our response to rejection or belittlement, or both. There are really only three negative emotions: anxiety, anger and despair, which are the emotional drivers of the three possible behaviours in the face of threat; flight, fight and freeze. These emotions spring from fear of death, because once upon a time to be unloved and powerless was to die. Now we are anxious if we feel we might be rejected, despairing if it finally happens and angry if we are belittled. Sometimes if we're rejected we use anger to escape our anxiety and despair.

Happiness is achievable, but not absolute happiness. There is no possibility that you will live your life without pain. The best you can hope for is to make sure you cause as little of your own pain as possible. If you practise effective damage control when life is being particularly outrageous, you will still hate what is happening, but you won't hate yourself.

Living your life intelligently is no more than trying to simultaneously find as much love as possible with as much dignity as possible. Care of yourself is care of your relationships. The better you do this, the better your self-esteem. The greatest happiness comes from being individually creative in the setting of love given and received.

Everybody wants to be loved. People are attracted to the people with whom they feel they belong; the forces of love and liking hold a tribe together. Self-interest motivates everybody to want to like everybody else, because that increases their sense of belonging and security. This means everybody will want to like you, unless you obviously belong to a different, totally unacceptable group or you behave in a way that makes you impossible to like. In everyday encounters with enlightened people, it is quite hard to get rejected for what you really are. You are most likely to earn rejection or belittlement for the things you do in expectation of rejection or belittlement.

Because everybody wants to like everybody else if they can, there is a golden rule for comfort. Treat every other person as if you believe they like you. Do this and you will never lose. Even if you have accurately identified rejection or put-down, you will be much more comfortable if you are slow to respond. To lose friends because you have treated them as enemies is a disaster, while failing to see a genuine attack or ignoring it frustrates an enemy and gives you some control, because you have taken the power from the attack.

If you want to feel good, you have to choose your actions well. If you want to feel like a self-respecting, equal adult, you need to behave as one. If you manage to look as if you like yourself, you will appear to have enough self-love to have love to spare for others. Therefore you are attractive because everybody wants to be loved.

Unfortunately, being nice is not enough; it has to be done with the power of dignity. To lean over backwards for other people is both generous and wise, but to fall over backwards is foolish. If you give more than you can afford you will be looking for payback and resentful when you don't get it. In this you will be neither kind nor dignified, which will make you unattractive to others and especially to yourself.

It is misleading to say you can't love others if you don't love yourself. To love and to be loved are inseparable and they grow together. If not loving yourself denies your ability to love, it would make it almost impossible for you to be loved by another. Fortunately neither is true. You can love and you can be loved if you don't love yourself, but you will need more self-understanding and skill to do it well than someone whose self-love is already established.

In the beginning it was different. Children can feel good about themselves simply by being given love by their parents; as an adult it's not so easy. A poor self-esteem makes you no less hungry to give and receive love, but means you see others as less likely to love you or want your love. Your heightened expectation of rejection or put-down can force you into defensiveness rather than openness, making you hostile or manipulative in the mistaken belief you are protecting yourself and serving your interests. If you do not love yourself enough, you must develop an active, reliable and reproducible system for earning love with dignity.

To live skilfully you must recognise it doesn't matter what you are feeling at the moment, it's what you do that is the major decider of the emotional outcome. Other people don't read minds; to them what you do is what you are. Thus the recipe for happiness is one of positive action, not just positive thinking. Actively trying to develop a healthy self-esteem depends on the principle that the only way to change feelings is through well-chosen behaviour.

You need to pit well chosen action and the positive responses of others against your self-doubt. Understanding that the ultimate criteria of human worth are kindness and dignity, you can script and choreograph behaviour that is attractive to you and to others. If your self-esteem has been poor but you do this consistently, you can set up a conflict between an established, anti-self prejudice and your active construction of the positive.

Inconsistency is disturbing to human beings, so having incompatible experiences automatically provokes an attempt to correct the inconsistency. It is possible to feel terrible about your looks, luck, brains or circumstances, but still manage to play the role of a self-respecting adult. By doing this, your behaviour can elicit signals of respect and liking, both from others and from the people in your head – the 'they and them' who are always watching you in the form of your Observing Self. Your feelings will initially rebel against acting like this to get positive responses from other people, but by harnessing your natural discomfort with inconsistency, the Gang of Three can be put to work: thoughts driving actions to get responses that change feelings.

To live happily doesn't mean you must or will be able to suddenly dispense with negative emotion. Not only have you no chance of getting rid of an unwanted emotion at will, you may not be able to prevent yourself from acting like a person who feels terrible. Then you need to act as a person who feels terrible but likes himself. You may be simulating self-like, but you are not trying to fake that you feel good, merely that while you feel terrible about what's happening, you still feel good about yourself.

When their world is falling apart, people who live intelligently may be angry, anxious and profoundly sad and their feelings may be visible, but they will still try to treat people with kindness and to conduct themselves with dignity. In short, they know that if they want to feel as good as they can when they feel bad, they have to be particularly careful to act the role of a good friend, reliable colleague, supportive partner and loving parent. Their vanities and fears will often cause them to fall short of the mark, but by making this their basic game plan, they'll feel as good as they can and may even find a little pride in the process.

Unfortunately, life may be simple, but it's not always easy and love won't fix everything. We want power as well, which can get in the way of love if territorial protection degenerates into aggressive invasion. In the jungle the aggressive and the violent win. In a civilised society, aggression is recognised as a fear of weakness and violence is forbidden, leaving assertion as the only option.

You will have disputes and disagreements, which are struggles over the territory of conflicting or incompatible truths. You could always hit the person foolish enough to disagree with you, but hitting someone only proves you're stronger, not cleverer. If you have the good sense not to be violent, you can never dominate another person unless he submits. All you can do is assert yourself, which is putting yourself in your place, not him in his.

An emotionally healthy person will want power with people, but not over them. You should respect the rights of others ahead of your wishes, but never put their wishes before your rights, which is buying love at huge expense. Sadly, you will occasionally meet people who see their wishes as being more important than your rights and you will need to deal with them as forcefully as necessary.

Fortunately, people who really want to tread on you are fairly rare and much less common than people whose wishes merely compete with your wishes. In these encounters, if you are armed with effective arguing techniques, you increase the chances of getting what you want. However, when you do argue it is prudent to remember you will rarely win and you may have to settle for equality. It will help guide your arguing strategy if you also bear in mind that you will always want to be liked.

That's all there is. Almost everything in this book is blindingly obvious, but people don't always see it. They see themselves in the mirror of other people, but don't know how to change their self-image. They don't always appreciate that hoping for their feelings to change before they change their behaviour will never work. They don't see that all the wisdom and self-knowledge in the world won't make anyone feel better if it doesn't lead to an improvement in the way they behave in their relationships.

Relationships are everything. There is no emotional problem that is not a function of rejection or belittlement, real or imagined. If you understand that every contact you have with another person is driven and shaped by your needs for love and individuality, and if you manage this balancing act with kindness and dignity, you will do very well.

I wish you good luck, but in a life lived intelligently, luck becomes less important.

About the Author

DR JULIAN SHORT graduated in medicine from the University of Sydney in 1970 and was admitted as a fellow of the Royal Australian and New Zealand College of Psychiatrists in 1976.

Julian's career has taken him all over the world; practising general medicine and giving anaesthetics in England and Nepal, working in general practice and studying in a number of psychiatric hospitals. His wanderlust has led him through the Far and Middle East, Scandinavia, Europe, Russia and the US. His fondness for the sea has taken him sailing in many places, including a break from medicine as cook and deck-hand on a yacht in the Atlantic.

Julian returned to Australia in 1978 to work as a staff specialist in a teaching hospital, before entering private practice. He is now a consultant to three teaching hospitals attached to the University of Sydney and works with the Royal Flying Doctor Service, providing psychiatric services to remote towns of Central Australia. He is a member of a hospital ethics committee and is an educator with the Black Dog Institute, an internationally recognised centre for the treatment of depression at the University of New South Wales. He specialises in the management of low self-esteem and relationship problems.

Index

Note: page numbers in **bold** refer to diagrams.